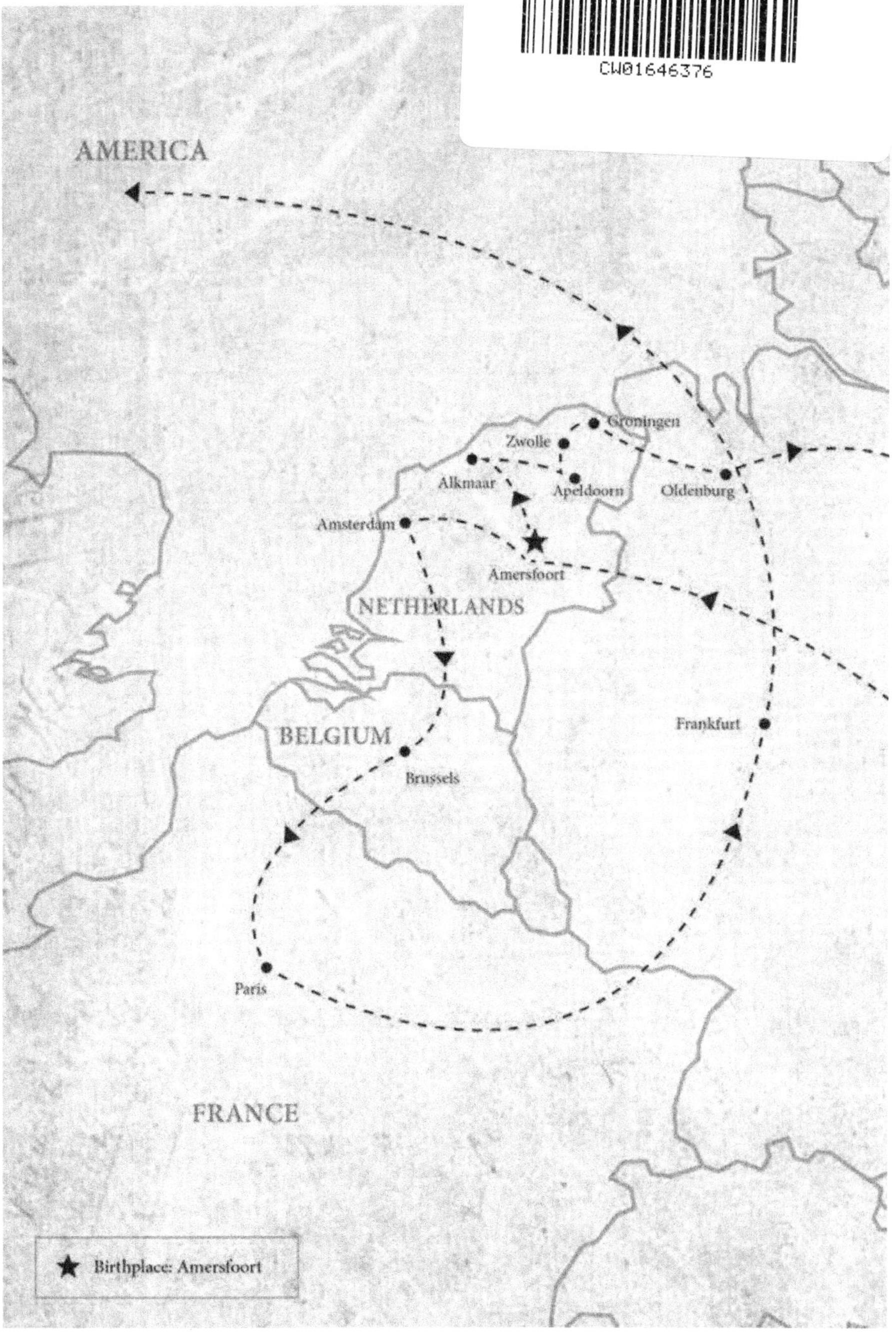

AMERICA
Groningen
Zwolle
Alkmaar
Apeldoorn
Oldenburg
Amsterdam
Amersfoort
NETHERLANDS
BELGIUM
Frankfurt
Brussels
Paris
FRANCE
Birthplace: Amersfoort

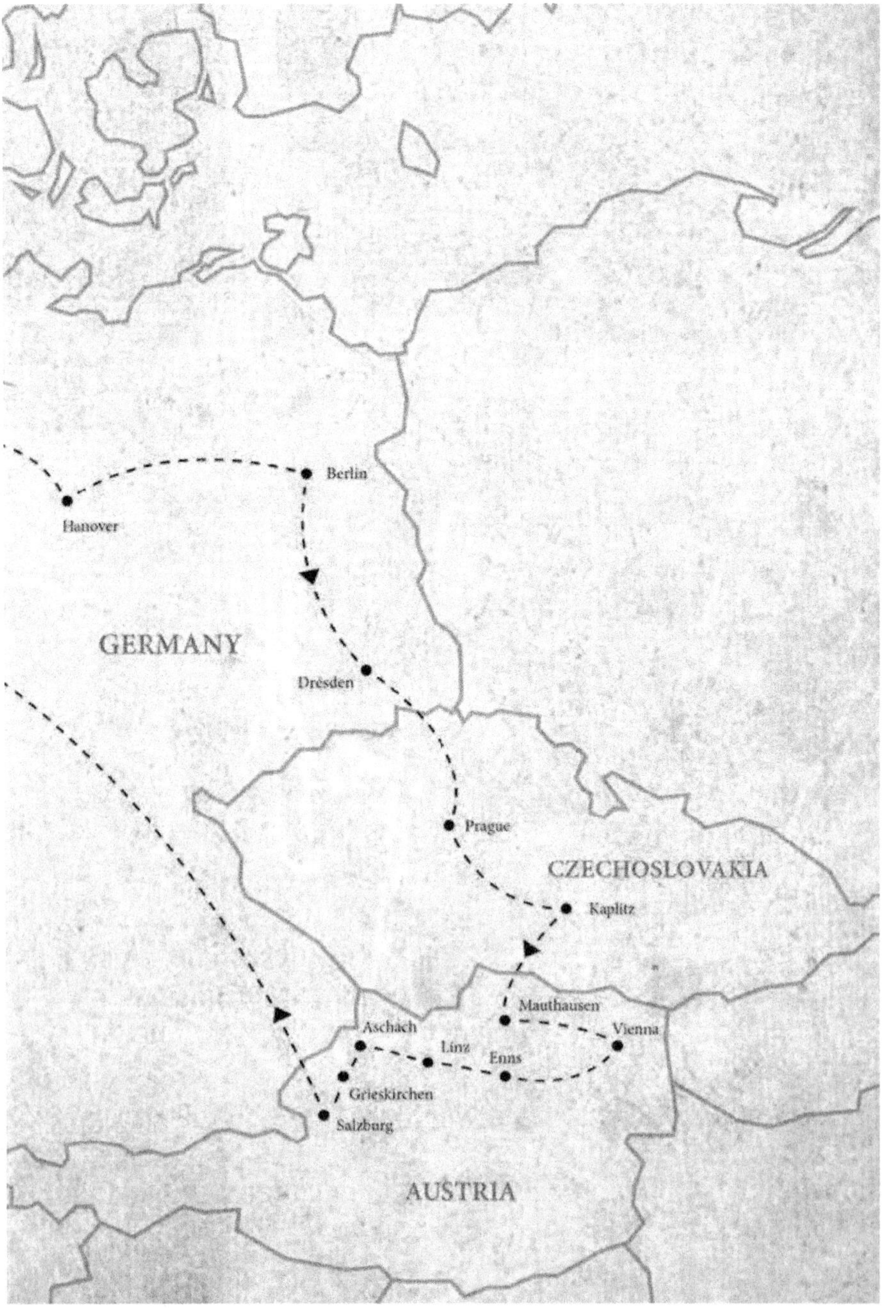

Berlin
Hanover
GERMANY
Dresden
Prague
CZECHOSLOVAKIA
Kaplitz
Mauthausen
Aschach
Linz
Vienna
Enns
Grieskirchen
Salzburg
AUSTRIA

Treasures of Sadness is a firsthand account of Cornelia Dykhorst (AKA: Corrie Smith), the War and the love that she found. Corrie died in 2003. She has one son, B. R. Smith, and two grandchildren, Chad and Kelli, who all reside in Tennessee. It was her son's dream to publish his mother's memoir. It was the gift that she gave him of her past.

Acknowledgements

First, I must thank my mother, Corrie Smith. She is not of this earth any longer, but her spirit is with us. I feel her most when I have difficult decisions involving character issues. I feel her push me in the right direction. Mom, thank you for writing this story of your life so I know who you were, who I am, why I am and where I am going.

I miss and love you very much.

This book would not have made it to print if not for my daughter, Kelli. Her involvement was unlimited from getting it copyrighted, multiple edits, multiple printouts and to cover design. Her tenacity and spirit are immeasurable.

Thank you, love Daddy.

I must thank my wife, Gail for all the edits, research, help with cover design and tolerating me through this long process. She never met my mother but feels she knew her through this memoir.

Thank you, with love.

I want to thank the Palmer Printing team. You took on our small project and gave it the time and attention that exceeded our expectations. I want to especially thank Michelle Meyers for her endless patience, professional insight and guidance throughout this process. I feel honored and privileged to have your assistance.

Thank you kindly.

Shemika Shackelford McCauley is the talented young woman who designed the book cover. She took the idea of what I imagined the cover could be and brought it to life.

Thank you.

To all my friends, family and all who helped me with this endeavor,

a sincere thank you.

B.R. Smith

Treasures of Sadness

By: Corrie Smith

ISBN 978-0-692-08820-3
Printed in the United States of America

For my son, Billy Ray.

Preface

From my window I look out into the street. How sad the sight. The gloomy November sky rises high above the ruins. Homes and buildings disfigured by the same wounds. Soldiers, women and children, disfigured bodies. People afraid of things seen and unseen, fears that do not show and never heal, crippling forever.

After surviving a rain of blood and fire that without mercy continued and continued, those who remain have an elementary fear, the creator we call Well Being. For that Well Being, we freeze. Is it over now? The war has ended. But the fear…to fear…there is no end. It is buried inside, deep into the heart, and it whispers constantly…from hunger, cold, or the next war.

I look out into the street, then turn around in this room in which I claim nothing. How we walk unconcerned, thoughtless, all alike into this ice-cold spacious world. The doors that are slightly open, do they all lead to despair and death? Is there hope that still there is an opening somewhere hidden, a promising star, a glow from heaven that in the darkness of our day some comfort brings? We do owe a debt, the debt of the living, to the dead. We must renew a love for our fellow man. Without it all hope is gone.

It is still dark, and I am alone in this bare cold room. I give way to my thoughts; I recall seeing the silent forms there suffering…gone… they are no more. But those that are no more, they comfort my soul and warm my heart. They console me, but they do not give me rest: the deaths of the Second World War.

When I was young and full of hope I believed in people. Now I doubt the sincerity of most people's words, the honesty of the tears that spring to their eyes. Now, I am standing helpless, too helpless to believe.

The only thing I will cling to and that is indestructible and everlasting is good will and compassion. With good will, you serve God and your fellow man. For that you get compensation and peace.

But it is still night, pitch black, and I have gone back...a long time back. My fear is not gone...it will always be. I want to be strong, but I am not...but I shall do my best and always have concern for others. Deep inside...always.

War

Amersfoort, a small town in Holland of about fifty-five thousand people, is the place where I was born. I lived there for the first twenty years of my life. We were an average family—my father and mother and four children. My brother, Albert, was the oldest; he was eighteen years old. I came next, sixteen years old; then, my sister, Annie, who was fourteen, and Tillie, the baby, was eight years old.

My father, a sergeant on the police force, provided well for us as a middle-class family. We lived in a comfortable house in one of the best sections in Amersfoort because my father was in charge of that vicinity. We always wore nice clothes because my mother managed her household economically. Our life was no different from any average family with a regular income and four children to support.

The war came while I attended high school. Germany, already at war with several countries, had now violated our neutrality. On May 10, 1940, we had been awakened early by the sounds of hundreds of planes—German planes, flying over Holland. The Dutch had already been under mobilization, but still had hoped to keep out of war. Now everyone was worried—people feared Germany. Then, Queen Wilhelmina had announced on the radio that Holland had now declared a state of war with Germany. The Germans were entering Holland with thirty divisions, hundreds of tanks and over two thousand airplanes.

The army of the Netherlands numbered nine divisions, and it also lacked planes and tanks. Dutch military qualities were untested because the Netherlands had enjoyed peace for generations. Because Amersfoort was considered a military target, the whole town was forced to evacuate. Each person was allowed forty pounds of luggage and all the clothes they could wear, and in addition, a blanket, which we carried rolled on our backs.

Arrangements were made earlier for each family to be lodged by individual families in a small town, Alkmaar, about seventy-five miles away. We left in organized groups by train, district by district, in alphabetical order. After our group arrived, we were concentrated at a church, and there the Netherland Red Cross served us cadetjes (small rolls of fresh Dutch bread) with ham or cheese and coffee, milk, oatmeal, and fresh fruit for children. The Red Cross then made arrangements for evacuees to be either collected or led to their quarters. The process took hours. Announcements were made that food for this district would be served daily in nearby schools for those who had no cooking facilities, and each person would also be supplied with a mattress of straw in case no beds were available.

Most of the people in Alkmaar were nice, but some had not yet realized we were at war and didn't like the idea of having to shelter strangers in their homes, even though we were their fellow citizens and of their own class.

The Civil Defense had taken nearly everything into consideration and tried to place people as near in their own social standing as possible; they even tried to place them according to their religion. The evacuation was well organized considering we were at war, but at the age of sixteen, it was hard to realize completely the full tragedy of leaving your home and all your possessions behind.

After about two hours of waiting, our family's name was called and a civil service man from Alkmaar told us he would lead us to our quarters. We followed behind him—the five of us, because my father was not with us. He had to remain in Amersfoort until the whole town would be evacuated. After a short distance, a walk of about ten minutes, our escort stopped in front of a large two-story brick house and rang the doorbell. An attractive, clean-looking woman of about thirty opened the door. The man explained that we were the people she was to shelter. She looked at us, and all the luggage; we looked depressed, with too many clothes on, and we were very tired. Without giving us any sign of compassion, she pressed her lips tight together and said, motioning with her head, "Follow me." The civil service man shook hands with my brother and said, in a sympathetic tone, "I hope you make out all right." My brother thanked him and we followed the woman up two flights of stairs, then entered an attic. It was bare except for a double bed and an old-fashioned washstand with a refillable water tank. There were no curtains for the small attic window. The floor was bare, unpainted, plain pine wood, but spotless. The woman turned around and said, "I have chosen the attic for your own privacy. You folks make yourselves at home. The bathroom is on the second floor."

After she left, we just looked at each other. Then, my mother sat down on her suitcase and she started to cry very softly. Thank God my brother was along. He just looked out from the little attic window, then composed himself and said, "Now, Mother, there is no reason for that; we are going to make out all right. It just seems so bad, but after things are arranged, it won't. It is true this way we do have our own privacy, and if it should take a long time, we can make other arrangements a little later."

My mother remained silent, sitting there on her suitcase, looking so forlorn. Then she said, "I know. It is just such a shock that people can be so unconcerned."

My brother told us he would go downstairs and talk with the woman and ask for some chairs and a table. We were all seated on our suitcases when Ab returned with the woman, Mrs. Palmer. She said we could have chairs, a table and also a dressing screen. She added when her husband came home he would help my brother get the things upstairs. My brother left to get three straw mattresses for Annie, himself, and me. My mother and sister, Tillie, would sleep in the bed.

Ab returned with our former neighbors, the Meesters, from Amersfoort. They came to see how we made out. They said they had to sleep on straw mattresses, too, but the people were so nice and considerate where they were staying. We felt much better as Mrs. Meester was such a nice person. She was a great comfort to my mother and reassured me that she would help us look after her. She knew all about my mother's illness which resulted from a fall in our home several years previously. She had fallen, head first, from the fifteen-step stairway and had seriously injured her skull. At first it had not seemed bad—that's why it had become so serious. Several days later dark blood had suddenly dribbled from her ear. She was then hospitalized for several months and underwent serious operations behind her ear and skull. Since that accident, she had spent more time in the hospital than at home. To look at my mother you would not think that there was anything wrong with her, though she had a rubber tube from her ear running to the affected place in her head. This required treatment by a doctor three times a week. She was forbidden to do work of any kind that required the slightest strain or bending of her head.

Mrs. Meester left, and we felt so much better since she had come to see us. Her place was only one block from where we were sheltered. Just think—Mrs. Meester sleeping on straw! They were people whom were considered "well to do." She had only two children, girls, ten and twelve years old. Her husband was a prominent businessman, and they owned a beautiful home in Amersfoort. They even had a car of their own but had not been allowed to take it to evacuate. Only doctors and government officials had been permitted to use their cars. There were not too many people in Holland who owned cars, but officials taking care of the evacuation claimed too many cars would cause a hazardous situation and add many other difficulties.

We were tired, and after washing up, we fixed our mattresses and covered them with our own sheets and blankets—they looked very inviting. Everything was quiet. Lying there in the dark attic, I thought how lucky we were. At least we were all together, except for Papa. Of course, he was a man who could well take care of himself. I could not imagine any one taking the upper hand over my father. My mind drifted back to the home we had to leave behind. I thought about my new dress, a semi-formal, my first one. The dress had been for a school party the next week, the pretty dress I had never worn. I had draped it over my bed, which was stupid. Someone might come in the house and get it, or lie down on the bed and get it all wrinkled, because everyone had been ordered to leave the doors unlocked so the Dutch soldiers could enter when there should be need for that. Oh well, poor Mama, all her pretty furniture…and here we were in a bare attic.

Suddenly someone knocked on the door; it was Mrs. Palmer. She told us to be sure not to turn any lights on. Tomorrow she would fix a black shade for the window. My brother assured her we would not turn on any lights. Everything was quiet again and we were alone with our own thoughts. No one said goodnight. We were afraid, I guess, that it would make us too sensitive. Sometimes it is better to remain silent.

Early the next morning, my brother went to a nearby store to get a loaf of bread, milk, preserves, and some fresh-sliced ham. Food was plentiful. Mrs. Palmer had supplied us with some plates, spoons, knives, and forks. We ate breakfast at the small table. We felt close without words, closer than we ever had been at home. How pitiful! There were people who had nobody. At least we had each other. There were so many people we knew around us as the whole of Amersfoort was evacuated!

The Dutch government reassured us there was enough food to keep the present population in Holland supplied with a sufficient amount of their customary rations of food for the period of at least seven years. The warehouses were stocked to the limit, loaded with provisions. Holland was small, but very rich. It had nearly everything because of the Dutch colonies. Of course, now there would soon be a shortage. All imports would be stopped: coffee, tea, rubber, oil, rice, tobacco, all kinds of nuts, spices, cocoa, and dried fruits, and of course, all imports from the Far East.

Mrs. Meester came and asked Mama to come with her to meet the people where she was staying. They were so nice! I encouraged Mama to go along, as there was nothing to do in the attic and the time passed better that way. There she could listen to the news on the radio and would know what was going on.

So, Mama and Tillie left. Annie and I straightened the "room." We hung some of our clothes on a makeshift clothesline. Ab refilled the water tank, then said he was going to look around town a little to see if he could find any of his school friends. Annie said she would like to look around too and see if she could find out where her girlfriend was staying; she said she should be near, also. They promised to return about two o'clock.

I went downstairs to see Mrs. Palmer. I knocked on the kitchen door and as she opened it she said, "Oh...it's you." She continued doing the dishes, not looking up. I asked her if I could come in and talk with her a minute.

"Yah," she said, but she said she did not have much time, as there was so much to do with such a big house with so many people. She could not do as my mother did, "already started loafing early in the morning."

I looked at her, shaking my head and I said, "You don't understand, you see, my mother is very sick and this has been a terrible strain on her. We want to help her all we can." Mrs. Palmer responded, "She does not look sick to me. She is just a small-frame woman, but I don't think there is anything wrong with her. I wish someone would help me—I am tired, too. I did not want this war."

I told her I knew we were bringing extra work—we were using her bathroom, her stairway, her entrance—and I could see she was a very good housekeeper, but if she would let us use her kitchen, I would promise to help her with all her work. She looked at me and said, "What could you do? You look like all you could do is primp."

I was glad I looked that good. I should have hated to look like a scrub girl, but I said, "Just tell me whether or not we may use your kitchen under those conditions."

She said, "You know I am frank about it. I did not want evacuees, but in war time that is your unquestioned duty. The government pays us three gulden a day per person if they eat here. Of course, they cook for themselves." (One gulden was then equivalent to one dollar). "We get $1.50 for just sleeping quarters per day per person." She said she had to think about it. She added she would like for me to start helping her, so she could see what I could do—and I could start with the ironing. I agreed. Three hours later she claimed she liked me and that my mother sure had taught me how to make myself useful. She was not so bad, after all, although far from being likeable.

Several days passed, then my father came to see us. He arrived so unexpectedly that it nearly frightened us. We were so glad to see him, but he could not stay long, but long enough to make it clear to Mrs. Palmer that indeed we were not on vacation. We were not guests in her home, and we were definitely to do our share of the additional work. But just because she had the advantage to remain in her home, she had no right to feel superior, because of our "due to the war" unfortunate circumstances. Should we have had the choice, we would have preferred to remain in our home and give shelter to evacuees from Alkmaar. Because my father was government employed and still receiving his pay, he offered to pay additional above what the government paid her. At that, Mrs. Palmer cleared one bedroom for my mother and Tillie on the second floor and we immediately had access to the kitchen.

Mr. Palmer was all right; he just had nothing to say. He really had a kind heart, but his wife dominated him, and he did not take his place as head of the house. There were two children, five and six years of age.

Papa left and told us he would be back soon to see how we made out. My sister and I helped Mrs. Palmer with her housework, and all in all, we were just fine, considering the circumstances.

It was soon announced on the radio that Queen Wilhelmina and other members of the royal household were taken to England by a British destroyer, after attempts had been made by the Germans to kidnap the Queen. Had it not been for the alertness of Prince Bernhard, the husband of Princess Juliana, they would have succeeded.

On May 13, government officials had fled, first to Paris and then to London. They had brought to safety all valuable documents and the country's gold, as well as diamonds and other gems the Germans would have liked to have taken.

On the morning of May 14, the Dutch army could only offer scattered resistance in isolated groups. The Germans had now set an ultimatum: either the Dutch would surrender before four p.m. or the city of Rotterdam would be bombed indiscriminately. The situation was now out of control, and General Winkelmann considered surrender of the Dutch army. While the city of Rotterdam was negotiating for capitulation, and before the Dutch army had a chance to carry out the surrender terms, Rotterdam was bombed, in less than one and a half hours almost thirty thousand civilian casualties were on the streets. Those who had tried to find shelter in the basements of large department stores had met their death by drowning, because most of the city's water pipes had burst from extreme pressure.

The Germans now set another ultimatum: either we would surrender or in three hours they would bomb the next city flat. That city would be Utrecht.

We were now in great danger. They had started bombing, and maybe we would be next. When the alarm came, we were so scared—we ran into stores, or into private homes, where in case of attack we would not been much safer than standing out in the open, except of course for the shooting of the defense, for sometimes parts of ammunition would come down with great force, and a small piece could kill you. Not being out in the open gave you a feeling of safety, because some people die of fear alone. The sound of dropping bombs could make some go into shock.

We realized Holland was not equipped to fight long against, what was at that time, powerful Germany. And before Utrecht was bombed, as the Germans had threatened, Holland capitulated. Queen Wilhelmina, in two broadcasts from London, stated that her government and her country proclaimed surrender in the struggle. Even though in Holland we had surrendered, the Dutch Foreign Minister Von Kleffens announced from Paris that the state of war continued, and that all Dutch overseas resources were placed at the disposal of the Allies. Now the fighting with Germany in Holland had ended, but the real hatred had just begun.

We were scheduled to return to Amersfoort, to our homes. Of course, it would take a little time, for at the present there was no water, gas, or electricity there. When we returned, it seemed that we had been gone much longer than a little over two weeks, and for the first few days, we appreciated our beds as never before. How fortunate we had been that our house was not damaged, and everything in place, just as we had left it. But, not everyone had been that lucky. Although Amersfoort had not been bombed at that time, mobilization had taken place and our own civilians had ransacked many homes and some of our own soldiers had misbehaved terribly.

Occupation

We were now under German occupation, for most of us a nearly unbearable situation. The Germans followed their method slowly. The Dutch army was disarmed, officials, officers, and service men were allowed to return home, but a short time later officials and officers forced to submit themselves, and then were placed in a prisoner of war camp.

A couple months later, my mother's illness made it necessary for me to quit school, much to my dislike, yet it was something I had to accept. My place was at home, being the oldest girl.

No one who was not there could really form a picture of what it was like in the following year under German occupation. Some people took it on their own to commit sabotage, much against the orders of the Allies, who in pamphlets thrown from planes told us not to resist the Germans, unless in underground organizations. Prince Bernhard, as head of the Dutch underground in Canada, under supervision of General Dwight Eisenhower, warned the Dutch underground against premature resistance.

Then, in the small village of Putten, some self-made hero took it on his own to shoot and kill a German high-ranking official. The Germans gave the villagers three days to find the brave man who did this foolish thing.

The town had about one hundred inhabitants. All were questioned; no one had seen or heard anything. Three days passed and the Germans took revenge to prevent it from ever happening again. All able-bodied men over twenty-one were gathered and transported to Germany to work in the war industry. The women and children were allowed to pack one suitcase each and then gathered in the church. Then their homes were burned.

We saw very little of the actual persecution of the Jews because most of the really bad treatment was camouflaged. However, we did notice that suddenly a Jewish family had disappeared, and their homes and businesses taken by the Germans, and we saw them packed in trains, or forced to labor for the Germans, on military grounds. The Germans tried to influence us, the Gentiles, by claiming that the Jews were taken to camps only long enough to teach them the art of work, to teach them handcrafts and skills because, according to the Germans, the Jews had no respect for labor. They said the Jews were moneylenders, loan sharks, and out to take advantage of the Gentiles. Therefore, the Germans were rehabilitating them until they would be qualified to make themselves useful in the labor world. We were disciplined and learned to keep our emotion under control, as well as our feelings of hatred, as we saw helpless Jewish women and children packed into trains and transported to Poland. We were not allowed to look at them, or even show the slightest sign of sympathy without endangering our own lives, and that of our relatives. We were careful what we said, and to whom.

Most of the Dutch people grieved when they heard of violence and unjust actions against helpless people.

Now, all able-bodied young men, if not making themselves useful in full-time employment, would be transported to Germany to work on farms or in the war industry. Often during the day, we had alarms, for now we were under German occupation and therefore, subject to bombing or invasion by the Allies.

Many people prayed for America to enter full-force in the battle and help us and other parts of Europe survive, but without result. They sent planes and supplies, but not anything that could put a stop to this hopeless situation. American civilians' viewpoint was "why should we get involved?"

Months passed, and I usually was so busy during the week that only on Sundays did I have time to visit with girlfriends or to go a few places. It was on one particular Sunday that I took Tillie with me to visit a girlfriend of mine who lived about ten or fifteen miles from us, in the small town of Soesterberg. We had to walk about three miles before catching the streetcar the rest of the way. Tillie looked forward to the little trip because she did not get to ride the streetcar very often, as it was on the outskirts of town. Had it been a pretty, sunny day, we would not have dared to go to Soesterberg, because now on clear days the Allies would bomb the airport, which was one of the largest military air bases in Holland. But, because it was drizzling rain, an attack would not likely take place, so my mother said it was all right to take Tillie along and we could stay for a few hours.

Jo Ponsen, the girl I wanted to visit, lived in Soesterberg with her widowed mother, a very religious, nearly middle-aged, woman, who still was wearing high-top shoes. Mrs. Ponsen was disappointed in her daughter who, though morally a very nice girl, absolutely did not take any interest in going to church, or even share in the least in her mother's ideas. In fact, shortly after the Germans took over Holland, against her mother's wishes, she took a trip to Germany and Austria, sponsored by a German youth organization, because it was free. The German group had encouraged several young Dutch people to take advantage of this educational tour. Under strict supervision, this had been a wonderful experience. Even though everyone had to make their own bed, help cook the meals, and keep their own clothes clean, they had been looked after with the greatest concern, and the food had been excellent (all for propaganda, of course), but it had not been without results. Several young Dutch people had been easily influenced and even came to think that Germany was right. They had brought out points against religion, of course, in a clever manner. They had not said that it was wrong or anything, but just not with reason, not facts, and that those people who leaned on religion were just weak, and therefore, inferior. They did not exactly close the doors on churches, as some had been led to believe, but just shrewdly instructed people against it. So, young people in general lost interest, and called religion "nonsense."

To a certain extent, I looked up to Jo, as she was very intelligent and had graduated from an excellent school for girls, for only those superior in mind and a visible desire to develop their abilities would have been accepted by the school as a student. When Tillie and I arrived at her house, Mrs. Ponsen was about to leave for church, but she said she still had time for a cup of coffee (imitation) with us.

Tillie was sitting close to me because she had never been there before. I explained to them that Tillie usually stayed close to home, but because the weather was so dreary, Mama had allowed her to come along. We sat there enjoying our hot drinks when I mentioned that I heard airplanes, but Jo and Mrs. Ponsen assured me they were German planes; they heard them all the time. But then suddenly the sirens began to scream...and we realized that these were not German planes. It all happened so fast, and so unexpectedly, that we did not have time to make it to the public shelter.

Mrs. Ponsen said, "Let's go in the closet under the stairway. "All four of us got in the closet. Mrs. Ponsen placed the vacuum cleaner in front of the door; otherwise, if the bombs dropped nearby, the door might close us in because of air pressure and we would smother to death. We sat huddled in the closet, listening to the planes flying over, then return and take a dive for their target. The whistling sound before the dropping of the bombs was nearly unbearable, then, the enormous thunder when they hit! We were sitting face down, on our knees. Tillie began to cry, whimpering, "I wish I had stayed at home." Then, before the next bomb hit, Mrs. Ponsen said, "Oh God, this is the end." She began to pray very softly and calmly in comforting, mumbling words.

The bombs kept dropping, one after the other. When the sound was closer than before, we were sure we were hit. Then, the sound of glass breaking, lots of glass, and then the roof...more glass...and more noise. We knew the outside was on fire. The bombs kept dropping; there must have been hundreds of them. I was sure this was the end, the end of us; we never would come out alive, we would never make it. I squeezed Tillie close to me. Tillie said, "Dear God, let us please live."

All in all, it must have lasted about ten minutes, which seemed a lifetime. We were afraid to move after the planes were gone, then Mrs. Ponsen, looking up, still on her knees, said, "I think it is over." But just then the planes had come back on a much larger scale and it started all over again. They never stopped. I thought we were all going to be killed, the whole city. We did not move. Finally, we could not believe that it really was over, and we were still alive. We did not move for a few minutes, then the safe signal was given. We crawled out from the closet, and looked around at the disaster. Every dish, decoration, lamp, and picture was broken, all the furniture was turned over, window glass was splattered everywhere—everything breakable was broken. Part of the roof was gone, and every four or five minutes we heard heavy explosions. As we went outside, we saw ambulances, and people running everywhere. Thank heavens Mrs. Ponsen's house was not on fire, even though at first, we had believed so. But, now we heard that the military barracks were on fire and that was not all, oil had been stored in large tanks under the ground, thousands and thousands of gallons, and the tanks had been hit. That's where the heavy explosions had come from.

Then there was my father, on his police motorcycle. He said Mama was nearly in hysterics. She was afraid that Tillie and I had been killed or badly hurt. So, Papa took Tillie home with him on the motorcycle. I told him that I would be home shortly after Mrs. Ponsen and Jo had decided what they were going to do and where they would stay for a few days. Of course, immediately I offered that they could stay at our house, but Mrs. Ponsen, thanking me for the invitation, said they would stay with some of her relatives.

The Germans were always nice and very helpful to Dutch people whose relatives were either killed or injured, or their property destroyed or damaged by the bombs the Allies had dropped. That, of course, was strictly for propaganda reasons. The German maintenance crew came and helped make temporary repairs, such as nailing planks over the broken windows. The Red Cross would help the wounded (then called luchtbeschermings dienst).

Mrs. Ponsen asked if I could keep Jo company until she returned from the evening services, because she missed the morning sermon. I told her I would be glad to. Jo asked me, smiling, if I believed prayer would help me during the bombing. Before I could answer, Mrs. Ponsen said, "That depends on what you pray for. Faithful Christians pray for spiritual strength and endurance, but," she added, "Jo does not pray anymore, she has outgrown it. She says she does not need God. Ever since she was on that trip to Germany, she has been convinced that prayer, and trusting in the power of God, is just for weak people, and very old-fashioned."

I did not answer, but I thought, "Well, I am in doubt myself and I have not been on a trip to Germany. If God answers prayers, and can do all things, why do helpless Jews have to suffer so much? In fact, some awful rumors are going around now, of course, maybe that was not all true, but some people claim some incredible things..."

So, I said, looking questioningly at Mrs. Ponsen: "If God does everything right, why do so many people have to suffer so? For instance, take the Jews?"

She gave me a strange look. She was an eccentric woman, I thought. And then she said, "It is written in the Bible that the Jews shall have no land to call their own, and that they will be persecuted, but woe unto the ones who persecute them because they are God's chosen people. The shepherd gathered his sheep before the storm which is surely to come, these earthly unfortunate people have now established a relationship that will remain unbroken, for they have felt the power of God's consoling love."

While Mrs. Ponsen was talking, Jo just looked at me, as if to say, "You see now what I put up with?"

I still did not answer, for I knew nothing to say. And then the doorbell rang and there were relatives of Mrs. Ponsen. So, instead of my staying with Jo, I asked her if she would walk me to the streetcar, but the streetcar did not run because of the bomb damage, so Jo walked me halfway home.

When I arrived, they were all pretty well in good spirits, not only because Tillie and I had survived the terrible bombing, but they also were excited, and glad that we finally had seen that the Allies had made some effort, and had attacked not with a few planes, but with hundreds, and might bring this war to an end soon.

Most of the Dutch civilians realized that we would have to sacrifice many of our own people, along with the destruction of lots of lovely homes and precious buildings. But Dutch people became so patriotic that many claimed they hoped that Allied bombing would continue at great force, even if it took their own lives. The radio announced that the Allies had attempted an attack at Soesterberg, and the Dutch civilians suffered severe damage, with many losing their lives and homes, but, as for the Germans, no military damage was inflicted, and they had suffered only one casualty. They always ended the broadcast with, "Wir hatte keine, or nur wenige ferluste." (We suffered no, or only slight damage.) Of course, that was only to keep the morale of the German soldiers high. The explosions lasted for four days, but they had suffered "no damage."

German looting had reduced civilian supplies to the bare necessities. Clothing and shoes were almost impossible to get, along with soap, toothpaste, toothbrushes, shampoo, cleansing cream, hair oil, shaving cream, coffee, tea, or cigarettes. From the beginning we had learned to do without meat, sugar, or enough of anything. The food situation began to worsen. Fuel was so scarce that people were now taking down wooden fences from their homes, trees in the parks and furniture that they possibly could do without. Because we were not allowed to be in the streets anyway, after nine o'clock at night, most of us went to bed early to keep from using our pitiful rations of coal or wood.

People got thinner and began to lose hope; there just wasn't enough of anything. The contents of our overstocked warehouses had been gradually transported to Germany, using our modern diesel trains, and they kept them there. The Dutch Railroad had to repair old long-discarded trains for transportation of civilians in Holland. Slowly everything disappeared from Holland into Germany: leather, rubber tires, canned meat. Only during certain hours could we get water, gas, or electricity. We were getting used to the hours that it was distributed.

Many young people and children failed to attend school, and young men stayed in hiding places (to avoid being sent to Germany), usually being kept by families without children, or where they just had girls.

Now the Dutch had to part with all their copper and brass articles. Nearly everyone was sensible enough to turn in some articles, but they were hiding most of it, things they did not want to part with. At least, they didn't want the Germans to make ammunition out of, but hiding it was dangerous. If caught, the penalty could possibly be shipment to Germany.

All Dutch people, including doctors, who were registered to own cars, now had to turn them in. Only those with extreme needs, or those who collaborated with the Germans, were allowed to keep their cars. They took everything—modern farm equipment, city buses—leaving us only long-discarded machinery.

Because our house was built in one of the most desirable suburbs in Amersfoort, which we called "Op de Berg" (On the Hillside), it so happened that we got as our neighbors the Germans. German officials, of course, chose the better sections for their quarters. On the right side of our house, a distance of about three hundred and fifty yards, was the former home of a rich Jewish family by the name of Ramselaar, now occupied by German officials of high rank, among them the German Commissioner, Artur von Seyss-Inquart. On the other side of our house, only a distance of about forty feet, we also had Germans for neighbors, but no high officials, just officers and under officers.

Nearly every day we would see them enter or leave the houses. When the summer came, they would sit in their yards, always greeting us with a very friendly attitude, saying rather loudly, "Guten morgen, Frauleins" (good morning, ladies).

My sister and I did not pay them any attention, because we knew better than to give the impression that we even were aware of them. My father would have given us a stern lecture if we as much as encouraged a conversation. Because my mother had been hospitalized again, my girlfriend often would spend the weekends at our home. On sunny days, she and I would lie in our yard taking a sunbath, and the Germans would look through their binoculars, and then whistle, or say, "Ooh, la la," but we never gave them a reply.

Weeks passed, and their water supply seemed scarcer than ours (or they were taking precautions, because lots of sabotage was taking place and their water might have been poisoned). Every morning one of their under-officers came to our kitchen to get several containers of water to use for various purposes, or perhaps to make tests to check if their water was the same as ours. We never carried on a conversation any more than necessary. But, without realizing it, I began to look forward to seeing the tall dark haired young man who was so well mannered, and who never tried to converse with me.

He usually knocked on the door, came in and filled several containers with water. He never failed to thank me before leaving. One morning, when he entered as usual, the radio was playing softly in the living room. The Vienna choir boys were singing "Brahm's Lullaby." He became aware that I was listening, and he said, "They sing well" in a tone as if an expert on judging them.

So, rather amused, I said, "Of course, they sing well, they are the Vienna choir boys, the best in the world!"

In a proud, but pleasant, voice he said, "How well I know; I used to sing with them. I traveled with the group all over the world: America, Australia, and every country in Europe, except Russia. It is really a privilege and an advantage to have been taught in their school."

I knew that only boys with good character and intense determination and musical inclination could have entered and stayed with the school, which was strictly disciplined and, of course, being in Austria, it was Catholic.

I looked admiringly at him. He smiled and said, "I was born near Vienna, and I love that city; that's where I plan to live some day." He picked up his water and said, "I like you, and believe me, I am just a human being. I have been watching you nearly every day for a month." He then stared out the window and said, "Where is your mother? I have not seen her here."

I told him in broken German that my mother had been in the hospital for nearly two months and that she was still very sick.

He looked at me with such kind eyes and said, "You are a very nice girl, you seem to me different from most girls that I have known, you have a big job here. I wish I could get to know you better." I told him my father would not permit me to talk with him any more than was necessary. He remained silent and slowly he picked up his water, smiled at me, and left.

For several days I did not see him. Then after that I saw him every day for nearly a month. He never lingered more than five minutes and our conversations were not personal.

My life was rather lonesome, as I seldom had anyone to talk to. My father and I never were close, and now he had so much on his mind, with my mother sick and four children at home. I did not have time for dates because there were always duties at home. No one realized how much I missed my mother to confide in.

I thought about this Austrian soldier constantly and I began to admire him more and more. I liked everything about him, his self-confidence, and his maturity. I liked him in spite of the fact that he was considered our enemy and I was not allowed to like him. One morning he entered and said, "This is my last day here." I never realized before how much seeing him every day meant to me. He asked me if I could see him that evening for a little while, that he wanted very much to talk to me. I promised him that if I did have a chance after my father had gone to see my mother in the hospital, that I would meet him after dark behind our house.

I met him at seven o'clock. I was nineteen years old and very inexperienced with boys. We talked, and he took my hand as we walked. Then he asked me if I trusted him. I answered that I felt very safe, and he squeezed my hand a little. He told me he was going home on leave. Then he said, "I want to tell my mother about you. I think she would like you." Then he said softly, "Corrie, I have always reasoned with my head. My head rules over my senses, but this time, my heart rules my head, because I want you as my wife in the future. I picture you as the mother of my children. I wish I were made of glass so you could see through me, then you could have no doubt of my love for you."

He then lightly kissed my hands. At that moment, I was completely happy. I believed in him and above all, I trusted him. He told me to never, never doubt him. He said he wanted to speak with my father the next day. I suggested he write him a letter, but he insisted he must see him because he had nothing to hide. I promised him that I would wait for him until the war had ended, and that I loved him very much. He then kissed me on my forehead and said, "I will see your father tomorrow at two o'clock." I left and slipped quietly into the kitchen.

After I completed the difficult task of telling my father about Victor, he said he would receive Victor the following day and that he would talk with him.

Victor arrived precisely at two o'clock, and I led him into the living room. My father, to my amazement, was very nice to him. When Victor promptly explained his reason for wanting to talk with him, my father told him that personally he had nothing against him and that he had no reason to believe his intentions were not honorable and that I, in Holland, probably could not find a nicer nor more upstanding young man. Then my father said, "Come back after the war as a civilian and I shall have no dislikes for you, because now your uniform is our enemy, and I must ask you, trouble us not."

Outside, Victor spoke with me a few minutes, telling me he admired my father's viewpoint. He told me he would write me at a certain address, because my father also forbade him to write. I told him I would be awaiting his letter eagerly.

Three months passed, during which I received five letters from Victor. Then, I received a letter from his parents. It was typewritten so that I could read it more easily, because my German was still very limited.

His mother explained that her son wrote her asking her to invite me to come to live with them so that we could see each other if he should get a leave. She said they did not question what type of girl Victor chose for his wife because she felt Victor would choose only a girl who would fit harmoniously into the family. They had already enfolded me into their hearts as their daughter-in-law. She said they would be looking for me from day to day, because under the present circumstances, it would not be advisable for me to remain in Holland, should anyone find out about my acquaintance with her son. She thought I should carefully consider leaving Holland.

I re-read the sentence. I did not have to consider, for I wanted to go over there very much and stay with his people. Judging by their letter, they must be a fine family, even though before the war, Hollanders had claimed that German and Austrian customs were so different that it would be unlikely that a Dutch girl would adjust happily. But I had no fear of that: Victor seemed enough like us, so I was reasonably sure that his parents would be of similar type.

Victor probably did not tell them that we never actually dated. I answered their letter, but I could not decide what to do. My mother was home now, not completely cured, but much better, and my sister, Annie, could take my place at home. But to leave home and perhaps never to return…Because the Americans had taken an active part in the war, there was no chance for German victory. And I doubted if German people after the war would be allowed to visit in Holland. Then, too, trains were constantly attacked by planes. I feared the bombing, hunger, and maybe disease in wartime, and it was some distance to Austria.

The telephone rang one morning, and I answered. It was Victor, and we had a short conversation, during which he asked me if I could leave Holland for the sake of our future and stay with his parents, because otherwise we might have to wait years to be together. I asked him if he thought it simple to travel that far. He answered that he already had the necessary papers for me and would send them to the address where I had been getting my mail. At that moment my father told me to get off the phone immediately, so I was forced to hang up. Papa lost his temper and said that if I ever attempted to communicate with Victor again either by phone or by letter, I would have to get out. I told him calmly that my mind was made up—I would leave for Austria. I added that because we never had seemed to understand each other, this might be best for both of us. He asked me how I expected to get to Austria under the circumstances: railroads demolished, bombings and fighter attacks on the trains? I replied that with God's guidance I feared nothing, because I was not leaving home for an evil cause, but for love.

The papers Victor had sent me arrived, so I was now preparing to leave for Austria. I sorted out my best clothes, as it would be impossible to take everything with me. I decided on my calf leather sport shoes and camel hair coat. I planned to wear my suit underneath and also my ski pants. I chose a pale green shawl for my head and carried soap, make-up, and a small towel in my shoulder bag. In my hand I should be able to carry a rather large suitcase, easier than two small ones. I hated to leave my books and my other personal belongings, and more so, I dreaded the thoughts of leaving my dearly beloved mother. She was so understanding and wanted my happiness. She gave me strength for she said she knew God would lead me all the way, but for me to contact them by mail as soon as possible.

Tillie, my baby sister, came to my room as I was packing, telling me how sorry she was that she had said so many terrible things to me about Victor, such as wishing he was already crushed under American tanks, and the like. She said, "Corrie, I hope and pray he will come out of this war alive and well." I told her to pray for herself because the ugly things she had wished for him were forgiven, but not forgotten by me.

But then she cried, and I told her she was a good child and that I didn't mean it.

Austria

The following day I left Amersfoort. My sister, Annie, and Jan, her fiancé, told me at the last moment that they wanted to take me to the train station. They did not want to remain at the station for fear of air attacks, as we usually had them daily. At seven o'clock my train departed, and I decided not to permit myself to think about anything concerning home. There were few civilians on the train, and not many soldiers. Few people talked; most were occupied with their own thoughts.

We traveled to Apeldoorn, where we changed trains. This train was much nicer and carried more passengers. They seemed friendlier, but that could be because it was getting so late. We spent as little time as was necessary at the stations, just long enough to pick up freight and passengers, for safety's sake. We passed Zwolle, but then as we entered Groningen, we were alarmed. As hundreds of airplanes flew over us, our train stopped, and everyone ran out of the train. Lights were thrown from the planes that dotted the sky, but no attack took place. In about twenty minutes we crawled out of the ditches and back into the train. At three o'clock in the morning we arrived in Wener, the borderline between Holland and Germany. There we had to leave the train with our luggage for inspection and to have our passports and other papers checked. Several passengers in my compartment said they would only take their handbag through the inspection to save time. I decided to do the same because I did have a few nice bars of soap and some other desirable articles that the German inspectors might take away.

I memorized my compartment number and left the train for the customs, but the officer at the control said, "You must have more luggage than just a handbag." He told me to get my other luggage, that he would keep my passport and other papers until I returned. The moment I entered the train, the signal for departure was given. There I was with my luggage, but without my passport and travel papers. I decided to leave the train at the next stop and return to get my passport. The next stop was Oldenburg, at 3:30 in the morning. I decided to wait in the waiting room for the next train back to Wener. As I was getting a cup of coffee, an officer of the Air Force started talking to me. In the conversation he told me that in a short while he would be in Holland. I asked him if I could give him an open letter to mail for me to my mother. He said he would be glad to. As I was waiting, completely unaware of all the commotion, the secret police were ordering all train departures stopped and no one to leave the platform. I asked the lieutenant standing near me what was going on. He said, "The police are looking for a woman spy. She went over the border without valid papers and escaped through the customs." Suddenly it dawned on me that they were looking for me. All that commotion frightened me and I felt some comfort in confiding in the friendly officer.

I told him what had happened in Wener, that I had no chance to leave the fast departing train. Luckily for me, he explained to the secret police about my leaving my passport in Wener and that I had fully intended to return for my papers. I was placed under arrest and two secret police officers accompanied me back to Wener. Every five minutes the train had to stop for a "non-safe" sign. The police were nice to me and they offered me a cup of coffee with bread, but I could eat nor drink anything because I was so nervous.

The secret police delivered me to the customs officials who were not very friendly. They told me I had entered Germany on a void passport and that I had been charged with several other violations. They told me to be on my way back to Holland in two hours. Then he handed me my passport. I stood helplessly at the platform in Wener, not knowing where to turn.

Then came an alarm. I didn't know where the shelters were. I just followed the people going in one direction and once I arrived in the bomb shelter, I saw the lieutenant I had met before in Oldenburg. He must have seen how lost I really was because he came over to me. I explained to him about my having to return to Holland, and he said that would probably be impossible for the next two weeks, because every railroad and highway was heavily damaged. He asked to see my passport, and we were still in the shelter when it was announced that the railway from Wener to Maastricht was for the most part destroyed. The lieutenant told me that the customs officials did not mark my passport "nonvalid," therefore I should easily be able to travel on as if no one had ever stopped me. He said that once in Germany (as I was now) all I would need was a train ticket. I still had my travel papers to permit me to travel through Germany to my destination.

Two hours later, everyone was allowed to leave the shelter. Outside there was no visible damage; only railroad connections had suffered. The lieutenant said he had some food tickets which was a relief. I was thankful for his help because I felt so lost and alone. He was quite nice and considerate of me. It was now nine o'clock at night. We had something to eat in a small gasthaus (restaurant) but I had no appetite, I was so nervous. He said he would not be able to travel as planned and to send my letter as promised. Letters, as all other connections into Holland, were temporarily at a standstill. I was very tired, but he told me I would not likely get lodgings for the night. He advised me to find a place in the waiting room and it would at least be warm and safe. He remained in the waiting room, too. It was now eleven o'clock Saturday night.

The next train would leave for Hanover at four o'clock Sunday afternoon. Of course, the train would be packed. The officer told me he would see to it that I got on the train. I asked him if there was any danger of my getting arrested, but he assured me that everything was going to be all right once I was over the border.

The train was hours late, so it was eight o'clock when it began to move forward to Hanover. The train was warm, which was unusual, because most trains were partly damaged—windows broken, doors missing, and other discomforts. But taking everything into consideration, all went fine. After my nerves settled a little, a civilian man who appeared to be traveling with his wife offered me a sandwich with bologna, and something resembling coffee. The train rolled on through the night, with people half sleeping. I was quiet with my own thoughts, wondering if I really had done the right thing, and hoping that my dear mother would not worry too much. Already I began to realize that I loved my family after all.

From Hanover to Berlin I got an immediate connection. The officer had to change over to a military train. He wished me a safe arrival at my destination. I was now on my way to Berlin, and as the train began to slow down about five miles before approaching a station, I noticed hundreds of barrage balloons anchored in the sky from which nets were hanging. If fighter planes would attempt to attack trains, they would become entangled in the nets. I had never seen them before, and they frightened me at first sight. Up to that time, I had no idea how scared I really was.

Luckily for me, we had only one attack on the way to Berlin. With the alarm signals screaming in my ears, I saw a young mother with three small children trying to make her way with her luggage to the shelter. Having only one suitcase, I told her I would carry one of the children. A soldier carried two suitcases for her. She carried one child and her suitcase, and the other child, about five years old, walked. After we arrived at the shelter, she thanked me. I just nodded my head, because I was rather overcome with some somber thoughts. People just sat around and waited with blank expressions on their faces. After the second safe signal (siren) was given, we returned to the train. I was helping the mother to the train with the children but was not allowed to travel in the same train car because there were special cars for mothers with small children. The young German mother said something to the conductor while I was standing in line to get a place in another car on the same train that was now nearly full. The conductor motioned for me to come to their compartment, and said that because of my assistance to the mother I would be permitted to travel in the same compartment. It made quite a difference in the icy cold weather to be traveling where there was heat.

As the train moved out, hardly anyone spoke, as we looked out of the windows, and miles and miles of destroyed homes met our eyes. Hundreds of women and children undoubtedly had found their deaths in those ruins. I soberly thought how awful war was. I stared into space. I did not want to see. I imagined this was my hometown, and those were my loved ones under the rubble. I kept asking myself, "Why did God not put a stop to all this? Why all this misery, for what purpose does all this take place?" When again I looked outside, I just held my breath. Up to this time I had never seen such disaster.

It was now Wednesday afternoon and we entered Berlin. I had been gone from home since Friday. I refused to let myself slumber in thought. I felt scared, and I was alone, but I was not going to let anything get me down. I decided to gain information at the Asukumpfs Bureau general information desk.

They told me there was no train going in the direction of Nuremberg; all connections in that direction had been temporarily discontinued. But I was told I could travel through Czechoslovakia (they called it "Das Protertorad"). I would have a through train to Prague, and from there I could make connections to Vienna, via Linz-aur-Gratz. I did not know that special travel papers were needed to travel through Czechoslovakia. I then took the subway to the Anhalter Station. I had never before been in a subway, and somehow it frightened me. Everyone seemed to be running. People did not like to remain any longer than necessary on the platforms, for fear of attack. When I arrived at the Anhalter Station, I went immediately to the waiting room and found out that my train for Prague would depart at six o'clock. It was now precisely three o'clock, so I was very lucky.

I bought a cup of coffee to calm my nerves. The people began to crowd in, and at five o'clock there was hardly any place in the waiting room. I decided to get on the platform; otherwise, I might have a hard time getting on the train. At 5:45 it rolled in, and it was not too difficult to get on. A young German soldier offered me a seat. I was so overjoyed at having been through Berlin without any attack, or even alarm, that I would have been able to stand all the way to Prague. In my compartment a lady and gentleman more or less took care of me. They generously shared their bread and other food they brought along with me. It was very cold, and the train was not heated. I thought I got a chill. The young soldier offered me his coat so I could get warm, and I told him I could not accept it. He insisted because I could not stop shivering.

In Dresden we got an alarm, and everyone left the train in a hurry; many people left their luggage in the train. We went past the railroad shelter to one of the city shelters. I suppose a bad attack was expected. I could not speak nor think; as I remember, we just ran in a daze. Inside the shelter we could hear the thunder of the bombs and the artillery shooting at the planes. We heard that the whole town was in flames. A half hour or so later, a short safe sign alarm was given. Then the young soldier told me we could get out of the shelter and return to our train because all trains were clearing the stations in a very short time. The attack was expected to return on a much larger scale. He said he was going to take a chance to leave for the station because there were short intervals of safety according to the alarm signals. I decided to leave the shelter when the soldier did, in the hope of reaching the train before they would strike again. Most travelers without children left the shelter to try to make it to the train and get away from Dresden before the expected heavier attack was to take place.

Once outside the shelter we saw unmentionable sights. People alive merely twenty minutes ago were now only a form of ashes. But no one spent any time looking around, we just ran to our trains. Some claimed the attack had been with bombs of phosphorous. The city was black with smoke and many buildings were on fire. Before the attack, our train had left the platform to return only in a case of a short safe period to pick up the passengers and then hurry away from the other attack to come. We had to walk about one mile to reach the train because the engineer did not intend to enter stations when the unsafe signal was on. Trains sometimes waited hours before entering a large town if an attack was forecast. Once in the train I felt safer and I was glad to know we were moving. It was near nightfall again, and everyone was quiet. Some tried to sleep; others stood stamping their feet to keep warm. Several people were talking in a language I did not understand.

Then two Wehrmacht officers came in. They kept standing, which was unusual to me, because in Holland civilian males would not be permitted to remain seated when German officers were standing. A German girl in uniform, a Wehrmacht angestehlte, asked them what their destination was. One of them, looking directly at the girl, said, "I am going home on leave." She replied, "On leave, at this critical time, you should be on the front, Herr Lieutenant." "All things have their purpose, Fraulein," he said, "even in wartime." "Not putting your own pleasure above serving your country at this time," she answered. "I am going home, with or without your approval, Fraulein," he said. The uniformed girl probably was of high rank, for she asked, "What is your name, Herr Lieutenant, and what place are you going? I feel it is my duty to investigate your furlough." Apathetically he looked at her and said, "It's my pleasure, Fraulein, Hans Fugen, destination Linz A/D Danube, to visit my wife and two children who were bombed out last week."

Sarcastically she said, "Never are personal matters more important than the welfare of your country, Herr Lieutenant." "Fraulein," he said, "if no furloughs were permitted in wartime, how would we continue our German generation?" She turned around to keep from facing him any longer. Then she began to look me over and said to me, "Fraulein, who are you, to be seated without a child, when I am standing?" She stared at me without really seeing anyone. I told her I was unaware of the regulations, but if such was necessary, I naturally would offer her my seat. Immediately she added, "I would like to see your travel papers."

A special permit was needed to travel through Czechoslovakia. I was very frightened but trying not to show it. I gave her my passport and other papers. She said they were all right, but she needed to see my "durchlasschein," a special permit to travel through Czechoslovakia. I told her I did not have such a permit. "You, then," she said, "must leave this car at the next stop and continue your destination in the sperwagon." I did not know what a "sperwagon" was. It was a railroad car used for transportation of animals, or freight. It would be packed with people, then the doors closed and locked. This was so no one could leave or throw out anything as would be possible in a regular passenger car. The sperwagon would be airtight, and in case of attack or fire, you would just be trapped. The officer with whom she had conversed previously spoke up and asked me, "Fraulein, what is your destination?" I told him my papers said Vienna, but I was really going near Linz Danube. He then spoke to the uniformed girl, "Fraulein, I take all responsibility for this young lady so she will not be forced to suffer the discomforts of the sperwagon. She gave him an icy cold look and said, "Whom, Herr Lieutenant, gave you the authority to take that responsibility?" "No one, Fraulein," he said. He did not look at me; neither did he smile. I was very uneasy and thought I should get up. But, as if reading my mind, he said, "She also has permission to remain in her seat." It was very cold, and we could see large snowflakes falling in the dark night. Lights were burning in the small towns we passed, which seemed so strange because Germany and Holland were under strict orders to let no light shine through anywhere.

It was so strange in Czechoslovakia to see lights burning in distant farmhouses and small railway stations. The snow kept falling and the wind blowing with more and more force. Everything outside looked so deserted, I could picture myself in Siberia.

At each stop, more people entered the train, all wrapped up in heavy woolen scarves covering their heads. They kept stamping their feet to keep warm and they talked rapidly in a Slavic language. I realized we were only a few hours from Prague and about one hundred eighty miles from Vienna. My feet felt as if they were frozen, so I started to move them as other people did. The snow fell much faster now, some of the windows were out, and if there had not been so many people standing close together, we all probably would have frozen. At times the train would stop for twenty minutes—no one knew why—then without giving a signal, it would roll on again with the same slow rhythm. Most people remained silent. Early in the morning we arrived in Prague.

Because we would have a layover of at least four hours, the Lieutenant asked me if I would like to see some of the city. He said usually people without a special permit and valid papers could not enter Prague, but because he would accompany me, it would be permissible. I felt very fortunate to have the opportunity of getting to see something of Prague.

We saw the most beautiful architectural masterpieces; gorgeous palaces which were to me breathtaking. Unfortunately, we did not have time to see the well-known church, Our Lady of Victory, which displayed the beautiful statuette of the infant Jesus called The Holy Child of Prague.

Prague was supposed to be one of the world's most beautiful cities. We were not permitted to pass over the Charles ridge, which connected the old part of the city with the new part. The Lieutenant was disappointed he could not take me to see some of the world-famous museums. We did admire some of the gorgeous churches that were only partly open to the public, except the local Czechs, because of the bejeweled statues set with brilliants and many other valuable jewels. I told him I did not understand the display of jewels and so much wealth in the Catholic churches. He then explained that many of the Catholic people had brought their most precious and valuable gems to their churches as a symbol of love, just as men give diamonds to their wives as symbols of their love. The diamond is supposed to stand for a light in their lives. These stones, expertly placed among masterpieces, painted by famous artists, formed a result so beautiful that it was truly breathtaking.

The rubies were placed to remind one of Jesus' suffering on the cross, for His love for the world. The blue sapphires stood for the promise of Heaven. The diamonds, arranged in the form of a star, stood for the bringing of good tidings, the Light into the world. Above this setting was standing a simple statue of the Lord Jesus from which shone a light so radiant that all the beauty below became meaningless and insignificant, except for the effect the guiding light from above had on it. I was amazed at his explanation and I was glad I had learned that much.

It was getting colder, so we returned to the waiting room at the railway station. The large room was heated, however sparsely, and I could not quit shivering, so he, Hans Fugen, took off his coat and draped it over my shoulders as I sat on the waiting room bench.

He explained that it was not necessary for me to travel all the way to Vienna, if my destination was in the vicinity of Linz. I informed him that I was expected in a small town, supposedly near Linz, the name of the town was Mauthausen." He said it would be better to travel by way of Kaplitz, that was a different route, but would get me there much quicker. I was glad not to have to go to Vienna or Linz because of the daily bombing. It was cold, but if it had not been for him, I probably would have frozen in the boxcar.

The train for Mesli-Most arrived at twelve o'clock and was also heated. This train was nice; no broken windows and not crowded. The snow kept coming down in large flakes, it was peaceful looking outside, not a sign of destruction. Now and then we passed a farmhouse, no mountains, just stretched-out snow-covered land.

At six p.m. we arrived in Mesli-Most, a small station occupied with nearly all Slavic people. Everything was very dirty. Soup was available in dirty bowls, but dirty or not, I was glad to get it. A hungry stomach pays no attention to a little dirt. The soup with carrots and potatoes cooked with caraway seed tasted good, and it was hot.

The restroom was filthy. I had never seen anything like that before.

The odor was unbearable, no cleaning facilities, no flushing or water available. It was just impossible to make use of the so-called "toilet."

Some time later I got a cup of something hot, sweet, wet, which was called "coffee," and it was appreciated by most all the people around us.

At eleven o'clock I would be on the train to Kaplitz. I was so glad everything worked out so smoothly. Hans Fugen wished me the best of luck as we parted. He was so nice and helpful, and he said that if on my arrival at Victor's parents I found things were not as I had been led to believe, then I should feel free to contact his wife. He said she was a fine person and would be glad to help me. He gave me his new address because as he told be before, their home had been bombed.

I was now alone and on my way to Kaplitz. I arrived there early in the morning. I seated myself in the small unheated waiting room for my last connection to Mauthausen. The trains were not on schedule; they came in whenever they pleased, it seemed. At last my train did arrive. I now was only a short distance from Mauthausen, but the train seemed to creep. Finally, at seven o'clock that night I saw the name "Mauthausen" on a small station. I was among the few people who were getting off the train. I decided to ask the station master about Professor Topitz, who lived on Heindle Kay. The station master seemed to be in his late fifties or early sixties. The platform was now almost deserted when I walked up to him. I asked him if he knew most of the townspeople. He said he did because it was a very small town. I asked him about the Family Topitz. He then took a long, curious look at me, looking over his glasses, and said, "You must be Herr Victor's bride from Holland" (bride is fiancée in Austria). I thought, "this is a very small town indeed." The Family Topitz had been expecting me for some time, he said, and had asked him to look for me in case I should arrive at night. He said he would take me there himself. It gave me a pleasant, comfortable feeling.

We did not talk much, and the walk seemed longer than it was over the heavily snow-covered streets. We came to a square, then on one side there was a high stucco wall. In the stucco wall there was a heavy wooden door on which was a door striker hanging on a chain. He picked it up and knocked loudly on the door. We waited, then a voice asked, "Who is there?" The station master said, "There is a guest here for the Topitz family, a fraulein from Holland." The woman who opened the door looked at me with great curiosity. She seemed at least eighty years old. She said she was Frau Shaumberger and the caretaker of the house in which there were several apartments. She and her eighteen-year-old grandchild lived in a small room by the gate. She intended to carry my suitcase, but I smiled and told her I would carry it myself. I thanked the station master for his help.

We went through the so-called courtyard, then up wide cement steps that led into a hall with several doors. She rang the bell on a large double door. A few seconds later, the door opened, and I stood facing Victor's mother. Frau Shaumberger went back down the stairs. I did not have to say a word. Victor's mother took me by the arm and pulled me in the door. She seemed excited and said warmly, "Come my child, Corrie, we have been expecting you for days. We were so worried and now, thank God, you are safe and with us."

She put down my suitcase, then I saw Albert, Victor's younger brother, who looked a lot like Victor, and Hedi, the thirteen-year old sister Victor had often told me about.

Mrs. Topitz, a handsome, dark-haired woman of average height and nice size, and spotlessly clean, said that as she could see I was exhausted, they would wait about asking me anything concerning my trip until I had had at least twelve hours' sleep. Immediately my bed was made. She said I would temporarily be in the living room on the couch since I had undoubtedly suffered severe cold on my trip and needed to sleep in a warm room, and all the other rooms in the house were unheated except the kitchen, which was heated only during the hour that meals were being prepared.

The most impressive room to me was the living room. I felt as I looked around as though I was in a museum. I thought it very beautiful; everything was so clean and well kept, and I liked it. It had Persian carpets, beautiful paintings, a large grand piano, and huge windows and heavy drapes. I had never been in so large a living room. One corner was arranged for a complete dining room. It had a buffet with silver and crystal and china sets. Everything there seemed to represent very fine and highly cultured tastes.

When my bed was ready, I just washed up, ate, and went to bed. Immediately I fell into a deep sleep. The following morning Hedi was sitting on the foot of my bed waiting for me to wake up. When at nearly eleven o'clock I finally opened my eyes, she smiled and said, "I thought you never would wake up." She reminded me of my sister, Tillie, so I liked her right away. She was thin and had dark brown hair in pigtails, and a rather pale complexion with freckles. She was so considerate and unspoiled.

When our late breakfast had been prepared and we were eating, I met Victor's father, a pleasant but solemn looking man of about forty-five years with large, penetrating eyes. As we were all sitting around the table, Victor's mother and younger brother, Albert, asked me many questions, most of them concerning my trip and Victor, when I had seen him last, etc. I told them of my trip and of my love for Victor. I considered myself a very lucky girl to have found such a fine person as Victor and with such a considerate family. After we finished eating, I helped with the dishes, then unpacked my clothes and became familiar with the rest of the house. Inge, Victor's oldest sister, would be home for the weekend, then I would meet her. I wrote a letter home and felt right away at home with the family, though we had just met. In the afternoon Mrs. Topitz introduced me to several people in the village. We also went to a variety of stores.

Many days had passed when, one day at the dinner table, Mr. Topitz, who was usually quiet, asked me point blank as he looked at me, what I thought of the war. I replied, "Mr. Topitz, I am afraid my knowledge about war and politics is very limited and I agree with Victor's saying that women should remain feminine and be satisfied with their womanly functions such as motherhood, which he considered "stardom of womanhood," and nursing, which comforts. Then all other things that bring forth beauty such as clothes designing, sewing, cooking, home decorating, music, painting, and so on. But not politics. A woman should always want to be led; she should not desire to become a leader. When she tries to lead, man will fail to be man, he will without doubt lose respect for woman and will no longer desire to support the woman. Therefore, Mr. Topitz, I can only say this much, I love peace and peace-loving people, I hate all injustice and cruelty and whoever is in the wrong will in due time suffer the consequences."

"I am beginning to see, Corrie, that you fit well into this family," he said. He looked up and smiled. I still did not know how he really felt, but one thing I was sure of, these were not Nazis. These were highly cultured and educated people, much respected in their community. I later sensed that Mrs. Topitz was a devout Catholic.

The days passed by quietly without any air attacks except those nearby in Linz.

I sent letters home explaining in detail what nice people Victor's parents were and how they treated me as if I were their own daughter. Mrs. Topitz said she was so glad I came because Inge, her own daughter, had such a different personality. Inge lived in Linz and came home on weekends and often more frequently. She was dark complexioned with straight, nearly black, hair. Her apartment in Linz was bombed, and twenty-six people lost their lives. She barely escaped. Her fiancé, Rudy, was killed in the same week on the front. She did not cry, she just became indifferent to other people's suffering and was very bitter about Rudy's death.

I mailed a card to the officer in Linz who had been so nice to me, telling him that indeed Victor's people were as I pictured them and very kind. I thanked him for being so concerned about my well-being. I was only a little homesick. I wrote three times a week to Victor and several times home. I did not know whether or not they would receive my letters. From Victor we received no mail and this disappointed all of us.

I had to learn to cook Austrian style, help clean house, learn to be a good hostess, all necessary for the future wife of a professor in Vienna where Victor planned to teach. I had to learn many things daily. They taught me how to speak correct German, things about the operas and about philosophy, Dante, Nietzsche, Schiller. At the time, Greek philosophers were prohibited. All books about Plato, Aristotle, Crito, and the like, were destroyed. In the afternoon many times Hedi and Albert, who was seventeen then, and I went skiing. In the beginning it was very difficult for me, but Albert was a good and patient instructor. He was so well mannered and more handsome than Victor. His admiration for me was very obvious, but of course he thought of me only as a future sister-in-law. He respected and adored Victor and of course I shared his feelings very much.

The first letter from Victor arrived in February. I longed to see him. There was a letter to his mother, also.

From the German officer I received a card saying he was glad I was in good hands, that all was well with him, his wife, and children. A true gentleman, I thought. How tactful to send an open card so everyone could read it. Mrs. Topitz agreed that he must have been a fine person.

Days passed with our doing the daily chores. We ate tasty food, some unknown dishes to me, numerous new varieties that were amazingly well prepared with limited ingredients. To watch Mrs. Topitz put together a tasty meal out of practically nothing was an unforgettable experience. She rolled the dough for crust so thin it looked like a table cloth. I knew I would never make a good cook in her eyes.

The war seemed to be less noticeable there than in Holland, except for one great horror. The concentration camp was only a few miles from where we lived. Victor had never mentioned it to me. I was there two weeks before I saw the pitiful prisoners passing on the street in the icy cold with nothing but the customary striped clothing. Some of them were without shoes and their feet were wrapped in rags. We were not allowed to show the least bit of sympathy, but silence can speak many words. One day Mrs. Topitz and I went to pay a visit to one of the farmers. The walk was about six kilometers of climbing up and down the mountain roads. On the way we met a group of pitiful prisoners. Hunger and death were written on their faces. I observed Mrs. Topitz as she looked at them with great compassion. One of the poor prisoners suddenly tried to escape—a man about thirty years of age. One of the SS guards shot him instantly. He fell to the ground and the other prisoners acted as if they were unaware of what had happened. They passed by him without a glance. Neither Mrs. Topitz nor I spoke for several minutes after we passed the place where the man fell. We walked on, each with our own thoughts, then she said, "There is so much pain and misery in the world today, and I hope Victor has not given himself for an evil pleasure or evil cause. When he left here he was such an exceptional young man, his principles so high, his ideas so wholesome, much richer than most young men his age."

She looked at me, staring out in space, then she continued, "You must know, Corrie, if by any chance my son has come to believe in all this horror and thinks it all right to kill a man for an unjust cause, then he is not worthy to return to my house." It was then that she cried, the only time I ever saw her in tears. I admired her; she was indeed as Victor said, "an extraordinary woman." I told her she had nothing to worry about there, as Victor had much of her character. "Mrs. Topitz," I said, "Victor has not changed; he is very capable of feeling the pain others suffer, and I should consider it a great loss if I were unable to feel this pain also." Then I told her of the time that Victor told me he despised a man that used power unjustly to take advantage of human weakness, against people mentally or physically inferior. He told me he would rather be the servant of a kind and just man than the hero of an unjust commander. She laid her hand lightly on my shoulder and said, "Thank you, dear, you are a comfort to me. So many girls are wasting time in frivolous doing and thinking. There is so much wrongdoing in the world, and all wrongdoing ends up in pain." She then added, "I am glad you came to us; Victor chose well."

When we came home neither of us mentioned what happened

that afternoon. Nearly every day we saw prisoners come and leave. Apparently, it did not affect the townspeople, but underneath there was a silent suffering, an inner compassion, a feeling that had no expression.

It was primarily Jews and Slavic people—men, women, and children—who we would pass on the streets. The hunger and hopelessness was written on those people's faces. Their faces did not even say "Help us, do something for us," for they knew their only hope was for the war to end, and to defeat Germany. Anger stirred up in me as I remembered my father saying, "Why didn't America come to help us sooner?" But they did not see this misery as I did not see it, until I came face to face with it. All the sorrow in the world has little effect on people who just hear about it. I remember the words, "By suffering, one gains an immense amount of wisdom." How true that was and is!

Our own food was getting scarce; potatoes became a delicacy. The thought of eating a good meal including a small piece of meat on Sunday was what kept our spirits up during the week.

Mr. Topitz received orders to leave immediately to serve as a military asset in a nearby village. The exact place was kept a secret. Albert, the seventeen-year-old son, received military orders to report to Linz. The length of time, and the reason, were both kept secret. Hedi, a thirteen-year-old girl, was ordered to a secret meeting that night at nine o'clock. The Youth Club, "The Young Wolves," which Hedi was forced to belong to, told her not to fail attendance. There were papers ordering all non-citizens of Austria to report immediately for work in a nearby iron plant. Mrs. Topitz was upset, but completely in control of herself. She said, "As for father and Albert, they have military orders. There is nothing they can do but obey them, but Corrie and Hedi are staying right here. They are under no military obligations."

She then looked at her husband and said, "Am I right, Albert?" Mr. Topitz said as he walked toward her, "Yes, Theresa, you are right." Then I saw that she found her strength in him. He embraced her as she said, "I could not stand it here all alone. Let them not take Corrie, too." "Sure, Theresa, I will do all I can. I will assure them at the Gemeente

Raad (courthouse) that you need Corrie and Hedi with you." He looked at Hedi and me with his arm still around his wife. He looked at us with eyes that were helpless, but full of compassion.

The following morning there were just the three of us, Mrs. Topitz, Hedi and me. Victor's mother was so depressed she could not eat. For nearly two months we received no mail from Victor.

We expected there would be a battle. Mrs. Topitz heard the Americans were approaching Craz and Wiener Newstadt; she said she hoped they would overtake Mauthausen. But we feared the Russians might beat them to it. She said we would pack away the valuables such as the silver, the Persian rugs, rings, and furs, because the soldiers, especially the Russians, took everything they could. We heard they cut off women's ears in order to get their earrings. We planned to hide in the attic in case they should enter the house before official authorities took over. She then gave Hedi and me a small pill, saying to take it in case of torture, because there were rumors that some soldiers were incredibly cruel.

We hoped in silence that the American troops would enter first, but we were on the left side of the Danube. We did not even care to eat. Mrs. Topitz went to the neighbors to gain information. They said we should get in the cellar. But for days we had not seen any planes; an attack was not likely to take place with the concentration camp so near. We also feared the prisoners who might have developed a great hatred and wanted to seek revenge. There were still some in fair condition and able to fight.

We spent four days in the attic and went from there to the cellar, two frightened women and a child. Everything seemed alarmingly quiet. Outside the windows people were hanging white sheets. I told Mrs. Topitz she should hang out a white sheet also, so they would not shoot at the house. She said she would do so.

Outside we could hear machine guns. Mr. Hafner, a sixty-year-old crippled man, told us to come to their cellar. Several of the neighbors were there, all huddled together like cattle in a storm. Mr. Hafner informed us that the prison camp was without SS guards and the prisoners were all over the roads. They were full of anger; looking for the SS guards to kill them. That was where the shooting came from. Mr. Hafner said that in two days the war would be over. The prisoners from the concentration camp told the civilians to have no fear of them, they had no intentions of harming us, they were only looking for SS guards.

There were no SS guards left in Mauthausen; they either killed themselves, or hid, or tried to escape. We were more afraid of the SS men in a desperate state of mind than of the prisoners.

All that day was calm, so we decided to take a look on the street. As we opened our gate and looked into the street, our eyes could not believe what we saw. Ex-prisoners, left unguarded, found the road open and just started walking, or actually crawling. Many young men were on crutches, or scuffling on little stubs of self-made blocks of wood, because some had no legs or arms, and others just part of each. How some made it those five miles was unbelievable. They just were so determined to get out of there. They asked us for food. Some were Russians and did not speak German. They just pointed at their stomachs.

Mrs. Topitz went inside and boiled some potatoes. When she took them outside, they grabbed them away in seconds and put them in their mouths whole, burning their mouths. They said the situation was unbelievable in the camp. They reassured us not to be afraid, that they did not hate or want to harm civilians, only SS guards they knew.

Then came the trustees. These were also prisoners, but in charge of the camp at the time. The trustees told these people that they had to return to the camp because there was no place to go yet.

The Americans were now entering Linz and would probably enter Mauthausen in a day or so, with food and medicine, but no one could leave the camp now before being checked by a doctor as there were many diseases rampant.

We were asked to give them no more food or water, as their stomachs would not be able to tolerate it. If they suddenly ate all they could, they would likely die.

By night most of the prisoners had returned to the camp, now void of SS guards, but still with closed gates because these people would need food, proper care, and medicine. The inhabitants of Mauthausen were absolutely unaware of the unspeakable horrors. We had heard that prisoners in the concentration camp were treated badly, but I can truthfully say that we, the family Topitz, and many other civilians in Mauthausen were just as disturbed about the horrors and conditions that were found there as the rest of the world.

It was some time in mid-April that with the Americans fighting on one side of the Elbe, and the Soviet army moving rapidly on the other side, we hoped things would come to an end soon. Then the 21st Infantry Division crossed the Danube and took over Mauthausen. We were relieved that the Americans took Mauthausen instead of the Russians. There had been very little fighting of any kind except between ex-prisoners and SS guards. They were still carrying machine guns. For days there were no planes in sight and no German defense near us. Austrian flags were already hanging out the windows, flags the Germans had ordered destroyed years ago. It was amazing how many people must have hidden them instead.

American Soldiers

As the Americans entered the village, I stood in the street watching the big trucks loaded with laughing soldiers pass by. They generously handed out candy bars, cocoa, and cigarettes. Some of them would throw me a candy bar when passing by. Candy was a special treat; we had not tasted any chocolate candy in years.

A few days later, Mr. Topitz and Albert returned safely home. Mr. Topitz was temporarily an assistant to the American authorities. Inge arrived home also. She spoke English fairly well and therefore made herself available to assist her father in his work with the Americans.

Every day I expected to either hear from Victor or see him appear off the ferry, or perhaps receive notice from the Red Cross. Many soldiers came home, but from Victor we heard nothing. Nearly every afternoon I looked out over the Danube watching the ferry cross. Every twenty minutes it went from one side of the Danube to the other. Often, I thought about home and my family. My mother was the dearest person in the world to me, so unselfish. I thought of how she tried not to cry the last day I was at home, how she wished me well, saying there was no wrong in my going and she would pray that the Lord may guide me all the way, because "your happiness is mine also" and she trusted me. In my heart I was so thankful for having been blessed with such an understanding and loving mother.

At those thought-filled moments I felt alone and lonely, and wished Victor would be home soon. There was nothing that could be done, but wait.

The next day, on Sunday, Mauthausen was completely occupied by Americans. The Catholic Church was to be officially re-opened for services with the American Commandant making an opening speech. Many people, young and old, were gathering at the square in front of the church. The priest and several nuns were present on the outside. The villagers applauded as the handsome young Lieutenant-Commandant made his appearance. He was undoubtedly the most handsome man I had seen up till then in my life. He spoke in perfect German, leading his speech in the direction of the wrong that had been done. He emphasized the greatest wrong of all, that of taking the lives of so many innocent people. He said, "A day of wrath, that day will be. Then will be brought out the book in which is written the complete record, that will decide each man's fate, and no sin will go without its due punishment."

He stood there tall and dark. When the priest entered, he made the sign of the cross and kneeled with the villagers. The voice of the priest then echoed:

"Agnus Dei, qui tollis peccáta mundi, miserére nobis." (Lamb of God, who takes away the sins of the world, have mercy on us).

Then he continued:

"Angus Dei, qui tollis peccáta mundi, dona nobis pacem." (Lamb of God, who takes away the sins of the world, grant us peace).

Many people were wiping their eyes. The Lieutenant had captured the hearts of most of the villagers. The people were very thankful for their American Catholic Commandant.

On June 11 we received the bad news that the right side of the Danube would be occupied by the Russians. The news was very disturbing, and at first, we refused to believe it. People who were not permanent residents of Mauthausen were already preparing to leave for the other side of the Danube. Many people, including Inge, said they were not taking any chances of remaining in Mauthausen in case it should be true that the Russians would take over that side of the Danube. I decided I would not make any plans until something definite was known. Where would I go anyway?

On June 17, it was announced in the paper that all non-Austrians had to report to the courthouse which was now occupied by American authorities. Immediate efforts would be made to return displaced persons to their homelands. Only if your country was now under Russian occupation would there be a possibility to remain. Of course, my reason for wanting to remain was strictly personal. I decided not to report to the courthouse at all. At that time, I was not interested in returning to Holland, as I was determined to wait for Victor's return. I would look out of the window watching the ferry take all non-Austrians to the other side of the Danube, to a small town named Enns. I asked Victor's parents for advice, but they said that was a matter I must decide for myself.

If I remained in Mauthausen and the Russians did take occupation, no one, not even the Austrian government, would be able to protect me because my own country, Holland, had ordered all her displaced citizens to return home.

Because I was not married to Victor, I would not be protected by the Austrian law. If he came home and we were married immediately, I would be an Austrian citizen protected by the Austrian government. Two weeks passed and the Americans were still occupying Mauthausen. We hoped they would stay instead of the Russians coming.

One day in July, the County Police sent a notice saying that Fraulein Cornelia Dykhorst was ordered to immediately make arrangements to return to Holland with a group transport leaving Linz in three days. Naturally, I was very upset. Inge decided she would go with me to talk to the American Commandant.

There were many people waiting at the courthouse, all trying to get permission to cross the Danube, as no one was permitted to cross the river without a permit. Some people were employed on the other side, others owned farmland, or had business reasons important enough to them to apply for a permit. The American commandant, Lieutenant Alex Berg, who spoke fluent German, was the only one in charge of these matters. I recognized him immediately because of the Sunday on the square when the Catholic Church was reopened to preach, as previously the German Nazi regime had censored the preaching in the churches. He was sitting behind his desk, with the top button of his uniform shirt unbuttoned, his tie loosened, and his feet on the desk, in a most relaxed position, and he was chewing gum in slow motion. We entered quietly but not unobserved. He didn't let on, but he was well aware of our presence. He told a young civilian employee who was not an American and who without doubt was not Austrian, to give us a seat. He said in German with an accent, that he would be with us in a moment. No one else was seated and in about twenty minutes, all the other people had gone. He was sitting there so relaxed that I calmed down also. Because he did speak German, Inge said for me to do my own explaining. I told him my reason for coming to his office, of my wish to remain in Mauthausen, and of the police order that I return home.

After I had explained all I thought was necessary, he looked somewhat amused, reared back in his chair, put away his gum, lit a cigarette, and said, "Okay, I will give you a permit to remain here if you are willing to make yourself useful." "Herr Lieutenant," I said, "I am not qualified for many things, what would you suggest I do?"

He looked at me with a puzzled expression, then said, "County officials suggest that all people who are not Austrian citizens and wish to remain here be willing to clean the streets."

I replied, "Herr Lieutenant, until I hear from my fiancé, it is important for me to remain here, but I have no intentions of cleaning streets. I am not a political refugee and I don't wish to be treated as such."

He inhaled the cigarette deeply, flipped his ashes in the ashtray and said, "Fraulein, I will give you permission to stay here, but everyone remaining here must work. That is the law." He paused, then looked at me, "You can work for me," he said.

I told him I could not do office work and also, I would like to discuss this with my prospective mother-in-law, Mrs. Topitz.

He got up from his chair and walked over to Inge. "Fraulein Topitz, would it be possible for me to explain everything to your mother myself tonight if it is convenient?"

Inge smiled and said that her mother would be honored to receive him at seven-thirty p.m.

As he walked us to the door, he said, "I will be very prompt."

Outside Inge said, "You really did make an impression on him, Corrie. I wonder if he really will show up tonight?"

At exactly 7:30 the doorbell rang, and Lieutenant Alex Berg stood there, very handsome in his beige uniform. Somehow, he seemed younger than I guessed him to be, about twenty-five years of age. He introduced himself to Mrs. Topitz, which was unnecessary because his position as Commandant of Mauthausen made him known to everyone. Gallantly he kissed Mrs. Topitz's hand, as is the custom in Austria, then told her he brought her a little gift. She blushed, but I knew she was flattered.

"You are very kind, Herr Lieutenant, will you have a seat please?"

She walked ahead of him into the living room as Inge and I followed. I noticed that he seemed impressed with the spacious living room, the tasteful arrangements, the beautiful oriental rugs, the grand piano, and the impressive velvet draperies.

He sat down, seeming comfortable and at ease.

Mrs. Topitz said, "I like the way Americans relax, they make themselves at home anywhere and they are so pleasant. He glanced at Inge and said, "We have reason to be pleasant; the war here has ended."

Mrs. Topitz opened the package he had brought. It contained two bars of Lux soap, two cans of peanuts, three small cans of ham and eggs, one large can of instant coffee, two Baby Ruth bars, and four packs of Lucky Strike cigarettes which were for Mr. Topitz, so the Lieutenant said.

Mrs. Topitz' eyes were filled with tears as she said, "May I offer you a glass of our oldest wine?"

He accepted.

When she walked across the room I was so proud of her, so glad that I was to become part of this fine family. With her large warm eyes and her olive complexion, she was a handsome woman.

After the Lieutenant finished his drink, he arose, complimented her on the good taste of the wine and asked her, flashing his charming smile, if she would give him permission to take Inge and me for an evening ride in his recently possessed convertible. The automobile had been taken from the Nazi village doctor. Mrs. Topitz looked at him with the eyes of a woman capable of a great deal of just observation as she said, "Very well, Herr Lieutenant, but not too late."

He kissed her hand. "Auf Wiedersehen, Mrs. Topitz," he said, "Miss Dykhorst may remain in Mauthausen as long as I am in command. How long we will be here I don't know; however, she must be willing to render small services."

"Just what would that consist of?" she asked.

"Well," he answered, "sometimes we do some entertaining and it would be nice to have a pleasant young lady to serve the refreshments."

"Would that mean keeping late hours?" she asked innocently.

"It could get late at times, but should that occur I will personally take full responsibility for her safety and welfare."

Mrs. Topitz smiled but did not answer.

I felt rather uneasy when Inge, Lieutenant Berg, and I walked to the car. It was quite a thrill to get to ride in a convertible and with a handsome American commandant. As we drove through the village, we brought forth some comment from the townspeople.

The lieutenant asked us to call him Alex, as that would sound so much friendlier. Then he asked Inge if she would mind the company of a good friend of his, Major Jimmy Taylor. She said she would love to brush up on her English. He was delighted to accompany Inge for a cool drive in the evening. He conversed with Inge in English because he did not speak German. Both Lieutenant Alex and Major Taylor were from Los Angeles. I told Lieutenant Alex that when I thought of California, I always pictured a beach with beautiful girls in bathing suits, lots of oranges and sunshine.

We returned home about eleven o'clock. Lieutenant Alex said he would pick me up at seven o'clock the following evening. He did not ask me; he just told me.

Quietly, Inge and I slipped up to our room and we talked a while about the very pleasant evening. The next day everything went as usual.

Inge helped with the daily chores, so we finished up earlier than usual. Mrs. Topitz did not mention the night before. However, she did ask me to go to the post office and ask for the mail. She said maybe there would be a letter from Victor or my parents. This was unusual because I had never been asked to pick up the mail. There was no mail for me.

I told Mrs. Topitz that the Lieutenant would call for me about seven o'clock and that I was to do some work for him. She said I might leave the table early to get dressed and Hedi was to help with the dishes this time. At seven o'clock on the dot, the Lieutenant announced himself. Mr. Topitz, who was home, received him. He was pleasant but very reserved. Mr. Topitz and the Lieutenant had met before at the courthouse, where Mr. Topitz was temporarily making himself useful because he was one of the few people in the village who spoke English. When we were about to leave, Mrs. Topitz said, in her calm pleasant voice, "Herr Lieutenant, I hope it won't be late before Corrie gets home."

"Dear Madam," (Genadige Frau) he said, "I will look after her and return her here myself, but we are expecting several guests and refreshments and drinks are to be served. Of course," he added, "I, myself, will help also."

"In that case, Herr Lieutenant, since that would be unfair to your guests, I insist that my daughter, Inge, render her service, also." She then handed me two small white aprons.

The Lieutenant laughed and said we would not need the aprons because they had many aprons, but he was delighted to have Inge help us out.

Somehow, I felt uncomfortable as we walked to the car.

Inge and I were really having a nice time before the guests were to arrive. The Lieutenant asked Inge to play something on the piano and he showed me some of the beautiful villa they temporarily occupied. While Inge was playing the piano, he said, "Corrie, I have a problem. I just wanted your company. I am not expecting any guests." I did not know what to say.

When Inge finished playing, she turned around and said, "Now, Herr Lieutenant, you might as well get me some company because you are going to be stuck with me all evening."

"I am very embarrassed," he said.

"My mother is a clever woman, Herr Lieutenant. She didn't believe a word you said about having people to entertain."

Lieutenant Alex arranged for Major Jimmy Taylor to join us. We ate crackers with cheese, drank champagne, Inge played the piano, and we danced. Lieutenant Alex said that the next day he had some business to attend to and that he wanted Inge and me to go along.

We went across the Danube to Enns, to the Red Cross; a few days later we went through the former concentration camp. The American Red Cross and the Swiss Red Cross, better known as the International Red Cross, had done as much as possible in the line of giving aid and food. Many people were transported in trucks on cots, then put on hospital-equipped ships and from there to hospitals. The situation was unbelievable, and I had to ask myself "why did God allow this incredible horror to go on for so long?"

For days I couldn't put the awful things out of my mind. We didn't talk much about it; we just kept our thoughts to ourselves. Inge, the Lieutenant, and I went to many other places where he had business to conduct.

Wednesday, the Lieutenant told me he would like to take Inge and me to the first dance that would be open to all girls in the village. I must admit I was flattered.

Mrs. Topitz said that as long as we stayed in the right place and conducted ourselves as was considered proper in the eyes of the townspeople, Inge and I had her permission to attend the dance. The Lieutenant was so gallant, and I felt so excited as if I were walking on air. Inge seemed to be having a good time, too. We came home rather late, but Inge and I had such a wonderful time that we were unaware of the hour.

The following morning, after breakfast, as we were putting away the dishes, Mrs. Topitz said, "And Corrie, tell me how does the Lieutenant kiss?"

The question was so unexpected, I was somewhat shocked.

"Well," I said, "not having been kissed very often, I do not know whether or not he kisses well."

"But he did kiss you?" she asked.

"Yes, he did," I answered. I felt most uncomfortable then.

"Did you think about Victor when he kissed you?" she inquired.

"I don't know what I thought about" I replied, hurt.

"Well, let's begin to think some then," she said. "Corrie, this is a small town, and it is important what the villagers think about you, but what is more important, is what you think of yourself. A kiss you may not consider much; but would you like for Victor to be kissing a girl?"

"No, I guess not," I replied nearly in a whisper.

She said then, "I am not angry with you, Corrie, I just don't want you to lose yourself before you give yourself a chance. I know it has not been easy for you since we have no assurance that Victor is...all right."

I said I meant no harm nor even wanted to cause her any worry. I knew she worried enough already.

I told her I thought I did understand and I wished that Victor would be home soon.

Weeks passed without any word from him and most of the Austrian soldiers had returned.

One afternoon Lieutenant Alex told me that at the end of the month Mauthausen would become Russian occupation territory. It was for sure and he could do nothing for me because the permission he had granted would not be valid under Russian occupation. He also said that because I was not a citizen of Austria and my own country had ordered all their landsmen back to Holland, it would be unwise for me to remain in Mauthausen. He said he would be stationed as Commandant of Aschach a/d Danube until he was to go to Linz to be the adjutant of General Mark Clark, who was now rumored to be either in Linz or Vienna. He said I could remain in Aschach if I wished, but he could not guarantee me any certain length of time.

I was very depressed from not knowing what to do. I decided to walk to the ferry and talk with some people who were leaving. They just had their suitcases, as the rumor had spread rapidly over the small town.

Inge said she definitely would not remain in Mauthausen. She spoke three languages, was a graduate nurse, and had special training in many fields. It would not be difficult for her to get a job, either for the Americans in an office or a hospital. Getting to work for the American authorities meant three meals a day and that of course was considered pure good fortune.

Saturday at four p.m. the ferry would quit operating by military order. Two American MPs were standing guard. A medical student from Vienna, a girl my own age, said to me, "Fraulein, are you not planning to leave here?" She had one large suitcase with her.

I told her I didn't know, but after talking with her fifteen minutes, I decided to get packed. She was going to Aschach, also.

Aschach, on the other side of Linz, a resort place on the Danube, still had some space for refugees traveling through. No one without a permit could remain in a town more than two days because of the food shortage. They did not welcome strangers there. The war was over, and they wanted people to go back to where they came from.

When I went to the house to pack my things, Hedi cried because she was so worried about me. Mr. and Mrs. Topitz were not at home, so I left them a note. Of course, they knew all about the disturbances. Many of the townspeople preferred to leave their homes taking just one suitcase, in order to live in the American or British zones. Many people thought Russia wanted to be friends, but they were wrong.

I decided to pack only my summer clothes. I just left my winter coat and dresses and snow boots with the Topitz family.

On the ferry we were offered a ride to Enns in a Jeep with Americans, which we gladly accepted. When we arrived in Enns we decided to go to the American Red Cross. It was nearly seven o'clock, and only Americans were allowed on the streets after nine o'clock. It was impossible for us to get to Linz that night, as there was no truck, train, or any other transportation. At the American Red Cross, they gave us some light bread and cheese to eat. As we were eating, an officer that we did not know had been observing us said, "Girls, for one night I am going to give you my room. I will sleep in the barracks with my men, but remember, one night only, tomorrow you both can come to the mess hall where we will give you some pancakes (we did not know what they were) and there will be a Jeep leaving for Linz at eight o'clock. You are to make sure you don't miss that Jeep. Otherwise, you'll have to walk to Linz."

Renate, who spoke pretty good English said, "Sir, America can be proud of a gentleman like you."

He said, "Well, we certainly can't let you stand on the street all night, and it is too late to get quarters anywhere."

Laughingly, he added, "We couldn't let you sleep in the barracks, so what can I do?"

Then he showed us his room, said good night, and told us to lock the door.

The next day we left at about eight thirty and were in Linz at eleven o'clock. We bought tickets for Everdingen. The train would depart about twelve o'clock noon. There was a sign on the train saying, "Off limit for all non-Austrians." But there was a far more depressing sign on the locomotive, placed there by Jews, displaced Poles, and other homeless people who could not return to their homeland because of Communism.

The sign read:

"Mann hatte Mich gefragt...was quelt dich denn so sehr...

Und Ich habe Ihn gesaght,

Wohin ist denn unser schicksal...

Wiz habe keine heimat mehr..."

It meant:

"They asked me, from whence cometh my woe?

And I answered them...there is no place for them

Where can my people go..."

There were hundreds of pitiful looking people at the stations with bundles and old suitcases, people who once had homes, and a country of belonging, they were not on transport and even they did not know where they were going.

I decided to ignore the sign about non-Austrians. I did not know anyone in Linz and I could not remain on the street. Luck was with me; no one seemed to doubt that I was Austrian. I just handed the conductor my ticket, he tore half off and handed it back to me. I did not talk in the train, not even to Renate. At five o'clock in the evening we arrived in Everdingen. We went to a gasthous to get a bite to eat. On our ration card we got one potato, one-half cucumber, and something like scrambled liver. It really tasted very good, but there was not enough of it.

It was still about six kilometers to Aschach. We just had to try to make it. We started out walking on the country road. It was getting very cloudy and after about twenty minutes, it started to rain. Then came a severe thunderstorm. The road was deserted and we were scared. We decided to make it to the next house. It was only about five hundred yards, just far enough to get us soaked. The people gave us shelter until the storm passed. We told them we had to go to Aschach. They said it would be difficult to travel with our suitcases because the roads were bad after rain.

We accepted their offer to keep our luggage there until maybe the following day or so when we would be less tired, and the weather would be better, we could come back and pick them up. When the rain had stopped, we took only a few things out of the suitcase, and we continued our walk to Aschach.

It was nearly 10:30 when we got there. We decided to wait until the next morning to contact Lieutenant Alex Berg, mainly because we looked like two drowned dogs. We went to the Burgemeister's home and some one there, very friendly, gave us permission to get a straw mattress and an army blanket in the school. The school was only five minutes away. There were many people from Mauthausen in the school. On the glass doors were signs saying, "Men only," "Women only," or "Women and children." We were on the second floor with about twenty other women. There were washbasins available and a curtain made from army blankets was hung to give some privacy, in case you desired to wash up. Downstairs in front of the school was a pump. Things were not too bad; it was clean, the war was over, and we could stretch out and have a good night's sleep.

The next day it was ten o'clock before we woke up to a beautiful day. I was just sitting on my mattress looking around in the classroom (things did not look as good in the daytime) when suddenly I was aware of someone standing near me. It was Lieutenant Alex Berg. I was so shocked and embarrassed that I began to cry. But he was so very nice. He said he would do all he could to get us, Renate and me, a room somewhere as soon as he had taken care of finding shelter for the aged, the sick, and the women expecting babies. He said he could take us after our luggage in about one hour.

In the meantime, Renate and I cleaned ourselves up as well as possible. No matter how difficult the circumstances, I always tried to look my best and take care of my clothes. Lieutenant Berg brought two bars of Lux soap and two army towels, one box of crackers, and a can of Nescafe.

When we first arrived at the home of the people who had been kind enough to keep our suitcases, they were frightened at the sight of Lieutenant Berg's convertible with an American official emblem on it. But Lieutenant Berg set them at ease and pleased them by giving them a jar of coffee for helping us.

When we returned, Lieutenant Berg had to return to the office and we went back to the school. The next morning, to my surprise and joy, who walked in but Inge! She seemed glad to see me and handed me a letter from her parents. The letter made me feel much better; it said even though we were several miles apart, the connection was still the same and if I should need any money, they had given Inge a sufficient amount to provide for my needs. Inge intended to stay in the school also until we could find a place with the help of Lieutenant Berg.

Inge brought with her most of her clothes, some books, blankets, sheets, and pillowcases. We fixed our own corner for Renate, Inge, and myself. It was separated by army blankets to give us privacy. We had a round, old dishpan we used for a wash pan. I used the precious Lux soap only for my face because soap was an extreme luxury. I had war soap that I used for bathing, but that didn't smell so good. We had very few food coupons. So far, we had managed to eat lunch and supper in the town's gasthouse. There were two places to eat. You gave them your weekly supply of food ration coupons and that gave you the right of eating two meals a day. Individuals could not possibly manage to cook and prepare a meal from the very small amount of food available for the coupons. For breakfast we just tried to sleep late and at twelve o'clock we would go to the nice clean gasthouse, where everyone sat at tables accommodating about twenty people. For lunch we were served soup with carrots, cabbage, and cream of wheat. The Austrians surely did have an art for making it taste good. They really knew how to cook, even with so few ingredients. We met several of the townspeople there as we picked our table carefully.

After about fourteen days in the school, Lieutenant Berg told me that he had found us a nice lodging, a room in the home of the druggist and his wife. They had no children, and they had one extra room that Lieutenant Berg ordered them to make available for refugees employed by the American officials.

We moved that same night. There were only two beds, so we had to take turns sleeping on the floor. But we were overjoyed with the nice room. There was no running water, but we could get water in the hall only a few steps away. We also had an iron and ironing board, and we used Inge's sheets.

I don't think the druggist and his wife were exactly happy about our moving in, but then again, they probably had to make the room available anyway. They should have been pleased to have three nice clean girls.

No company of any kind was allowed in the room, not even the Lieutenant. That was all right with me, but the following week, Renate disobeyed the house rule and Inge caught her in an embarrassing situation with her soldier boyfriend. Inge immediately became very indignant and told her that she could not remain there. Renate was not angry, for she said her boyfriend, "Hank" from New York, had a much better place already. So, the girl who was studying to become a doctor, moved out with my only pair of silk stockings and my precious bar of Lux soap. Inge said not to worry about the soap, and that we should just be glad to be rid of her before she might take off with our suitcases.

That night Inge and I were invited to a dinner party in the officers' mess hall. We really looked forward to it, but we decided to eat first our regular rations in the gasthouse, so we would be more able to control our desire for good food. Arriving at the party at 7:30, after eating in the gasthouse at six o'clock, we still found it rather difficult to act lady-like and refrain from loading up our plates. The food was still limited, the Lieutenant said, because much of their supplies went to the ex-prisoners in the concentration camp. They had sufficient food for their occupation troops, but usually, he said, they had fried chicken and dessert. Nevertheless, we were happy with what they gave us, cold meat, white bread, coffee with cream. We did eat too much because we thought this occasion might never arise again. It was rather embarrassing when Lieutenant Alex said, when he brought us home, that he never saw two women eat so much. Once in our room, Inge asked me if I ate all I wanted. I said, "no, I could have eaten twice that much." She said she could have, too.

The following day, I passed Renate on the street and she stopped to talk to me. She said she had a nice place to live, on a ship on the Danube with a Yugoslavian family. I told her I was glad for her and to try to overlook Inge. She had turned bitter on many things since her fiancé, Rudi, was killed just before the war had ended. She hardly ever talked about him and her mother had told me she didn't even cry when she received word of his death.

I had asked Inge, "you didn't cry or anything when you heard about him getting killed?"

She just looked at me with so much sadness and said, "Corrie, if crying could bring him back, I'd gladly cry a tub full."

Renate said she lost everyone dear to her. Both her parents were killed in an air attack in Vienna, and her sister was trapped for three weeks in a shelter and starved to death. She said she didn't care what happened to her anymore.

There was nothing I could think of to say that would even make sense in such a dreadful situation. Then I said, "Renate, maybe your friend, you know, your Hank, maybe everything will work out for you and him."

She suddenly turned around and said, "Nothing is going to work out for me. I have been cheated, I did not want to lose them all and survive alone."

She left. I felt miserable about that poor, unhappy girl. I thought how I would feel if I had lost all my loved ones. What would my attitude be toward a new life? The war had ended, but the aftereffects were just beginning.

When I returned to the house, Inge and I had a few words over Renate.

Daily we ate in the gasthouse. At our table I met a young woman named Mary Albrecht. She had a very well behaved six-year-old son, Reino. I liked her from the beginning; she was pleasant, attractive, and dressed well. She asked me to visit her in her small two-room apartment right by the Danube in Aschach, a summer resort.

The following day I went to see the young woman I had met. She was from Vienna, and because of the daily bombing, she had been evacuated during the war. Mothers with small children were urged to do so. She had married a German dentist seven years before and had lived in Berlin during the first three years of her marriage, in a nice suburb called Wilhelmstadt." Then when the bombing began, Reino and she moved back to Vienna to be with her parents for as long as her husband had to serve in the army. She said, nearly crying as she did, that she had heard nothing from him in sixteen months, except a letter from his commanding officer saying he was missing.

Again, I felt words inadequate, so I just remained silent.

Then she spoke again, "Now, Reino and I are making out fine in this small town, it restores my nerves, except I do worry very much about the well-being of my parents. She made the sign of the cross and said, "I am Catholic; I'll pray God guides over them." She said she expected to hear from them any day now. Three days later she was all smiles when she told me her parents were all right, that they wrote and told her to stay where she was, because in Vienna most people were close to starvation, but they would do all they could to survive. With tears dripping down her face, she said, “I am so thankful; those dear, dear souls.”

I liked her, she was so responsive, so different from the distant Inge. I admired her pleasantness and she carried herself as if she had not a worry in the world.

Inge told me she had the promise of a job at the American Headquarters in Linz, because of her acquaintance with a young Lithuanian woman, a mother of two little girls, five and six years old. The mother, who was employed as an interpreter at the American headquarters, had not been able to find adequate living accommodations in Linz for herself and her little girls, Modithe and Maja. They now lodged temporarily with relatives until the end of the month. Inge had offered that at the end of the month, if she had not found anything, the two girls could come to stay with us in that one room. We would manage somehow, Inge had said.

The rumor went that Lieutenant Alex Berg was to become Adjutant to General Mark Clark. This he never denied nor admitted. He told me he was leaving Aschach in about two weeks. I thought I would not be permitted to remain in the nice room. It was only because of the kindness of Lieutenant Berg that Inge and I had been allowed the room in the first place. And sure enough, three days after it became known that the Lieutenant had left Aschach, I was called to the Burgemeister’s office. He explained that because I was not employed by the American authorities, he thought it was his duty to look after people more in need of a private room than I, because pregnant women, sick people, and the aged were still living in the school. He said I would be permitted to remain in Aschach, but I would have to move back in the school or in barracks provided for refugees.

At once I went home and told Inge. She remained annoyingly calm and said, with her nose in the air, “we will manage the best way we can.”

The next day Lieutenant Berg came just to see us and said he was leaving permanently and advised me to go to the Netherlands consulate in Linz. He said he could take me that day in the car. He said I should look into that immediately in case something should be wrong, he meant in case Victor should not return, I wouldn't become "Staatenlos," that is, no citizen of any country.

I asked Inge to go along, but she said she had too much to do. So, I asked Mary, and she said she would enjoy the trip very much. At the Netherlands consulate I got permission to remain in Aschach for three months. I certainly was relieved. Then I went to see Victor's grandfather, who was a retired professor and lived in Linz.

When I rang the doorbell, the old professor's housekeeper, Mitzi, apparently in her sixties, opened the door. Lieutenant Berg had given me several candy bars, which I had saved for Mitzi's grandchildren, but the 80-year old man began to cry and said the candy was for him, that the children didn't know what candy tasted like anyway. I told him I had brought him two fine cigars, but he insisted the candy was to be his also. The housekeeper said to give the candy to him; he had become so childish. I asked if they had any mail from Victor because we expected that Victor would write to an American occupied town before writing to his parents in the Russian occupation zone. They had no mail from Victor.

During my visit, Lieutenant Berg had been patiently waiting, and Mary had been looking after some business concerning her return to Vienna.

When we returned to Aschach, Lieutenant Berg told us goodbye because he would not be back in Aschach; in fact, officially he had already left there.

In the afternoon, as I was coming out of the bakery from getting our bread rations, I noticed Mary waiting on me. She asked me if I had found a new place to live or if we intended to live in the barracks. I told her we planned to look for a room or someplace the next day. She then said that in the house where she rented, there was a large front room that was empty, that maybe I could persuade the landlady into renting the room to us. Mary said she would be willing to share the small kitchen which was in between the large front room and Mary's room.

The landlady agreed to let us have the room for twenty marks a month. It contained two beds, a wash table, and an old stove. There was no glass in the windows. Of course, with the coming winter, that was going to be bad. But at the moment, that was of no importance as we could hang army blankets to keep the dust and sun out. For safety there were heavy iron bars across, like in prison. I liked that protection.

The house rule was that no one could enter after ten o'clock. The landlady kept the outdoor key, so no one could enter through the main door after hours. If we expected relatives, she would give us an extra key. She was a retired old maid schoolteacher, she appeared to be about 75 years old.

There also was a Mrs. Hartel who lived upstairs. She told Mary she had not been with a man since her husband left to fight in the war and had not heard from him in four years.

Inge and I moved that night. We had several extra army blankets and put them to serve as rugs on the floor. The floor was wood and spotless. The landlady gave us four chairs, a wooden table, and a large mirror. We also hung the blankets over the windows, and after everything was placed, we liked it very much under the circumstances. There was a pump in the back yard and a laundry room to wash clothes. We were provided with a tub and scrub board, and a clothesline put up in the completely private yard. In our room we put up a line so we could empty our suitcases and hang our dresses.

Of course, when Inge moved to Linz, I would have the room all to myself. At the moment, all the money I had was about 80 marks. I would just have to ask Inge for a little money in case she should go to Linz.

We became acquainted with several nice people in the gasthouse.

Most of the homeless refugees had left Aschach to stay in camps because the small town could only quarter at the most 200 refugees. We met a Greek doctor, Milto Dimitriano, and a Greek diplomat, Gova Dacosta. The two had spent six years in concentration camps as political undesirables. Gove Dacosta apparently liked me because he insisted daily that I eat half his ration of food. I certainly was embarrassed, but Inge insisted, saying he would be deeply hurt if I refused to eat it. Until I had finished my plate, he would keep his eyes on me like a mother watching her child eat. It made me very uncomfortable.

There were nights when Inge and I were in bed that he would knock on our window. Inge always answered his knock, and he would be standing under the window with a bunch of grapes and then would say, "For Fraulein Corrie, for the hunger." He had stolen them somewhere that night from a grape orchard. Inge would thank him and then tell him he could not keep standing there, it was late and he must go away. He would just look and then walk away. It seemed rather pitiful because neither of us could speak his language. I felt sorry for him, but after all it was his own doing, and it would please me if he stopped it.

The days passed in the same routine way. We would try to sleep as late as possible—that way it would not be long until time for lunch and we didn't need anything for breakfast. After Mary, Inge, and I would return from the gasthouse where we ate our meager lunch, we would take our army blankets and stretch out by the Danube in the sun trying to get a tan. It was so pleasant, about 78 degrees. The three of us looked all right, and if it hadn't been for a miserable, hungry feeling most of the time, we could have been pretty content, except of course that each of us had our personal troubles.

Mary's husband was missing, Inge's Rudy was killed in the war, and I had a daily longing to hear from Victor. Sometimes I began to lose hope, for people told me that more than likely he would have written if he were in an American (our Allies) prisoner of war camp. Inge offered little encouragement. She would say, "I suppose in time we will know."

She then told me that she had been notified that the two little girls, Modithe and Maja, were due to arrive any day.

One night when we were in bed, she talked about the time she and Rudi were together, of how she had looked forward to be his wife. They had made so many plans and now everything seemed so meaningless. I felt deeply sympathetic toward her; fate had played an unkind part on her. She showed no emotion except that she began to talk faster and faster. I just let her talk; it would be better if she did talk about him now and then.

Modithe and Maja arrived the following day. Their mother brought them. She said as soon as the job came open for Inge, she would make efforts to find an adequate place for all of them in Linz. She brought some American supplies such as powdered milk, powdered eggs, ham and eggs in cans, cheese and crackers, soap, and toothpaste. She definitely was well-educated, but her two pretty, little blond-haired girls were obviously neglected. Every stitch of clothes they wore needed mending, laundering, and ironing. All week Inge and I were busy repairing and laundering the girls' clothes. It was fun to look after Modithe and Maja, they were so obedient and undemanding. At night, before going to bed, Inge prepared a little snack for them from the things their mother had brought. On their rations they would eat with us in the gasthouse.

Later in the month the first dance for American soldiers and Austrian girls was to take place. Mary and Inge planned to attend. They asked me if I would take care of the children, Mary's son, Reino, and Modithe and Maja. When Saturday night came, they were prettied up in their best outfits, and in good spirits, prepared to have a good time. They instructed me to take good care of the children, to give them their little snack they had prepared, and put them to bed at eight o'clock.

When Inge and Mary left, I thought neither of them had been kind enough to offer me as much as one cracker. After giving the children their snack and putting them to bed at eight, I went to bed also. I felt sorry for myself and there was nothing to do.

I pretended to be asleep when I heard Mary and Inge come in. I overheard that they had had a liquid named "Coca-Cola" and peanuts mixed with other nuts, and big hunks of cheese with crackers. My eyes filled with tears; they had not even offered me a few crackers. I wondered if they maybe had forgotten, and finally I fell asleep.

The following morning, Inge asked me if the children had been any trouble. I told her all three of them were well-behaved children. I asked her if she had enjoyed the evening before and she said they had had a nice time, and she told me about this drink, "Coca-Cola," which Mary and she said was delicious. She said that the next Saturday night there would be another dance that they both would attend. I felt very much left out, but after all, I was engaged, even if not officially. I still was waiting for Victor's return.

I began to wonder about Victor, and at times became very confused. Mary and Inge were going to the dances twice a week now while I tended to the three children. Then one day I became seriously ill. I fainted in the bathroom and Inge went for the doctor. He said it was my stomach, that I needed more substantial food such as bread, butter, potatoes, and if possible, meat.

For weeks I had lived on a diet of cucumbers, soup, and cabbage, and about 400 grams of bread for a week. Inge told me I should get bread at least one week old because it would have more food value. I told her she did not buy bread that was one week old. Then she explained that she did not have to because she was fortunate to have an American soldier friend who supplied her with some food.

When they left the following Saturday night for the dance, I asked if they could bring me back a so-called Coca-Cola. But they said that no one was allowed to take anything out.

That night after I put the children to bed, I felt so hungry and forlorn that I decided to make myself a cracker sandwich, so I took two crackers and put a very little ham and eggs on them. I felt justified in eating them since I kept the children for them and they gave me nothing to eat.

Again, I pretended to be asleep when Inge and Mary came home. The next morning Inge accused me of getting into the crackers and that a heaping spoonful of ham and eggs had disappeared out of the can. I looked at her and said, "How are you so sure how many crackers are missing?"

She said that she had counted them and that I was the only one to be tempted by the crackers. I told her she should think it her place to share some of the food with me now and then; after all I did look after the children for her while she was out having fun.

She said from then on, I had better learn to look after myself, and she would look after the children. She said then, "Corrie, in this time of food shortage, everyone does look out for themselves only, and I certainly do not intend to share what little food I get with anyone."

I said nothing, but I thought plenty, and I made up my mind to go to the dances myself and get something to eat, too.

Mary never interfered between Inge and me.

I went to the bakery a few days later to get my bread rations. Kurt, the eighteen-year old son of the bakery owner, had told me several times before that he would like to take me as his guest to the American dance. He was given the privilege of taking one person because he played the piano for the band. He was so nice and treated me quite casually. Because he was a local boy and only eighteen, I saw no harm in accepting. So that day I told him I would like to accept if his invitation still stood. He said he would pick me up at eight o'clock Saturday night.

On Thursday afternoon before the dance, I was in the yard attempting to start a fire to heat a tub of water to do some laundry. Suddenly I became aware that someone was watching me. A handsome American soldier was looking out of Frau Hartel's window. He said in a pleasing manner, "Would you like me to start that fire for you?"

I was almost ready to give up all hope of getting it started, so I gratefully accepted. The reason for him being upstairs in Frau Hartel's house was that she took in washings for American soldiers. That way she received enough soap to do her own laundry, also.

He started the fire without any trouble. He then asked me if I was "frau" or "fraulein." I said, "something in between," because I did not know how to explain being engaged. He spoke hardly any German and I spoke very little English. Apparently, he took it differently because he laughed and said, "Good, frau, nix good, I like frauleins."

There was something about his manner that was very appealing, and he was very nice and clean-cut looking. He didn't seem so sure of himself as did most American soldiers in Austria. They just seemed to take girls for granted.

I thanked him nicely and went inside to get my laundry. I waited there until I saw him leave the house. When I was back in the yard finishing my laundry, Mary came outside and said, "Now, Corrie, how would you like him?"

I told her I didn't like him, which was not true. Then I told her that I planned to go to the Saturday night dance with Kurt, the son of the owner of the bakery, had asked me to be his guest. Mary did not answer. Then after a minute or so, she said, "Who will look after the children?"

I did not want to speak sharply because after all that was the only home I had for the moment, so I said maybe she and Inge could get someone.

Mary smiled. She was pleasant about it, and said, "Oh, well, I don't blame you, Corrie, and don't worry about the children. We'll make a way."

Saturday afternoon I learned that they had arranged for Frau Hartel to look in on the children every now and then after they were first put to bed.

All three of us were getting prettied up for the dance. Then to my great surprise who walked in but the soldier I had been talking to in the yard on the Thursday before. He gave me an approving look and followed Mary into her room. Mary's American friend, Sammy, arrived a few minutes later.

Then Mary invited us, Inge and me, to join them for a highball.

When at eight o'clock Kurt arrived to pick me up, the American gave him a strange look but did not say anything. After instructions were given to Frau Hartel and the three children were put to bed, Mary and Sammy, Inge with the handsome soldier, and Kurt and I left for the dance.

I looked forward to drinking a bottle of the often talked about Coca-Cola which the Americans referred to as a "soft drink." I had been told they also served crackers with cheese and all sorts of fancy nuts.

The six of us were seated at a round table, all of us in pretty good spirits. The band was about to start, so Kurt had to leave the table to play the piano. They started playing "Lady Be Good" and Mary was on the dance floor melting away in the arms of her American, but more Italian looking, friend. Also, Inge and her friend made for the dance floor. Shortly several American soldiers asked me to dance, but I did not accept because I thought that unfair to Kurt, who was so considerate. Then I heard the remark that one of the soldiers made, "I guess she thinks herself too good for enlisted men. She has been the girl of Lieutenant Berg." So, when Inge's friend, Roland, asked me to dance, I accepted.

While we were dancing, he told me that Mary had led him to believe that I was to be his date, rather than Inge, and he had been so confused when he saw me with a date. Mary then had explained that I had not been interested, but that another girl who lived in the house also would like for him to take her to the dance. Inge and he had not been acquainted formerly, but Inge apparently liked him. I told him that, but he only said, "Inge is alright, but I have no intentions of dating her. Of course, I could not have backed out tonight after I was already at the house."

I explained that I was at the dance just to be getting out of the house and I was with a local friend, not a date, because I did not go out with anyone as I was engaged to Inge's brother, and whether I would ever hear from him, I didn't know. All of this I explained in a combination of self-made words of English, German, and many motions of the hands.

Inge was sitting at the table alone, so I told him we must return to our table. We did not dance any more that night, but I made sure I got my share of cheese, crackers, and Coca-Colas.

At eleven o'clock the place closed and the six of us walked home. I told Kurt good night at the door and thanked him for having me as his guest. Mary, Sammy, Inge, and Roland were gone to play cards in Mary's room. After I said good night and went to bed, I lay there wondering if Victor were alive and in a prison camp. If so, why didn't he write???

Mary told me a few days later that Roland had asked her to let him know whenever I wanted him to take me to the dance.

Inge told us she would be leaving for Linz the middle of next month. The mother of Modithe and Maja had found Inge a job and housing for the four of them.

Mary said she had given up hope of ever hearing anything definite about her husband and that she would go to Linz to apply for her native Austrian citizenship.

I received a card from the Red Cross informing me that my parents were alive and well and that they had received my Red Cross message.

That week Mary and I went to Linz. She had asked me to go along as she intended to apply for her former Austrian citizenship, and I would inquire again about Victor. She suggested that we take the Danube cruiser instead of the bus. It would be slow but relaxing and inexpensive. I enjoyed that very much.

At the information desk concerned with missing German soldiers, they knew nothing of Victor. Mary put in her application for citizenship. The following day as we discussed our trip at the gasthouse, the Greek doctor said I had just as well give up hope, that I lived in a nightmare thinking of Victor. He said that after the first World War, some mothers, wives, and fiancées had tied themselves down for the rest of their lives hoping and believing in the return of their loved ones. It was not that he was personally interested in me, but he said it was time I faced the facts. After that I fell into a state of depression.

Inge and Mary were invited regularly to the American dance and often to dinner. But Inge was not what one could call "dating" any one in particular.

The time for Inge to leave for Linz drew nigh. I asked her one morning if she could leave me a little money, as her parents had told me in a letter that they had given her some money to give to me.

"Well," she said, "first of all, I have paid the rent up for the next two weeks and also paid for food in the gasthouse for two more weeks, and by that time the money was gone. Look, Corrie, I told you before that in this world we must take care of ourselves and I do just that. It will be my brother, Victor, who must look after you, not me; and when I leave for Linz in a few days, you are on your own."

That evening I was talking to Mary and told her I did not know what to do. Three days later Inge left with her books, linens, blankets, and Modithe and Maja. I was alone with the room rent and my food paid for two more weeks. I felt blue. Mary talked very kindly to me. She said life is full of unpredictable, unpleasant times. We just have to pass through it from day to day. So, many after effects of the war we had to learn to live with.

On Thursday noon, the day after Inge left for Linz, as I was eating in the gasthouse, the village clerk brought me a message. The burgemeister wanted to see me at once. I was worried because I probably would have to leave the room, and within six weeks cold weather would arrive.

The burgemeister was pleasant; he asked me to take a seat and said he hoped I would cooperate concerning my room. He explained that a couple, man and wife, who were now living in the school, were very much in need of a room and if I would be willing to share my room with them, he would refurnish it with new army furniture, two new beds, two wardrobes, and a cook stove. He added that they were nice people. The man was a political ex-prisoner, released from the concentration camp, and his wife was an eighteen-year old refugee from Sudetenland.

I asked him if I could meet them. Immediately he sent the clerk to the school. The man, Will Muller, came alone; he explained that his wife was, because she was pregnant, not feeling well. Her condition was the reason the burgemeister was trying to find them a more private lodging than the school. The man seemed to be about forty years old and had the appearance and manner of a gentleman.

I told the burgemeister it was all right with me if the landlady agreed. He said the landlady had praised me highly and if I agreed, persuading her would be no problem.

The couple agreed to pay fifteen shillings a month, which left me only five shilling a month to pay. The landlady did not raise the rent. The new furniture was sent out immediately and Friedel and Will moved in that night. They were nice and agreeable people and really an asset to me. Friedel, a country girl out of a family of eleven, was used to long hours of hard work and considered herself very fortunate to have such a nice clean room. She said she would prepare meals at home every day since she had a stove to cook on. They received two American Red Cross food parcels a month; they had a small supply of food, some beans, a sack of flour, and several cans of U.S. meat. She said she would like to cook for me also, if I gave her my rations.

I told her that my food supply was just that which I got from my ration card. I explained that I had no money and that even if I did have money, I had no connections to get anything in the black market. Will asked me if I had a green D.P. (displaced person's) card. I told him I did. He said I had a political "safe" card, all I needed to do was to go to Linz to the Netherlands consulate and have a stamp put on my card saying I had been given permission to remain in Austria for the time being. Then I would be entitled to two American Red Cross food parcels a month, a gift from American civilians for a starving nation except for German Nazi collaborators. He said he was sure I would be eligible and that I should apply for them before the month was out.

The next day Mary and I went to Linz. I had no difficulties getting my card stamped. All green cards were given the parcels, they said. The Red Cross Headquarters for food parcels was established in a small town, Grieskirchen. I would have to go there to receive them.

We took the bus early the next morning for Grieskirchen. Many people were lined up and only with a lot of pushing and elbow twisting did we manage to get a standing place on the overloaded bus. During the two-and-a-half hours of driving over dusty roads, we had three flats. But it was fun; most of the passengers seemed not to mind at all and carried on pleasant conversations.

When we arrived in Grieskirchen, I expected to receive my American Red Cross food parcels without any trouble. But I had to sign up and then after a week when my new supplies arrived, I would receive two food parcels. We left very disappointed.

Our eyes caught a sign on a small gasthouse, "Soup Today," no ration card required. We went inside. As was true of most Austrian cafes in the country, this one was clean and friendly, and besides, the smells coming from the kitchen were promising. We sat down at a table by a young man in work clothes who was enjoying his soup, making a loud sipping noise. Looking up at us he said, soup dripping from his chin, "Mensch, (folks), this soup is good." At which Mary answered smiling, "Yes, we noticed by the sound." I thought perhaps he would be embarrassed, but he just laughed, showing a flash of most beautiful teeth. Mary and I ordered our soup, wondering what it was made of, but we decided we would rather not ask—it might ruin the taste if we knew.

Our bus was scheduled for three p.m. to return to Aschach, and we remained in the café until we saw people lining up. The old bus was right on time and hobbled faithfully all the way.

I hated to tell Will and Friedel that it would be another week before I would receive my food parcels. But when I told them, Friedel said she wanted to fix my meals anyway. I told her how nice and considerate she was. She, as young as she was and short, made for an odd match beside the nearly bald, six foot, 200-pound, jovial looking Will. He was so considerate and pleasant to his expecting little wife that I enjoyed them being there.

The following week after I returned with my food parcels, I told them half of the food was theirs, and with the other Friedel would prepare my meals now and then. She claimed she enjoyed cooking since she had more ingredients. There was also in each parcel one carton of cigarettes. I did not smoke; therefore, I sold one carton of cigarettes in the black market for 200 shillings, clearing my money shortage. The other carton I used to exchange for stockings, shampoo, a couple packs to have my shoes repaired, and then some to get an extra potato or a piece of meat in the gasthouse.

Roland

The first signs of fall began to appear; the days seemed longer and more lonesome. Mary and her boyfriend, Sammy, who were becoming very attached, asked my permission to bring this American soldier, Roland, to the house one evening to play cards. I agreed, remembering the nice clean-cut looking American. We had a good time and I accepted his invitation for the Saturday night dance.

On the following Wednesday he took me to an American movie.

I enjoyed going to movies, but I could not understand much of the English spoken in the movie. This handsome American soldier was different from any person I had ever known before, soft-spoken, full of life, and easy to get along with.

My memories of Victor were fading somewhat.

We got along, the four of us, Sammy and Mary, Roland and me. Every Saturday night we went to the American dance and on Wednesday to the American movie, taking Reino along then, also. Roland and I did not carry on much of a conversation because of the language difference. We just exchanged expressions and of course we continued going places together, including taking walks along the beautiful Danube. After a while we began to develop an affectionate romance.

On most Sundays Roland managed to get a military Jeep and we would spend the whole day riding around. Of course, we included Mary, Sammy, and Reino every time we had the Jeep. When Roland was sitting behind the steering wheel, looking at me, and now and then and winking, I felt as if I were floating on a cloud and didn't have a care in the world. I realized that Victor was being pushed more and more to the background.

Then came November: wet, cold, and gloomy. We had to wear our coats in the house. After dark, Sammy and Roland would sneak over to the railroad track several times a week and get a couple of sacks of coal out of the loaded boxcars. In Mary's room there was a little monkey heater. Sammy had a pipe connected from it to the window. We had the luxury of a fire. The room would be warming up, but the smoke would force us to open the windows to let the smoke out and the ice-cold air in. We would just close the windows, enjoying the fire with tears running down our cheeks.

Will and Friedel always remained in the front room. Boards were partly nailed over the windows where once there had been glass. So immediately after supper, when their cook stove had not gone out completely, they would just go to bed. Often, they were reading in bed with their coats on because the wind coming in from the Danube was cold and nippy.

Christmas came. For dinner, Roland and Sammy tried their luck and killed a wild rabbit. Sammy cleaned it expertly. Friedel promised to do the cooking with all the trimmings. She said we would have potatoes, relish, gravy, beets, the rabbit, and an apple strudel. Sammy said he would bring a bottle of wine.

I had to tell Roland that I would not be permitted to remain much longer in Austria. My three months were up.

I still thought about Victor now and then and could not understand, even if the worst had happened, why I could not find out anything concerning him at the information office in Linz. Even though I realized that I had begun to care for Roland more and more, I knew I had never felt anything in the least like it for Victor. Roland's gaiety, high spirits, and his wonderful smile had me utterly defenseless. Victor's intelligence and principles were admirable; it was part of his charm. Of course, I looked at Roland from a sort of different angle.

Mary asked us if we would attend midnight Mass with her on Christmas Eve. We went just to please her. As Mary and Sammy walked in front of us, she slipping her arm through his, she carried herself so gracefully that somehow, she reminded me of a bird spreading wings through the sky. The villagers were standing outside wrapped up in shawls and heavy coats. They started their singing, "Auf, Glaugibe Leelen" (Awake Believing Souls). They sang so well and with such obvious deep feeling that it was impossible not to be moved by it. I noticed Sammy watching Mary with pride and love shining through his eyes.

When I returned to my room, Will and Friedel were sound asleep. I lay awake a long time thinking how strange it was that Victor became more and more in the background. I could not understand myself.

The next day Roland and Sammy arrived early for Christmas

dinner. We had a white sheet on the old, long kitchen table and placed a ring of holly in the center and added two candles Frau Hartel had loaned us. Dinner was expertly prepared, and we had a joyful atmosphere. We realized we had much to be thankful for. Mary and I talked after Roland and Sammy left and gave sincere thanks for the first peaceful Christmas in a long time and that we would be able to go to sleep and be undisturbed and have no fear of bombs.

A few days later I received a card that my resident permit had expired, and I was ordered without delay to sign up for my return to Holland. When Roland arrived that evening, I showed him the card. He immediately said he did not want me to leave, and added that he loved me and asked if I would go with him to the chaplain to gain information concerning papers to get married. I told him I knew that our time was limited, but I was very confused, and I needed to know more about him and his background. He said he had told me all there was to know about him. But I insisted I wanted his mother to write to me because I should like to know their attitude toward their son marrying a European girl. He readily agreed to write home about me.

A few days later we went to his chaplain. He asked us how long we had known each other, our ages, and if we were of the same faith. He explained that at this time American soldiers were only given permission to marry European girls when they could prove by two American witnesses that the couple had known each other at least six months. In the meantime, he said we should get all the necessary papers in order.

I needed a political "safe" certificate dated since 1940 stating each town in which I had lived since that time, and a certificate showing that I had no police record, also from each place or town in which I had lived since the age of eighteen. Then, I needed proof of my nationality. A passport was not sufficient because as of now, German girls were not permitted to marry Americans. I needed proof of Dutch nationality, then proof of no hereditary of malignant disease in our family. He said when these papers were in order, then I must consent to a complete physical by an American military doctor.

After we returned from this interesting trip, I wrote a letter to the Netherlands consulate explaining my situation and asked them to prolong my permit to remain in Austria.

That afternoon when Roland and I had tea after returning from a walk by the Danube, everything was quiet and peaceful, and he told me about his boyhood. He was born in Bessemer, Alabama, but moved with his parents, four brothers and two sisters to a small four-room frame house in Mentone, Alabama. He was six years old then and finished grammar school and managed two years of high school. When he was seventeen, he went to work as a welder in Panama City, Florida, and one year later at eighteen, he enlisted in the army and up until that time he never smoked or drank beer.

His brother, Melvin, was killed the year before in combat in Belgium. He then said, "I am not pretending to be something that I am not, Corrie. I am a country boy, brought up very poor. I quit school because I didn't have the right clothes. We didn't have electricity until recently; we often had cornbread over beans for breakfast on Sundays and then beans all through the week. We had to carry our water 500 yards for the house. Now," he said, "do you think you still want me?" He looked at me, his eyes sparkling.

I suppose a young heart is flexible because Victor never entered my mind. I looked at Roland and said, "I love you very much, Roland, and more every day, no matter how poor you were, or how far you had to carry your water."

He said, "I am not afraid to work, Corrie. I'll provide for you as long as I am able."

He looked so kind and handsome, there was something so loving and forlorn about him, that my heart overflowed with compassion and tenderness.

Mary and Sammy apparently felt much the same way about each other. At night when we were sitting in Mary's smoke-filled but warm room, we sat around the little heater listening to Mary singing old Vienna folksongs. We loved to hear her sing:

> "Mei Mutter was a Weinerin
> Drum habe ich Wien so gern."
>
> "My Mother is a Viennese
> That's why I love Vienna so."

While we were listening, we ate the usual leftovers that Sammy and Roland had brought from the mess hall. We shared part of it with Friedel and Will.

Roland had brought me several yards of parachute silk to make something for myself. But instead I made some little dresses for Friedel's baby. I made them by hand. Also, Friedel and I made several diapers from used army sheets. Many people were wearing coats made of army blankets and with expert tailoring they looked surprisingly good.

One morning, unusually early, Roland came to see me. Immediately I sensed that something was wrong. He told me his division company was leaving Austria for occupation in Germany, and he feared he was soon to leave for the U.S. I felt as if the world was falling apart. He promised me to do what he could, he was going to Linz to see if he could transfer to a remaining division. He was now in the Yankee division. Even though I worried, I had to laugh—a Southern Alabamian in the Yankee division.

After three hours, which seemed endless, he returned and told me that the following week he would be an MP in the Rainbow division and remain in Austria for three more months, not in Aschach, but in Salzburg. He said he could make arrangements for me to come to Salzburg, as a buddy of his, also planning to marry a girl in Austria, had connections with a Salzburg family who were willing to rent a room in exchange for food. Roland told me not to worry because the Rainbow division would remain in Salzburg for quite awhile. But I was worried; without him, I just felt lost.

Mary had the blues because she had not succeeded in getting her Austrian citizenship back, and as a German citizen, she could as of yet not get permission to marry an American soldier. She was notified that more documented proof was needed if her husband had been killed, for as of now he was still listed as missing. So, she had to fill out a long form answering many questions concerning her German husband. The authorities said they would make a thorough investigation; because he was a dentist in the army, it was unlikely he had been killed in combat.

Roland left for Salzburg. Friedel and Will made plans to move to Linz as soon as possible, because with all the snow here and Friedel pregnant, the roads might be getting worse and Will wanted Friedel near a hospital. Friedel hated leaving Aschach, but she needed to be near a hospital.

Roland drove to Aschach several times a week whenever he managed to get a Jeep. It was so good to see him, no matter how unexpected!

One day Roland and I had just returned from a walk by the Danube when we found Mary very upset and her eyes swollen with big red rims. It took a moment before she could tell us what was the matter. Finally, in between sobs, as she covered her eyes and mouth with her hands, she said, "they found Hans, my husband; he is alive and well and waiting for me in Berlin. He wants Reino and me to come as soon as we can. He had difficulties locating me, and only because of my applying for Austrian citizenship, they made contact." She cried softly, saying, "I did not hear from him in nearly two years and now I don't know what to do." She broke down completely and sobbed, "I cannot go to him; I love Sammy." She looked up at us as a child expecting help from someone, "I just cannot go, I must have time to think about all of this." Then she cried quietly, accusing herself of having fallen into wickedness all because of this cruel war. She said, "Of course, I am glad and thankful that he was not killed; God only knows how thankful I am for that."

All this time Reino just sat with his little arms tight around his mother's waist, not about to turn her loose. Reino was an unusually intelligent boy with his finely drawn face and deep-set eyes. He looked beautiful.

Suddenly Mary got up and said," I am going to the priest." She put on her coat and dressed Reino. I made no comment, but my eyes filled with tears as I watched them leave, hand in hand.

When they returned she said, "Tomorrow morning I will go to Holy Communion."

When Roland looked at me I saw that he was deeply moved. He told me shortly after that that he had to return to Salzburg. He told me he could get a place for me now, but thought I would want to be with Mary this week.

Mary said she needed me to stay with her for a little while if I could, but she intended to make arrangements as soon as possible to leave for Berlin to see her husband. She told me there was no point in making any future plans concerning Sammy, for "I know I am still married, for better or for worse." She continued, "Sunday morning I intend to hear Mass and say the rosary and benediction in the evening. It will be difficult for me to realize I have to get along without Sammy, but we could never be happy now. If we could marry, I would live with a burden, the burden of having wronged Hans." Sammy came in, so I left for my room.

"War," I thought, "is the destroyer of mankind, it does not only take the lives of those who are dead, it crushes the good that is left in the souls of the living." But how could one explain the pain and chaos of the "after war" to any outsider; it would be as if explaining colors to a blind man.

Later that night after Sammy left, I talked to Mary and she said that she planned to go to Vienna first to talk with her parents. She asked me, because of the still unpredictable trains running off schedule, if I would keep Reino for about a week. Of course, she said, she hoped to get back in less than a week. I told her I would be glad to take care of Reino. She said she did not intend to see Sammy again, it would make it more difficult for both of them. After all, she said, there is the difference between right and wrong, and right is not easy, but wrong has its consequences.

Because she was a resident of Vienna she had no difficulties getting a visepass (travel permit) to pass through the Russian zone, and because Vienna was occupied by the French, the British, the Russians, and Americans, she was very fortunate that her parents lived in the American zone.

For the week she was in Vienna, Reino and I ate our meals daily at the gasthouse. Fraulein Mitzi, who usually served our food, putting his plate before him, said, "Now, Reino, that sure does look delicious, doesn't it?" She then smacked her mouth and said, "mmmmm..mm…! I know," she said, "Reino just can't wait to start eating, can you, Reino?"

"Yes Ma'am," Reino said politely. He just sat there looking at his food, taking little tiny bites. Then without a sound, he placed his fork on the table, bowed his head deep and folding his hands, after making the sign of the cross, he said, "Lord, I cannot eat this crummy stuff." Then he frowned and looked at me. "Fraulein Corrie," he said, tears welling up in his eyes, "I never could eat this kind of a mess."

He was not in the habit of refusing to eat what was put before him, so I told him maybe for this one time we could fix him something at home. I was amazed how well behaved he was, so obedient, it was the only incident that occurred during the week his mother was in Vienna.

When Mary returned, she told me her parents had advised her to remain in Aschach where she had at least a certain amount of food, and Reino being a frail boy, needed all the food he could get, as well as the country air. People now had to be sensible above all to survive, and if Berlin had a food shortage anything like Vienna, it would be as good as suicide to let your emotions overrule practical reasoning. Then she said she had to think about her poor aged parents because she said many people were near starvation in Vienna.

When I let myself think about everything, the whole world seemed to be a mess of hopelessly misled people.

The days were long and dreary and with Roland and Sammy gone, there was not much to look forward to. Mary said she explained to her husband in a letter the situation and asked him to come to Aschach, if possible.

One afternoon Mary and I went to a religious meeting. She only went, she said, because while she was in Vienna, she ran into an old acquaintance of her husband, a doctor in Christian Science. He had told her that he would be in Aschach on a certain date to give a lecture on the Bible. She said he was not a Catholic, but it might be interesting because there was nowhere to go anyway. He had asked her to bring children, for the reading would be so simple that any school child could understand it. So, we picked up Reino at school and went to the building and into one of the rooms occupied by about twenty women and several children.

Dr. Helmut Weis was standing behind a desk making his introductions. While he was explaining a story from the Old Testament, Reino tapped his mother very lightly on the shoulder, but Mary ignored him. Disgusted, he took a deep breath, shrugged his shoulders and quietly left his seat. Mary then looked at him, raising her eyebrows, and he whispered, "I already know that story, I've heard it before," and he tiptoed very quietly out of the room.

When the meeting was over, and Mary and I returned home, Reino was very occupied with doing his homework. But Mary did not let him off that easily. She ordered him in a demanding voice, "In the corner, on your knees, facing the wall." He obeyed. Then she added, "Put your hands behind you."

She made him sit there at least ten minutes. Of course, I had left her room. I felt so sorry for him, but having had no experience with children of my own, I didn't know whether she was right or wrong.

Roland arrived in the middle of the week, and said they had the room for us. The girlfriend of the mess sergeant, Stephanie, a girl from Belgrade, and I would share the room. I hated leaving Mary, and at Mary's insistence, kept my room in Aschach. Perhaps I would get tired of staying in Salzburg in a room with another girl, and with Austrian people who rented us the room only because of food and who hated to live with two girls in the house, because very few people had any extra room and maintained their own privacy.

So, I promised Mary I would be back in a few days to wash my clothes and do my hair.

I enjoyed the trip to Salzburg, riding in the Jeep, just Roland and me, taking in the peaceful mountainside and each other's company. He was so pleasant and agreeable. He took me to a clean, modern-looking apartment house and introduced me to Stephanie, the girl from Belgrade.

I had pictured her to be dark and pretty, being from the Balkan states, but she was small with strawberry blonde hair, and not pretty. She was very fair complexioned and had a large thin-lipped mouth. I was not especially fond of her; somehow, she reminded me of Renate. But we got along.

After Roland left, I put my things up and observed the room. Just two small narrow beds, one old-fashioned commode, one large closet for our clothes, and a window looking out on the street side. We talked about our experiences in Austria. Her brother was in Austria. He had been in the German army, and her parents were in Belgrade. She said she had no reason to be uneasy about them. I knew we would never be close because we were two completely different types. Anyway, during the hours that I was not with Roland, she was company.

Roland brought my food twice a day from the mess hall in a mess kit. We looked forward to that good food as if going to a party. Those

Americans were spoiled. On Sundays Roland said the food was better. We already thought it so delicious, but he said on Sundays they had chicken, and it was the most delicious meal I had ever eaten since the war.

Salzburg was such a lovely place. We drove on Sundays through the outskirts of town, looking down from the mountains at the Salsach River. The lovely wooden houses had deep eaves and balconies, in the early spring covered with geraniums. The snow-topped mountains in the background seemed nearly unreal with snow still there. Sometimes at night we would take the street car and find a place provided for Americans to entertain their dates, such as the Roxy Bar. Not far from it was the monument of Mozart in the house in which he was born. This musical town was so beautiful and peacefully surrounded.

Usually after four days I returned to Aschach and sometimes Stephanie would come along, and when Roland was unable to get a Jeep, we would take the train or bus.

Roland told me when I returned that he had been interviewed concerning his pending marriage to me and that he had filled out many papers. I was expected to take my physical examination and was due to be interviewed by one of his superior officers. So, one day that week, Roland took me to the military hospital to get my physical. They started with the dentist. I knew that I was blessed with a set of very pretty teeth, even and white, but when I was seated in the dentist's chair, the dentist looking them over one by one, left and returned with his assistant, also a young man in uniform. They talked to each other in medical terms, tapping every one of my teeth with a small hammer. He then looked at me and said, "You are hoping to marry one of our soldiers as I understand it?"

"Yes," I said, "I am here to get my papers in order," making a mess out of my English. He said, "You will have to make some sacrifices to come up to our requirements."

"Oh, I do?" I asked.

"I'm sorry," he said, "but we will have to pull every one of your teeth!"

I protested that I had never had any trouble with my teeth at all, in fact I had only had the toothache once.

"OK," he said, "we might as well start now, if you want to marry this fine boy."

"Well," I said, as I got up from the chair, "I do want to marry him, but I have no intentions of letting you pull my teeth."

They both laughed then and said there was not anything wrong with my teeth. They just were teasing me.

Then another young man in uniform entered the room. He talked so fast in English that I could not understand a word he said to the other two men. The dentist and his assistant left. I asked the young man where I was to go next, and he told me to remain in the room.

"But," I said, "I was to see a doctor for a physical."

He laughed and said to my astonishment, "Yes, I know." Then while he picked up some papers, he said "I am your doctor."

He did not look more than twenty-three years old. Even though he was very professional, his carefree manner had made me rather uncomfortable, but I am sure he meant to set me at ease.

When he completed the examination, he opened the door and Roland was in the adjoining waiting room. The military doctor winked at Roland and said, "you lucky man, in a few weeks this fine young lady will be all yours." He then extended his hand to Roland.

"Thank you, Sir," Roland said, blushing a little.

In the streetcar on the way home, I told Roland about the teeth incident. He said that I would have to get used to American humor. But I did not have to get used to it, I told him, I liked it already. He squeezed me close, sitting side by side in the streetcar. I could not have felt happier if I had been sitting beside a king. I felt so glorious! Roland said it could be arranged for the Colonel to interview me that same week.

The Colonel who interviewed me said promptly that he was not in favor of any marriage between service men and girls away from home. "People are often more drawn to each other because of loneliness, and often young couples think themselves in love," he said. I asked him if I were an American WAC away from home if that would make a difference.

He said, "Yes, being from the same country makes a big difference. When two people marry and must adjust to different customs as well as to each other, that often brings more problems than they are able to handle." He asked me if I pictured life in the U.S. as very different from life in Europe. I said, "possibly from life in Europe, but not too different from life in Holland. I know you have to eat, sleep, and work everywhere, and I realize Roland is an ordinary man who would have to use his hands to make a living."

He did not say much, and up until the last moment, I did not know whether he would approve and sign the papers. But then when I was about to leave, he said, "Good luck to both of you and God bless you!"

I returned happily to Aschach that weekend and Mary was glad to see me, she said it had been lonesome without me. She said her husband wrote her several times a week and thought it best for her to remain up there until things began to look better in Berlin.

The Return

The days passed without any excitement. We tried sleeping late, as there was no use getting up early. We spent much time reading and mending our clothes, besides the daily household routines. Then on Tuesday in the afternoon, the mailman brought a telegram-letter. Excitedly I looked at it, thinking it to be a message from Roland. But it was not. It was from Victor!!! My hand trembled so badly I could hardly open it. It read:

Dear Corrie,

Plan to meet me at 4 o'clock in Cafe Enzelberger in Linz.

Yours, Victor

I just felt numb. I did not know whether to cry or feel happy. I felt sort of uneasy. That night Mary and I talked until late, and of course I planned to be in Linz at the set time.

I was rather nervous when I went to Linz to meet Victor. When I entered the Cafe Enzelberger at 4 o'clock, it took me a few seconds before I saw him because of the dim lights inside. He saw me and, smiling, he came toward me with outstretched hand, pressing my hands in his for a moment. Then said, "You have not changed any, Corrie!" Warmly, he asked, "How are you?"

I could not keep from thinking how much different he was from Roland, even though not less handsome, but very precise and reserved. He did not have any of the casual nonchalant manner that had attracted me to Roland so much.

He politely pulled out my chair, and when we were seated at a small round table, he motioned for the waiter, then asked my permission to order wine. We were sitting there, each taking little sips from our glasses, avoiding looking at each other. I noticed his hand, the long, sensitive fingers, turning the stem of the now nearly empty glass around and around. I had an impulse to put my hand over his and stop him, but instead, I said, "It is good to see you, Victor," and I meant it!

He kept looking at his glass and said, "For months and months I have been thinking of our being together, Corrie." He then added, looking at me, "Not like this, of course."

I looked at him, "Victor, you got here four days ago; why didn't you get in touch with me immediately?"

"I was so shocked not to find you with my parents, and then I wanted to talk with them about several things. I also was very tired, Corrie."

"Have you seen Inge yet?" I asked.

"Yes, I talked with Inge."

"She told you a lot about me."

"No," he said, "but she said there is a lot you have to tell me."

"Perhaps there is, Victor. You said I had not changed, but I have—I have changed a lot."

"I'll expect you to be honest with me, Corrie."

"Well, I'll expect from you the same. There is something that keeps bothering me, Victor. Why didn't you write more often when you were in Holland before the war ended?"

He answered me rather indifferently, "Oh, well, I knew you were staying with my parents. I knew you were in good care, and I did not worry."

"Oh," I said, "only your peace of mind was important. Keeping in touch with me was not really necessary then."

"No, Corrie, it was war and I didn't think my letters would reach you and I guess I should have tried more, and I am truly sorry that I did not make more effort."

"Victor, did you during all that time ever date another girl?"

"Naturally not," he said. "After you left Holland, I had my mind on no other girl but you, because I had already enclosed you in my heart as if you were my wife, which you would have been should I have been home on leave. And after the war, I was in a Canadian P.O.W. camp in Holland until two weeks ago."

The waiter came and we ordered some more wine. A small orchestra was playing "Es gehet alles foruger" (Everything will pass).

We remained silent, then he looked at me and said, "And how about you, Corrie?"

I thought "I cannot tell him, not now, anyway," and so I said, "I cannot say the same for myself, Victor. I have been very blue and alone, and it is not easy to always keep up your spirits when things point in a different direction. No, I cannot say that I have been all that faithful as you expected me to be," I said bluntly.

"Did you go out with Americans?" he asked in a soft tone.

"Why? Did Inge tell you so?"

"No, Inge told me nothing, but mother said I should ask you how you felt about a certain Lieutenant Berg!"

"Before I go into that Victor, promise that you don't doubt my answer, because there wasn't anything between Lieutenant Berg and me. I liked him, and oh, yes, he kissed me once and it didn't mean a thing. He flattered me. He said I was pretty and that was all."

Victor smiled, seemingly relieved, he said, "I believe you, Corrie, I could not lose faith in you easily."

I thought how much I hated to hurt him, but I could not lead him on, so I said, "It is true, Victor, there was no romance between Lieutenant Berg and me, but there was someone else."

He looked at me, biting his lower lip. He asked, "An American soldier?"

I felt awful, but I had to tell him.

"Yes," I said, "he was an American."

I used the past tense because I realized it would be most cruel if I had said, "He is still here."

I hoped Victor would break off with me, not I with him. The least I could do was to save his pride.

He closed his eyes and said, "Good God, Corrie, how could you!"

"Understand, Victor, my situation was not so good, and I know it is not possible for you to see my side, and I want you to know I wasn't in search of seeking cheap amusement. For awhile I lived like a gypsy, no place to stay, hardly anything nourishing to eat, and no bath for weeks."

He remained silent, just looking into space.

I then added, "I know, Victor, everyone who is imprisoned always thinks that on the outside there is no hardship. There has been much suffering, not only in the prison camps." I looked at him and my heart overflowed with compassion.

I asked softly, "Did they treat you badly in the P.O.W. Camp?"

"Bad," he said, frowning, "when is bad...bad? It is all a matter of comparison."

"Yes," he said, "the Americans were filled with horror when Pearl Harbor was bombed, but what about the Allied Air Force bombing Berlin, Dresden, and Vienna? They burned the people alive in Dresden!"

"I know that was awful, Victor. But that was only to put a stop to all the gruesome things that happened to the Jews in the concentration camps."

"No, Corrie, if the Americans had really been concerned about that, they would have entered the war long before they did, it could have all been prevented. The Allies are just as guilty. Look, Corrie, war is all rotten politics, it is calculated murder. You don't love your fellow man by dropping bombs on cities and deliberately killing their women and children, the innocent! You cannot blame individuals in war. People, not only soldiers, are used to settle international conflicts. The world over, people have turned away from all principles. Any nation will fall unless they teach high principles and morals, and enforce the right kind of discipline; any country will face their own damnation."

I hadn't meant for all this to enter our conversation. I realized he must have been through plenty of hell. I thought when I looked at him, "he is quite a man. Even when defeated, he has pride and maintains an amount of power. Perhaps, I thought, who is to judge, who really is defeated and astray from principles?"

He got up from his seat, his lips pressed together. He motioned to the waiter, paid him, then straightened his coat and looked at me, a strange fire glowing in his eyes. He said, "Corrie, I need to be alone, away from my family, I will go up in the mountains and I will write you before the week is out to the same address in Aschach." Rather distantly, he asked, "Do you need anything...money or food, anything I could help you with?"

"No, Victor. I am all right now, you see I have been receiving, as a displaced person, American Red Cross food parcels."

"Oh, I see," he said slightly sarcastically, "the Americans are good to you." And he left.

I did not answer and remained at the table in the cafe until I was sure he was gone. I did not know whether to feel sorry for him or for myself. I rode the bus back to Aschach. It was late when I got there, but Mary was still awake. She asked me how things worked out. I told her it was awful, I really did not know how he felt, and what was worse, I did not know how I felt.

"Do you think you still love him?" Mary asked.

"I don't know. While talking to Victor I only thought about Roland and wondered what he was doing."

"Was there anything about Victor, in his looks or behavior, that you did not like?" she asked.

"No, he is every bit as nice looking as Roland; he is very reserved and sure of himself, somehow superior, he is really worthy of admiration."

"Yes," she said, "I gathered that much." She then shook her head and added, "I hope you know what you are doing, Corrie."

I stayed in Aschach that week. Roland came by Jeep just for a few hours in the afternoon. I told him about receiving the telegram and my meeting Victor in Linz and that I should hear from him again later in the week. Roland seemed worried. I told him I felt sure Victor would break completely with me once he thought things over and realized that I was not the strong, steadfast person that he dreamed me to be. I knew I didn't have any supernatural strength; those people exist only in story books. I needed someone to care for me when I was cold and hungry. Some people call that weakness, but perhaps that is human—to want someone who cares.

Roland made me promise I would not allow Victor to kiss me. I nearly had to laugh because Victor had not shown in the least any inclination that he had wanted to kiss me.

I realized that I was completely captured by Roland's charm. When I looked at him I knew life would be meaningless without him. Roland appeared very concerned and uneasy when he left for Salzburg. I told him my meeting Victor was a matter of decency, not wrongdoing.

A few days passed, and I received a card from Victor just signed, "Love, Victor."

The days were passing slowly. We slept late as there was no reason to get up early. As for the rest of the days we busied ourselves with the daily chores, doing our laundry and mending our clothes because we had to take good care of what few nice things we had. Mary promised if she should return soon to Vienna, she would bring me in exchange for food for her parents, several nice dresses. She said she had many nice clothes in Vienna. She then explained that her father was head tailor at the opera house and many of the well-known artists left gowns, dresses, and coats at the theater for alterations and then never picked them up. After a period of time the clothes were considered discards and her father would take them home. When she evacuated from Vienna, she said she had only packed practical things.

Early on Thursday morning the mailman brought a letter. He said he delivered the letter special, appreciating the usual cigarette. The letter was from Victor, a small poem written on a piece of paper. There was no heading, and it read:

"Und aus all dem finsternissen
Trehed der Herr, so weit Er Kann,
Und die fahden, die Zurisshen
Knopft Er-alle wieder an.

"From beneath all darkness
Forward I come as far as I can
and all the strings
that had been broken
I'll tie them stronger...one by one."

I did not know whether to feel happy or sad. In small print it said, "I will be in Linz at the railroad station at 10 a.m. Friday. Looking forward to seeing you. As always, your Victor."

"Why," I thought, "at the railway station?"

I suppose it was just my female pride because I did take pains to look my best.

At eight o'clock in the morning, I took the bus to Linz. As I walked toward the station, I saw him standing at the platform waiting for me. He was nicely sun-tanned; a handsome man, I thought. He smiled as he came to meet me. He was wearing a nice green tweed dark suit. It was the first time I had seen him in civilian clothes. Even in his at least three-year-old suit, he was a man of distinction. He always walked somewhat with his nose in the air, sort of looking down on people. I had made a remark about that once in Holland, but he had laughed and explained that he could not help it, that was to blame on his Adam's apple. So, I knew he was not trying to be conceited.

He seemed so happy when he walked beside me, taking my hand. I asked him where we were going, but he did not answer, he just squeezed my hand, then said, "Let's go in the compartment of the train." I argued that I could not, but he insisted, saying he only had a short while. The train was almost empty. I did not know what to expect of him.

Once in the compartment he asked me to sit down, and he sat down beside me. He took both my hands in his and said, “Corrie, I have thought things over. I reasoned with myself and I know I am willing to forgive you much more than I could forget you. I know, Corrie, dear, I cannot forget you.”

I wanted to say something, but he placed his forefinger over my lips, pointing to my nose and said, “Never a word about the past, Corrie, dear, we talk about the future, our future only.”

Suddenly I noticed the train moving and I told him so. He laughed and said he knew. He bought tickets all the way to Zell am See.

“Well, now, Victor, I don’t appreciate that, that is not right, I need to be back in Aschach this afternoon,” I said angrily.

He just sat there looking out of the window and making remarks about the beautiful scenery. I became truly angry and decided to get off at the next stop.

“Why do you have to be back?” he asked, still looking out of the window.

What could I say? I thought to myself that I was sorry, at least I could spare that much.

“Well, you see, Victor,” I said hesitatingly, “you didn’t let me talk awhile ago, but this American soldier I told you I dated, well, he is still here. I don’t know how to begin to tell you, because I have become very attached to him.”

“You mean you have been dating him for a long time?” he asked, his face turning red.

“For nearly seven months,” I admitted.

“Is that the one my sister Inge knows?”

“I thought you said she had not discussed me with you!”

"Oh, yes, she told me about that one after I talked to you in Linz."

"Corrie," he said, "I had planned to spend the day in Zell am See with you". We can have dinner there and return on the last train and you will be back in Aschach by midnight. Let's spend this one day together," he pleaded.

"Well," I thought, "I could not be so cruel as to refuse him that." Therefore, I agreed.

So, the train moving on to Zell am See, I told him how Inge, Mary and I lived in Aschach, then how I met Roland and many things concerning my stay in Aschach. He listened without interruption.

It was shortly past noon, and we were seated on one of the nice terraces in Zell am See, looking out over the beautiful lake surrounded by mountains. As we sat there enjoying the view, Victor turned and looked at me, studying my face, and said, "You have not changed, Corrie, only the environment made you think so. I am certain you won't find happiness with this American soldier. You have told me he gambles a little and drinks a little. Those are very bad habits, Corrie."

"Oh, well, when he is back in civilian life he will be different about drinking and gambling, and then maybe all that is not so bad. Perhaps I am somewhat different from what you thought me to be, Victor."

"I could not imagine you living in an atmosphere in conflict with your upbringing, Corrie" he said.

"You know, Victor, perhaps some day you may be doing things, or desire to do things, in conflict with your character. You think you will always be doing exactly that which is right?" I asked.

"Yes, I shall always do what I think is right, I certainly will not do that which I know is wrong," he said. "Of course, it may not seem right to others."

I thought how all this deep conversation, this much talk, makes happy people unhappy, and unhappy people probably happy.

"You know, Corrie," he said, "I know you pretty well, but your

American soldier does not know the real you. The circumstances he met you under were different from when I met you in Holland, even though we were both men in uniform."

I thought how Victor had character, high morals, and was a reliable person, but I was sitting there thinking about Roland the whole time.

The effect Roland had on me was so different, I just could not explain it, not even to myself.

"What is it that attracted you so to him?" Victor asked solemnly.

I thought for a moment, then I said, "I guess it is his pleasant carefree manner. You see, Victor, he is so easy going, so happy-go-lucky."

"Is that what you want in a husband?" he asked surprisingly. "People like that have no ambition or self-discipline. They don't live to amount to something, they just live to get all the pleasure and amusement out of life they can."

"Do you think it is wrong to want pleasure out of life, Victor?"

"No, Corrie, I am fond of pleasure, but only of the kind well-chosen. There are tremendous distinctions in one's finding of amusement, and your American friend, having met you under those unfortunate circumstances, has mistaken you for a light-hearted girl. He is no match for you, Corrie, and once you are married to him for several years, you will see what I mean. Then the time will come that you see him for what he is because there are many men like him, likeable, pleasure-seeking, good-looking men. After his physical desire for you is fulfilled, he will blame you for all his dissatisfactions. And there is really no one to blame, because he is empty of understanding, that is, of understanding you. Because you enjoy intellectual exercise, your needs are beyond what he can give you."

"Maybe my needs are just a pleasant, uncomplicated, good-looking husband, Victor."

Victor gave me a pitying look, then said, "You are more lost that I realized, and I am sorry for you, Corrie, about getting hurt."

"Victor, it is not easy for me, I wish I could understand myself."

"Corrie, some people think love is all that is necessary to make a lasting marriage, but love without compatibility, decency, sacrifices, and character, is like forgetting to give water to a flower, and you don't love him, Corrie, all you had together is good times; you cannot judge when everything is so pleasant."

"Victor," I said, "he is thoughtful and considerate of me."

"For his own pleasure, does that prove love to you? Do you think in time of sorrow that he would deny himself and comfort you?" Victor said.

"Oh, Victor, you want a pattern of your life lined out ahead of you. If we should have troubles, I'll manage them then, not before."

Victor looked at me and said, "That is why I worry about you; you have nothing in common with this American soldier, he is no match for you. Now you are infatuated by his charm and you find comfort in being with him because of your unsettled circumstances at the present. Corrie, I know your true nature."

I looked at him and said, "Perhaps this is my true nature, Victor, reckless, adventuresome, and pleasure seeking?"

"No, Corrie," he said, "you are just out of balance."

He bent over the table toward me, his face flushed and his eyes full of warmth, and he almost whispered, "I care so much for you."

"I am really miserable, Victor, I am so mixed up, I know I do want to marry him, no matter what anyone says about him, and I know he loves me," I added cruelly.

Victor, who looked pale now, asked, "If you become crippled and an invalid, do you think he would care for you?"

I thought awhile, then I said, "There you are, you see you are always running ahead of things, solving problems which probably never happen. After all, if such things occur, no one knows their reactions. You know, Victor, I don't like creating problems, I try solving them if I can when they happen."

He stood up and got behind my chair, putting his hands on my shoulders and said, "I'll always want you, even if I had to push you in a wheelchair, if that should be necessary. The difference is that I know you have a quality that he will never recognize, in fact he is not capable of making you a suitable husband no matter how hard he would try. You are not meant for each other, Corrie, dear," he added in a soft voice.

I asked him how he formed all his opinions on "that American soldier" whose name is Roland, and "please, Victor, do call him by his name."

He said, "Inge and I formed these opinions. He's not a bad fellow, but insincere, and too happy-go-lucky."

"What does Inge know about him, and you, Victor, you see him through jealous eyes, and so does Inge!"

"Corrie, please understand me," Victor spoke sharply now, "if you had met an American whom I thought would make you a more suitable husband than I, believe me, I would accept it as a man, but as it stands, I see only unhappiness can come forth out of your marrying him and I see a lonely time ahead of you, alone in America."

"You don't like America," I blurted out.

"I was in America as a boy, fourteen-years-old; I stayed six months. I know little about American people and their customs, but I think if you had the right man, then of course things would be different. You would learn to love his country as well as his people. I am only discussing the individual as in your case. But since you feel this way, I must know one thing: in case it doesn't turn out as planned between you and your American...I mean Roland, then what will you do?"

"Then I will return to Holland."

His eyes softened, and he added, "I will look you up in Holland and perhaps you will be pleased to see me."

We remained silent for a while. He then looked at his watch and said it was time to go. In our conversation, Roland was not mentioned anymore. Victor told me about the time when he was in Holland, taken prisoner by the Canadians and placed in a P.O.W. Camp. He said he filled out several International Red Cross cards and they must have gotten lost, because at that time very few people received mail in the Russian-occupied zones. Later the cards would have gone through, but he did not know that the first cards he had sent never had reached his parents.

When we arrived in Linz, he took me to the bus, shook my hand and said, "Auf Wiedersehen, Corrie."

Riding back on the bus to Aschach, I felt depressed.

I talked with Mary for a few minutes, then went into my lonely room. I went to bed immediately, burying my face in the pillow and weeping, not for myself, but for the grief that I caused Victor. I was painfully aware that he suffered, and I realized that forgiveness had not come easy for him. I had robbed him of all his hope and was deserting him in the midst of his pain.

The days that followed were only made bearable because of short visits from Roland. Then in the middle of the week, he suddenly declared that he most likely would be shipped back to the U.S. in approximately one month. He told me that I was not to worry because he had no intentions to return to the U.S. until I could come with him. Every time he left Aschach for Salzburg, I felt very depressed and uneasy. After all, Roland was still in the service and everything would not be in his power. They could send him home if they wanted to.

Then I received a note from Victor saying he still thought about me, and asking if I remembered the piece of philosophy he once had read by one of German's great philosophers, he enclosed it. It read:

> "The world is a palace with many doors, and behind each door, God kept a secret hidden. The human walks through this

palace, each with a key in his hand in search for the door which his key will fit. Early in life he is very carefree and fearless, life stretches endlessly before him. He has no haste to look for the door which his key will fit. He passes the simple ones without taking notice. This search is for one of luster with golden trimmings and massive columns.

His hair has turned gray and his step is tired, his mind confused. He sees that there are no doors left. There must be one door somewhere to fit his key.

Could it be that he had overlooked the right one......?

Perhaps just a simple one......

No lock of golden trimmings, or maybe had he taken the wrong way.....?

His heart beats faster and in fear he looks around. Then he sees a door......But the last one......In front of it sits a giant in burning rags.

'Who are you?' he cries in despair.

'I am the dead,' answered the giant."

Sometimes when I was alone, I thought I had perhaps gone past the right door. Is that what Victor meant? But then I wiped these confusing thoughts out of my mind; after all things were going to work out fine. It wouldn't be long until Roland and I were married. Then our biggest struggle would be over, and we could plan safely on the future. I felt I had many reasons to be happy and thankful. The war was over, people could now go to bed and sleep all night, and there were no more bombs to fear. I was feeling quite happy, but almost guilty, when I came to think of so many good things always happening to me. Everything seemed peaceful living beside the blue Danube. Many people thought of the Danube as being really blue, but it wasn't blue; in fact, it was not even clear. Maybe the water seemed to be the color according to the mood people were in.

Mary, after receiving a depressing letter from her parents in Vienna, became heartbroken. They wrote that after standing in line for hours, even with their ration card, they often came home empty handed. You had to be strong and ruthless. People were fighting shoulder to shoulder; they would trample over each other for some shriveled apples, or a small sack of rice. The people's fight in the city was no longer against enemies, it was now for food. They advised Mary to remain in the country, in Aschach. In Vienna there was nothing to hope for, only fighting for food. Now more people were losing their lives in the battle for survival, than had been killed by bombs. There were no potatoes, no eggs, no butter, no fat of any kind in the stores. Shopping had become an exhausting matter, a matter of life and death. Being civilized at their age was plainly a misfortune. They were tired and had become bitter. Mary said that no matter what the risk, she would have to try to get to Vienna and bring them some food.

After that it was difficult for her to enjoy eating, even the most necessary things, and without doubt I knew she was often preoccupied, thinking about her aged starving parents.

Roland continued visiting me as often as he could. I preferred that to my visiting him in Salzburg. He always carried with him a nice supply of food, such as crackers, cheese, milk powder, egg powder, chocolate, ham and eggs in cans, salmon in cans, and other "goodies."

Mary and I were getting along so well that I became very attached to her.

Two months passed, and we still were awaiting the papers concerning our marriage. When Roland arrived unexpectedly one day, I sensed immediately that something was wrong. He told me that he had received orders to return to America to be discharged there. I refused to believe this. He tried convincing me that there was not anything more important to him right now than for us to be married and he promised me he would not return to America unless we were married. He told me he planned to discharge in Salzburg and he would place an application now and in about ten days he would know whether he was accepted.

Again, another long ten days.

But then came the good news. He would be placed as a file clerk working for the RD and R Division in Vienna. Its headquarters were there.

Immediately after his discharge he had to leave for Vienna. He promised to make arrangements as soon as he could to get the necessary papers for me to join him there because we should get our marriage papers any day.

Mary was very excited and a great help and comfort to me. She said she would make plans to return to Vienna with me if Roland and I could not be married right away, I would be welcome to stay with her parents temporarily. Of course, I understood; it was expected of Roland to supply them with some American rations. A PX had been set up in Vienna and many things we had not tasted for years were to be purchased there, all American products of course, and only for payment with American money.

In less than a week I received a letter signed by one of his superiors, and by presenting this letter to the American official in charge of issuing travel papers necessary to travel through Russian occupied territory, I was to receive such a permit. We learned that such matters were handled in Grieskirchen.

After Mary and I boarded the bus, other Austrian people informed us that passes could be obtained for non-Vienna residents only in very special cases. It would be difficult for personal affairs to even get admittance to the officer in charge.

After arriving at the square, we noticed many people already lined up in front of the courthouse, now used for American headquarters for that district. We just took our place in line. Several hours later a U.S. military police on duty as a guard told the remaining crowd, including us, that for today the limit had been surpassed, and for those who for very important business matters had to have a pass, to return next Thursday when more applications would be issued.

I barely kept from crying, but Mary said not to give up so easily. She waited until most of the people had left, then walked to the guard and asked him, "Twice a week the office is open to the public?"

"Yes," he answered, "on Mondays and Thursdays from ten until two o'clock."

"Oh," she said, "and on other days the commandant remains in Linz?" rather questioningly.

He said, "No, he usually comes in every day except on Saturday, but only on those two days the public can apply for papers."

The guard was friendly but not talkative, but Mary tried her best saying, "I think I have met him at a party once in Linz."

That seemed to make no impression on him, he just shrugged his shoulders and said, "He's a nice guy and enjoys a good time."

Mary did not answer right away, but she smiled, then after a moment she said, "We'll probably see you again Thursday, are you on duty every day?"

"No," he said, laughing now, "tomorrow is my last day for this week. We're on duty two days and off three."

"Well, so long then," we said.

He answered pleasantly, "Auf Wiedersehen."

The bus was about to depart so we hurried and were lucky to find a seat. Riding along, Mary told me that instead of on a day open to the public, we would return on a day he usually did not see anyone. We planned to go Wednesday. The same guard would not be there, we would just gamble on trying to get to speak with the commandant. If it didn't work out, we hadn't lost much, we just had to come back on regular office days.

Mary was always so sure of herself that I usually left everything up to her.

So, early Wednesday morning we again took off to Grieskirchen.

There was another soldier on duty now by the entrance and Mary asked him if the captain would be in by ten o'clock. The soldier looked at us indifferently, then said, "possibly." He was looking up in the sky as if watching a bird or something when he added, still looking at the sky, "But he won't see anybody today, that is no Austrians."

"Yes, I know," Mary said, reassuring herself. She then smiled and added, "The captain is expecting us. We are not Austrians; we are from Holland."

The soldier agreed for us to wait then until he came. It could be as late as eleven or twelve o'clock, he had said.

We remained silent, but then a few minutes later a Jeep stopped, and an officer stepped out. The soldier said to us, "Well, you're in luck; he is on time today."

The captain saluted back to the guard and was about to pass us when Mary fell in step beside him, looking up at him in her most charming manner.

"How are you, Captain? You act as if you do not remember me."

He stopped, and she extended her hand. Again, she repeated in a softer tone,

"How are you, Captain?"

He took her hand and held it as she introduced me, "My Dutch girlfriend, Corrie. Remember I told you about her in Linz?" she added.

"Yes...yes...," he frowned a little as if he seemed not to remember.

"Come along, ladies," he said, "and let's recall what that was again that I promised you."

He was obviously straining his brain as to where and what he promised her. We had to practically skip beside him to keep in step, he walked so fast. Standing in front of his office, he took his key and opened the door, leading us inside.

Most Americans were pleasant mannered, especially when in

company of two young women. He took his place behind the desk, offering us a seat.

Mary crossed her legs so that the effect could not be unnoticed. She then offered him a cigarette, only to remind him to offer us one instead, which he promptly did. I lit mine and then posed with it because I did not smoke, but holding the cigarette gave me more assurance. Mary waited until he had inhaled several good puffs before approaching him with our wishes. Then, as he sat completely at ease, observing that he had two nice looking young ladies present, he asked, "What can I do for you?"

Mary looked at me and said, "Corrie, show the Captain the letter."

I handed him the letter, and after reading a sentence or so he handed it back to me, "and now what is it you want me to do?"

So Mary explained that all plans were made for me to marry this American, and in order to get to Vienna I needed a geallierte reisepass to be permitted to travel through Russian occupied Austria. Slowly he looked me over, then said, "Do you know that it takes from six to eight weeks to get such a pass?"

"But, Captain," Mary pleaded, "Could you possibly speed it up some now just for old friends' sake?" Mary then looked at him so pleadingly.

He took out an application sheet and started asking my name, age, and other particulars. Then after he finished writing, he said, "Let's see now, today is Wednesday; with luck I could have it for you Friday, but come back next Monday, be here at ten o'clock and it will be fixed up."

Mary arose from her seat and walked over to the desk, looking very grateful to him as she said, "Thank you, Captain, I knew you would not let me down. Thank you again!" She then extended both hands, which he took, claiming it was a pleasure to be of help to two such charming ladies. We left feeling very pleased.

Outside I asked Mary if she really had met him somewhere before. She said, "Of course not, but I nearly convinced myself that I had met him before, but men are generally so flattered that they like the idea themselves, and rather than find out for sure, they convince themselves also."

It was a good day for us and I felt with reasonable good luck that soon I would be in Vienna. But it was not until the following Friday that I received my travel papers.

Mary and I immediately made arrangements for our trip to Vienna. All Mary needed was a seal on her evacuation papers to return to her place of residence. We wasted no time and planned to travel by bus, leaving Linz on Monday morning.

It had been several weeks since I had seen Roland. I wrote him, telling him our plans, and to expect us some time that following week.

Mary said my staying with her in the home of her parents was all arranged. Roland had been there and had brought them a few American articles. They had become fond of "Smitty" as they called him in their letter. My heart warmed for him, a sweet, thoughtful boy. Everyone would like him, he was so gentle and kind. I realized how lucky I was to be able to find lodging with Mary's parents, and if it had not been for them, I could not have obtained a pass so easily.

Several of the villagers in Aschach wished us well, and the Burgemeister personally offered me his help if I should need any references. In the gasthaus where we had eaten our meals for the last year and four months, they prepared for us a special "good luck" meal.

It certainly was a coincidence that now I should go to Mary's place of birth. Mary smiled and said, "I could not think of anyone whom I should like to introduce more to my parents and my beloved Vienna."

The next morning, we left for Linz, and from there boarded the bus for Vienna. We were tired when we arrived, but Mary and Reino were so happy to be with their loved ones. Meeting Mary's parents was pleasant, but it saddened my heart; they were older than I had pictured them. Mr. Richter, Mary's father, was not quite fifty, yet his eyes were deeply sunken, and he must have aged rapidly to judge from his picture two years ago that Mary had shown me. Broken down physically and mentally, they seemed so humble and so grateful for small things.

Immediately we began unpacking the things we had been able to bring over the border through the Russian occupied area. Mary's mother prepared to cook some noodles, the water now boiling and bubbling, forecasting delicious moments. She could not wait to take out one package after another, looking at them as a child opening Christmas toys. Mary had opened a can of Nestle's milk, and was now making them a hot chocolate. She then ordered them into the living room to sit down. As Mary carried two cups on a small tray, her mother sat restlessly in an easy chair, her hands folded on her lap, already licking her lips. Mary handed them the steaming hot chocolate and Mrs. Richter brought the cup tenderly to her lips, then said, "how delicious!" Mary looked at her father who had made himself comfortable for this great treat, taking little sips, leaning forward in his chair.

"Magnificent," he said, quietly enjoying it. When Mary smiled at her mother, tears rose in my eyes. I left for the bedroom...Those stupid tears!

Yes, the war had ended. These people—how they had struggled to keep out of the cemetery. It was all so awful, it just seemed a nightmare!

When I returned to the living room, they were talking about hunger-mad parents, who made their young daughters get acquainted with allied soldiers, knowing what awaited them, but silently praying that the saints would stand by. Hunger—dying of it—made many go mad.

They treated me not as an outsider; they were so nice. Mary had told them in her letters so much about me that they felt they had known me a long time.

Mary's mother was preparing a bite for us to eat. She seemed so thrilled, busying about in the tiny kitchen. After we ate, we freshened up, then Mary and I took the streetcar to Roland's quarters. But an MP on duty told us that Smith was not there, and he did not know what hour he would return. We left a message. I was a little disappointed, but then again, I could not expect him to stay home; after all I only said in my letter I would arrive some time that week.

We returned to Mary's house in the Schadekgasse 2/9 on the second floor. The apartment was small: two bedrooms, one living room, a small kitchen joining a small workroom for her father, then a storage room in the hall. A place was made for me in the living room on the ottoman (a daybed). It was customary for the caretaker to lock the front door after ten p.m. But at eleven o'clock, Roland rang the doorbell and had the caretaker let him in. I was overjoyed to see him, even though it was so late.

Roland was sweeter and more affectionate than ever before, but I also knew he had been drinking. I forgave him easily enough, but I also was embarrassed. Mary's mother suggested Roland better spend the night. He could sleep on the ottoman, and I with Mary, all for the sake of keeping the apartment quiet.

Roland promised to bring cigarettes for the caretaker. He also gave Mary's mother twenty shillings to give five of it to the caretaker. Everything seemed to be settled now.

When I awakened the next morning, Roland had already left, and he told Mrs. Richter that he would be back after work around five o'clock that evening. Arriving at the said time, he told us that each U.S. civilian employed for the U.S. Service in Austria or any U.S. officer was permitted to take a guest twice a week to dinner in the officers' mess hall. Roland had a friend, John P. Alexander, also a civilian, but in a higher classification than Roland. He took Mary as his guest only as a favor to Roland. Each American had to pay fifty cents in U.S. scrip for his guest.

Mary and I were overjoyed to be taken to dinner in Cafe Beethoven, a very up-to-date and classy restaurant, specially used for U.S. officers, U.S. civilians and their dependents or guests. It seemed as if a dream had come true to me and I found Vienna the most wonderful city I had seen. In the restaurant a small orchestra of violins and piano was playing old Vienna waltzes. I felt so comfortable and happy. Roland was so dear to me and I so completely dependent on him. He was so pleasant, winking at me now and then and smiling when he suddenly said, "our marriage papers will arrive any day now." I felt so blessed, so fortunate, perhaps it was because I was in love, or maybe it was Vienna.

After we ate and boarded the streetcar, I realized it was not Vienna... at least not now. I observed the people on the overcrowded streetcars. It was disturbing how the friendly, lighthearted Viennese people were now ill-tempered and constantly at each others' throats. Half-empty stomachs, too many families living together in too small quarters, nothing to smoke, etc. It was not uncommon to see once well to-do-people in ragged, faded overcoats. It really took acrobatic movements to get on a streetcar. You had to be rough; otherwise you were pushed and elbowed out of the way.

Mary explained that her father had been temporarily (they hoped) dismissed from his job at the state opera house as head tailor because during the war he had been a member of the Nazi Party. She said it had been compulsory, or otherwise he would have lost his job then. So, what were they to do? For the present time he just did some part-time work at home, and of course their income was very little. I felt compassion for her parents—poor, misled people. Roland said he liked them both and that he had been bringing several packs of cigarettes weekly for her father. But, during my stay in their home, it came to my attention that the poor man had to sell the cigarettes in the black market to help support the family. One night after Roland left, I noticed that he immediately emptied the ashtray, where four cigarette butts were left. A few minutes later, leaning back in his chair, he was putting together the leftovers and he rolled himself a cigarette which he then smoked, looking very satisfied. He did not know that I had been observing him.

The next day I told Roland we must give him some more cigarettes and I told him of the incident. I also suggested that I should pay a certain amount of board, even though I did not eat there. Food was so scarce that most families in Vienna ate at restaurants, or at least had them cook for them and then went there to pick up the scanty meal to eat it at home. Small families could not prepare a meal on the small amount of food one could buy on the ration card. It helped out for Mary and I to eat twice a week with Roland. We gave our portion of food to her parents.

The following day when Roland came to see me, I knew the moment he entered that something pleasant had happened. He did not keep me guessing long. He kissed me, then picked me up from the floor and said, "How would you like to be Mrs. Smith?"

"Oh, Roland! You got the papers," I said excitedly.

He looked so handsome in his tailor-made U.S. civilian uniform that I could hardly stand it.

"When do you want to set the date, Miss, to-be Mrs. Smith?"

"I don't know, Roland, you set the date," I said, kind of bashful.

"All right then, Monday. Today is Friday, we'll plan everything for Monday."

Mary's mother told us we needed to go to the Standesamt (courthouse) and sign up so that everything could be arranged. She explained that we had to sign up in the district where Roland lived. Roland told us that he had already arranged for an apartment, that he would be eligible for private quarters as soon as his marriage papers came through. We would, however, share the apartment with John P. Alexander, John's classification being higher than Roland's. Together they could arrange to get a nicer and larger place. After we were married, I would be permitted to eat two meals a day in the officers' mess hall. The restaurant where I would eat was even nicer than Roland's. The reason that I was to eat there was because all other places were full. One had to be captain or of higher rank to get a mess hall card for that restaurant. But, Alexander had it arranged for me. There I would see U.S. female civilians employed for the War and State

Department. But I had rather not eat so formal and be with Roland. I was allowed to take a guest twice a week, and of course, every evening I would eat with Roland and Alexander, each taking me twice as their guest. They had found two more colleagues who worked in the same office to sign up so Mary could eat with us on Sunday nights. Of course, Roland would pay the required fifty cents.

I promised my food ration card to Mrs. Richter as soon as we would be married.

Roland had asked his folks to send a package, and it had arrived. For him there were two suits, two pairs of pants, shirts, and accessories. Mary, who had lots of nice clothes in comparison with others, wanted to exchange some clothes of hers for some coffee, sugar, etc. So, we both were made happy that way.

During the hours that Roland worked, Mary and I often went to shows, plays, or sightseeing, taking the streetcar instead of a subway. We went above the city, a streetcar on a speedway, and in only a few minutes it was possible to travel from one end of town to the other. Vienna was supposed to have the second-best streetcar service in the world; Chicago had the best, it was said.

Some afternoons we would drink a soft drink (colored sweet water with an artificial taste), sitting leisurely on one of the sidewalk cafe's terraces. Mary's mother did not mind that we left the house early. We always helped first with tidying up around the house. Mary showed me nearly everything there was to see in Vienna. We looked forward to seeing some of the operas. Soon the Staatsopera House would be reopened.

After Roland arrived early that day, we left to make preparations for our wedding. Because our new address would be in the Gershover Strasse 19, we would have to register in that district. Roland seemed as happy as I was, because every time he looked at me he winked and squeezed my hand. I thought myself the luckiest girl in the world.

We both were nervous as we entered the Standesamt "Whearing." A clerk showed us where to go after Roland explained in English what we came for. A Justice of the Peace, or a Judge, whatever he was, inspected Roland's papers, then gave us each a paper to fill out. Watching me sign my name and place of birth, he stopped me and asked me if I was not Austrian. "I am from Holland," I said.

"Hollandish," he said, shaking his head. "I am sorry, fraulein, but a girl from Holland cannot marry unless she has her parents' consent."

"I am twenty-one," I stated.

"That makes no difference," he said, then added, "are they here in Vienna?"

"No," I said, "they are in Holland."

"Ach," he said, sympathetically, "Those Dutch people have a law that females under thirty years of age cannot marry unless permitted by both parents."

"Is that some kind of a joke?" Roland asked, laughing.

"No, sir," he said seriously, "that is true."

Roland asked him if there was anything he could do about it.

"She needs a notarized letter or statement from her parents consenting to her marriage, then I can marry you."

"I never heard of any country having such a law," Roland said, still doubting.

"That's right," he said, "Holland is the only country in Europe which has that restriction on marriage."

After returning to Mary's parents, I mailed a letter home explaining my plans and asking for permission. Roland also enclosed a nice, but formal, letter asking for my father's consent. It took another three weeks before I received an answer.

My father wrote for me to come back home, talk things over sensibly, and he enclosed no permission for me to get married. Leaving home to marry an Austrian and then asking permission to marry an

American was beyond his understanding. Then the letter was signed, "Your father." Roland said he wanted to go to the Dutch consulate and see what could be done. There a young Dutch officer listened to Roland explain everything. He then got up and said, looking straight at Roland, "I understand you once had a letter of consent and it has gotten lost, so I can write out a consent for the court." Roland smiled and we both understood that we had to sign a paper to that effect. Strangely enough, we were so pleased that Roland and I really agreed to each other it happened that way.

But still the help of the court was needed. A small fee had to be paid, then in three days we could be married.

The Dutch officer told us to repeat our plea for consent. He told me to write another letter right there, he would officially stamp it, then when consent was received we could be married by the American chaplain and he would keep the records on file as the last date showed. That way my father could not say that we were married before we received his consent. He explained that that was necessary also because of my passport. In Holland, all marriages are announced in your place of birth, if you want it on record in Holland.

Roland and I decided to marry quietly the following week with just Mary and a friend of Roland's as witnesses. We would plan a nicer, larger wedding when we would marry in the chapel by the U.S. chaplain. Of course, I was just as happy as if we had a large wedding. Also, now I could eat at the American mess hall and move to the Gersthover Strasse. I knew European girls were not eligible for allotment checks, except when they lived in the U.S. I also knew I had no more rights as a Dutch citizen and that it would be years before I could become an American citizen. Roland said as soon as I received my letter of consent from home, we would be married by the U.S. chaplain in the chapel. In Austria, marriages must take place in the courthouse first; being married in the church alone is not considered legal.

John P. Alexander said when our chapel ceremony would take place he would take care of all necessary arrangements. Alexander, as we called him, was such a nice person, so considerate and helpful. Without him we would have run into many obstacles. He was the one who saw to it that I received my mess hall card, my streetcar and theater pass.

Roland surprised me with a pretty, printed house coat, a beautiful Swiss gold wrist watch (my first watch), toilet soap to bathe in, and two pairs of nylons, all purchased at the PX. I was so happy and told him I must give Mary one pair of the nylons. He did not mind. I told him I felt partly American.

Eating daily in the "For Americans Only" restaurant, I observed several American girls. They ignored me completely. They were so stuck-up, and acted superior. I noticed that most girls were reserved even to each other. Roland explained that some worked for the State Department, others for the War Department, and that in America, women who did not know each other would not take a seat at the same table in a restaurant as in Holland or Austria, where this would be acceptable.

American women were too reserved and sophisticated. Mary, who was allowed to be my guest twice a week, decided because I ate in the American restaurant that we would not let the Austrian waiter know that we were not American. Therefore, we concentrated on speaking English only. Of course, we did not talk much except to give him our order. Two American civilian girls sitting a short distance from us at a small table, were eating very appetizing looking dishes of ice cream. Mary asked if I could order that for us. Proudly I told her that I was given the privilege of ordering anything on the menu, at no extra charge. She suggested that I order the same thing. When the waiter came to ask what we wanted for dessert, I said, "two ice creams, please." He then said, "a dish?" and I said, "Yes, for two, please." A few minutes later he brought two dips of plain ice cream in two silver cups.

Our disappointment must have shown for he asked if everything was all right. He was Austrian and of course spoke only a few words of English. We did not want to speak German with him because we thought he would not wait on our table so promptly. So, I said, trying my best English, "No, Sir, we ordered the same as served at the next table."

"Oh," he said, without a smile, "you mean a sundae."

"No," I said, my face turning red, "not Sunday."

"I'm sorry," he said and left.

I didn't want it Sunday because I eat with Roland on Sundays, I told Mary.

Mary whispered, "you see, Corrie, they know you are not an American and you are not getting that fancy stuff."

I was embarrassed and told her I would ask Roland. So, we quietly ate our plain ice cream, which was still a delicacy because Austrians could not get any at that time, but we felt we were treated inferior. I told Roland about it immediately, right when he entered the door. I told him how humiliated I had been. I explained that those fancy dishes of ice cream are only served on Sunday to people like Mary and me, but American girls could have them any day.

Roland was about to laugh but when he saw that I tried hard not to cry, he said very gently, "Come here, Corrie, let me explain it to you. A sundae is a name for a certain dish of specially prepared ice cream. The waiter did not understand you. Why didn't you tell him in German what you wanted?"

Stubbornly I said, "I am going to act as an American girl. He thinks I am an American girl."

"Corrie, he knows you are not an American girl," Roland said casually.

"I don't see how," I said, "I have an American dress on, nylon hose, a dependent card, a streetcar pass. Even the conductor on the street says to me, 'good morning' and to Mary he says, 'guten morgen, fraulein,' so there must be something American looking about me." Mary just listened.

Roland then laughed out loud and said, "Corrie," then he added, as he did when he wanted to be extra kind, "Cornelia Maria Chatarina Dykhorst, you look European. Your hair and your face—it is just a European face, and you walk like a European. American girls walk different. You and Mary are acting silly trying to pass for American girls for no reason at all, and you are not fooling anybody."

"All right," I said, "so you mean to tell me I always will look European?"

"Oh no," he said, "Probably after you live in America for some time you will look more American."

"OK," I said, "show me, then, how American girls walk. Show me how!"

He was lying on the bed, but he got up, then walked with short, prissy steps through the room, sticking his nose in the air and holding his elbows close to his body, his hands in front.

"I intend to start practicing a little like that every day, and Roland, I want to find out how American girls roll their hair because you are right, my hair does not look right."

"I did not say it didn't look right, Corrie, because you have pretty hair, real pretty hair," he said, obviously overdoing it, "but it doesn't look American."

"Well, you find out how I am going to get that American look."

Mary then agreed with me and insisted Roland should help me more. Roland shrugged his shoulders and said, "Now, listen, I want her as she is, so don't bother about all the nonsense."

"Well, I'll find out from Alexander if you don't want to help me."

From then on Mary and I agreed we were not going through town carrying shopping bags anymore, but we would carry our supplies "the American way," in a large paper sack, which became real unhandy when you carried it right in front of you with both arms locked around it. All American women carried their stuff like that. It maybe wasn't handy, but it sure gave you that American look.

I made Roland promise to bring me a bright lipstick and nail polish. Roland shook his head, telling me it would not look right on me, but I insisted by telling him, "just give me a chance and you'll be surprised." As I was looking at Mary, I then suddenly remembered, "Mary, what was the name of those coats I saw several American girls wearing?"

"Oh," Mary said, "let me think...I believe they call them Chesterfield coats."

"That's what I want, Roland, a Chesterfield coat someday when I live in America. I'd love to have a coat like that!"

Roland looked at me, his eyes soft and loving. "Honey," he got up, putting his arms around me, "when we get to the States, you will see much nicer looking coats than Chesterfields."

"No!" I was determined they were the prettiest coats I had ever seen. I could just see myself in one, red with a black velvet collar. I would look just beautiful!

"The only thing, Roland—you said those girls working as U.S. civilians are making plenty of money and I must say they wear nice clothes. But Mary and I saw an American girl looking awful, she was dressed all right, but those shoes she was wearing, those awful looking shoes!"

"You know, Roland," Mary added, "the shoes were probably too short for her feet, so she cut the tip of her toes off, her big toes were sticking out of her shoes, and you know, they were winter shoes, not sandals."

"Yes," I added, "why so stingy on shoes, I'd like to know?"

Of course, I thought it could have been her feet were hurting and she just had to cut her shoes, but I would rather hurt than look so funny, especially as an American girl who was supposed to have everything, pocketbook and shoes to match, and all that sort of extravagance, or so we heard.

Roland looked at us and explained simply. "Those shoes are made like that; there are many girls wearing shoes with the tip of the toes cut out."

Mary and I looked at each other, then we both said in disbelief, "What for?"

"Well, just stylish, I suppose." He then added, "I don't know for what reason."

"Stylish!" I said again, "I think it doesn't look right."

Mary agreed it didn't look right at all, in fact, it looked poor. But a couple weeks later when Roland had a chance to buy a pair of patent leather shoes with the toes out, from a girl who worked in the same office with him, I decided they didn't look bad at all, and I wanted them. Of course, they were much prettier than the ones I saw on that American girl. When I showed them proudly to Mary, she asked if it would be possible to get her a pair also. Roland promised Mary he would do his best, and if he could not get them through some office girl in Vienna, he would ask his sister to send a pair of the right size for Mary.

Things really were changed now, eating every day in a fancy place in the evenings cozy with Roland, dignified waiters in split coat tails, serving us the best of food, accompanied by soft playing violinists creating an even more delightful atmosphere. Sometimes after dinner we would stop at one of the "For Officers and U.S. Civilians Only" nightclubs, either the Regina, or the Bristol. There I tasted my first liquor and some delicious delicatessen things, completely new to me. We danced to the Austrian waltzes, the English waltz, and tangoed to the beautiful German song "Horst du mein heimliches rufen" (Do you hear me calling at home?) a war song about a young soldier fighting and being homesick, a song at which nearly everyone became sentimental.

A few nights later we went to a night club which had a sign beside the entrance "Strictly prohibited for all U.S. personnel." The American authorities had ordered the sign put up. But Roland, wearing civilian clothes, could not stand the temptation. We, and another couple, a U.S. civilian and his date, an Austrian girl, entered the club Orient. Once inside, we found the place packed by Americans and their dates. Evidently the sign had just stimulated the desire to go inside where scantily dressed oriental looking girls performed the snake dance, the belly dance, and other exotic dances. I felt that I was now seeing the peak of nightlife. But, we also enjoyed the more cultured side of Vienna's nightlife, such as the operas and famous plays.

I will never forget the first play we saw called, "Gederman" meaning "Everyone," taken from the original Dutch play, "Elkerlik." It concerns the story of every human, the struggle of the soul between the Devil and God.

Vienna, being already the musical capital of the world, had many varieties of beauty to offer. On Sunday afternoons we would take the streetcar and go sightseeing. We stood quietly observing the beauty of the partly destroyed Saint Stephens Cathedral, the Karlskirche (Church) which was built in the Roman style. On other days we saw the Belvedere, the Garden Palace designed for Prince Eugene of Savoy, one of the heroes over the Turks. The Palace is a masterpiece of Carouge architecture. What impressed us most were the elaborately decorated interiors of the palaces, churches, and theaters, many gorgeous fountains, beautiful gardens, and sweeping stairways.

I began to feel part of this beautiful city with its love for music of great composers, memories of whom still linger; Brahms, Johann Strauss, Wolfgang Mozart, Shubert, and Beethoven, plus the folk music which is appreciated as well. Every inn has a violinist and the moods of the people change so easily according to surroundings. From the inn to the church they immediately embrace the reverence of the glories and mysteries of God. I liked the way the Austrians expressed their religious feelings in a sincere, but casual manner as a positive accepted part of life. I began to like it, my life there in Vienna.

After Roland went to work, there was not much to do except read and help tidy up the house. We had a nice Austrian cleaning woman daily from 9 until 12. The apartment we occupied was on the third floor, a nice, clean and modern place with bath. All Austrian occupants had to vacate the whole building to make places for American personnel working in Austria and their families. The caretaker and his wife were the only Austrians still living in the building. They could remain if they kept their job as caretaker, keeping halls, stairways, and entrance clean and, of course, in the winter taking care of the furnace.

The cleaning woman who came every day except Sunday, took unusual pride and effort in polishing and cleaning the furniture. When I asked her to sit down and have a cup of coffee, she seemed out of breath. I told her there was no need to take so much pain with everything. She then explained that this was her place, her own furniture. Of course, she had been allowed to take her linens, silver, china, rugs, lamps and books among all other personal belongings out and store them away. Her piano, she said, they allowed her to take, but she had no place to store it. She worried about her things, to think that she had been blessed not to lose them during the bombings, and now it had not been easy to give them up for others to use. I sympathized and promised that as long as I lived there, her things would remain in perfect order.

"Ah," she said, "the Americans in this building are so nice and courteous." And then she said a complete inventory had been made including every picture and nail in the wall. Before anyone could move out, the caretaker, together with an American in charge of such matters, would check everything. She said it seemed bad at first, but then she had accepted the job offered to her to look after her own place and keep it clean. In this way she could keep an eye on her things and get paid as well, plus American food rations. She was glad I had come to live there. She explained this was not only her apartment, she owned this unit of four rooms in the apartment building. I did not know that people could own their own place in such an arrangement. We got along fine;

she was company for me, someone to have coffee with, even though she made sure not to neglect her work. Now and then I gave her little extras to take home such as instant coffee, a bar of toilet soap, or a box of Kleenex.

Besides Mary, I knew no one. Therefore, just to pass the time I went with Mary on some errands she did for her father. When he tailored clothes for long-time customers he had known from the theater, Mary now often made these deliveries for him. This is how we met a wealthy lady who still was somehow connected with the opera. Mary was in no way related to her, but as a little girl she had started calling her Aunt Erika, and referred to her still that way. Though Mary's parents were musical in their way, it was Aunt Erika who had developed in Mary a very appreciative ear for opera music; that's how Aunt Erika had become fonder of Mary and eventually had taken part in her musical education, for Mary could play the piano, classical as well as a waltz or beer garden music.

To judge from childhood pictures, Mary had been a lovely pansy-eyed, dark-haired little girl. I could easily imagine that Aunt Erika became very fond of her and insisted that she call her "aunt." There were times that I envied Mary her dark good looks, her easy manner, and her well-rounded personality.

Roland and I accompanied her one day to see her Aunt Erika. Mary said she still lived in the big magnificent penthouse, though only occupying the first floor. The rest of this enormous house had been, because of the war, rented to several different Austrian families. After Mary rang the bell, the door was opened by Aunt Erika. She appeared to be about sixty years of age, a pale figure, her hair nearly white, wearing a faded, but evidently once expensive, green silk wrapper. I realized then that one need not be pretty to be elegant and charming. Mary greeted her warmly, then she observed us close, too close I thought, as if we came for hire of something.

But, Roland as if he were a born gentleman, bowed slightly and introduced us as if he had been accustomed to these fine surroundings all his life. Entering through a vestibule, we followed her into a large room. I was overwhelmed by the size and furnishings completely in French style. But she soon set me at ease, asking us if we would give her the pleasure to stay for tea.

I had noticed her walking with some difficulty, leaning slightly on a cane which, so Mary said, she did not need, but used it as an escort to give her moral support, a feeling of security and poise.

Before we answered, she clapped her hands three times, quick and short, and a Zimmermadschen (chambermaid) entered the room. Frau Erika gave her the order for tea.

I was impressed. I had never been a guest in such elegant surroundings.

She sat down, just observing us, looking from Roland to me, then she said, shaking her head in an agreeable manner, "Thon ist es nevei so hupsche menschen nusommen ne sehn" (it is nice to see two handsome people together). I was embarrassed. Of course, Roland did not understand her, he just knew something nice had been said. He smiled, showing a row of beautiful white teeth. Looking at his profile, I noticed how nearly perfect the lines in his face were. I could hardly believe that he really belonged to me. The Zimmermadschen (chambermaid) knocked on the door, pushing a small bamboo tea wagon.

Frau Erika served us tea, remarking how lucky we were to be treated to a Russian tea (considered the best). As we sat, drinking our tea out of small china cups, we talked little, mostly because Roland could not understand us. Frau Erika asked me some questions about Holland, my family, and how I liked Vienna. She asked me if I would come back with Mary to visit with her, saying that she enjoyed talking with young people.

We finished our tea and got up to leave. Mary embraced her, kissing her lightly but with affection. Frau Erika smiled as we shook hands. She then raised her hand to Roland and Roland courteously bowed slightly and gently kissed her hand. He did it so naturally; there was nothing awkward about him.

As we walked toward the streetcar stop, Mary linked her arm through Roland's and she said, "Aunt Erika thinks you are adorable, Roland. She usually thinks of Americans as good sports, wholesome, pleasant people, but they have no elegance. You have demonstrated something she would only expect from a Frenchman or an English gentleman perhaps."

Really, I was a little jealous. I did not like Mary hanging on Roland's arm, so I just linked my arm through his on the other side, and he squeezed my arm. I hoped he was not squeezing hers.

In the following weeks, Mary and I went to see Aunt Erika several times. She was a clever woman and I began to develop a great deal of admiration for her. On one afternoon, she invited Mary, Roland, and me to one of her small house parties, consisting mostly of people connected with the theater and a few intimate friends. Mary insisted that we should not miss it; it would be a new experience. We accepted. Mary would be accompanied by an acquaintance of Roland's, a Mr. Newman, who worked for the U.S. State Department, and Roland referred to him as a "big shot."

As a result of that acquaintance, we were privileged to ride to Aunt Erika's in a large, chauffeur-driven black limousine, courtesy of the U.S. State Department. Riding in a car during that time was something very special; that is, a car like that.

I took extreme pride in my appearance that night and liked the result. I looked beautiful in my American pale green crepe de chine dress. Mary and Roland commented on how becoming the dress was with my light blonde hair. But I became less sure of myself after Mary dressed. Standing in the door, she made a stunning appearance, of which she was well aware. Wearing a burgundy gown of smooth crepe, touching the floor, she smiled, standing there. Roland looked admiringly at her and whistled, a long whistle!

I said, with genuine admiration, "Mary, you look beautiful!" There was something exotic, tempting, and daring about her. She resembled Ava Gardner. It made my blondeness seem innocent, too lovely, too pure. Roland seemed very proud of me and secretly I hope that he only liked blondes. And I thought that Roland looked more handsome than ever in his uniform.

Mr. Newman arrived, admiring us openly. American men are nice that way. Mr. Newman, wearing a dark brown tailored suit, looked very distinguished.

Roland made us a drink. He said, "Since we look like somebody, let's feel like somebody." We then left riding in Mr. Newman's chauffeur-driven State Department limousine. Secretly I pretended that I was rich.

Arriving at the party, Aunt Erika welcomed us warmly, introducing us casually to most of the people there. I smiled and said, "How do you do," nodding my head politely to each in turn. Roland's appearance had not gone unnoticed, partly because anyone in uniform usually stands out.

Frau Erika, as I called her, made us a drink. Roland had a whiskey and soda, and I had a brandy. As we sat there sipping our drinks, Mary took Mr. Newman by the hand and introduced him to several people we had not met. I noticed one of the women sitting with a much older man, now and then focusing her eyes directly upon Roland. He acted as if he was unaware of it, but then he finished his drink in one swallow. He got up, looked around in every direction, then turned to me and said, "Corrie, I will see if I can find Mary and Mr. Newman, if you don't mind." I did mind that he left me there, but I didn't say anything, I just smiled.

When Roland did not return after ten minutes, I began to feel uncomfortable and neglected. Then one of the guests, a man who appeared to be in his fifties, reached for my glass and asked if I wanted a refill. Before I thought, I said, "No thank you, I seldom drink," in a too-cool tone. I realized immediately that I had made a blunder. After all, he had tried to be nice, and someone to talk to would make my aloneness more bearable and less noticeable. But, I had come to the party to show myself with my husband, and now he was nowhere in sight.

I looked around as casually as possible, then I spotted him. He was standing by a group of people with a glass in his hand, completely absorbed in their conversation, obviously enjoying himself. I was getting very uncomfortable. I was tired of looking pure and sweet and being refined; it was getting me nowhere, sitting there all alone while my husband was keeping himself occupied paying attention to other women. But of course, a nice woman did not have the same privilege as a man. In the first place I had not been to any parties like this one, and I knew no one except Mary. Then, I consoled myself thinking that once in America, married to Roland, we would not associate in circles as this where people were far beyond our financial, as well as intellectual, capacity.

I must have looked unhappy because I felt a hand lightly laid upon my arm, and looking up I saw the delicate face of Frau Erika. She placed herself on Roland's seat and said in a pleasant tone, speaking German, "Ein shones gesicht sall doch frah sein, mein Ziebes kind." (A pretty face must be pleasant, my dear child). As she made herself more comfortable, she added, "Tch magte mir etwas mit dir unterhalten du bist doch so hubfch und suze." (I came to talk with you a little, you are so pretty and sweet.) I had the urge to be very rude, but then after all it was Roland I should be angry with. My reply was not very polite for a young woman to a dignified older lady.

"G'nadige Frau, Leider bin ich nur hupsch und Liez wie die kinder, liebee moghe ich rafineerd sein, wie eine schone Frau" (pretty and sweet are children, I would rather be a cunning, beautiful woman who knows what card is up.) She said softly, "Was ist den mit dir mein kind......das Du so unge mutlich bist heute abent." (What ails you, Dear, that you seem so sad tonight?)

"But," I said bluntly, "my husband has been taken completely from me by your guests."

She then said, "You will not be the only one to find him attractive, but you must challenge him; just being pretty is not enough."

"What does it take besides," I asked boldly.

"No one could say, it takes different types for different people, and for some men, a variety of types, unless they really discipline their minds."

"But he is such an unpretentious, humble person," I said, more or less assuring myself.

She looked at me somewhat puzzled, then said: "That's what makes him so appealing. Often a weak man is more attractive to a woman than a strong-willed man."

"You say that the less attractive a man is, the stronger his character?"

"Concerning women, a handsome man has many more temptations. Of course, plain men sometimes cultivate charm because success in anything lies in careful development of anyone's capacities." She then added, softly, "To be married to a handsome, very charming man has often proven an extravagant luxury for any sensitive woman. Of course, women who have capital or a profession, they have some security, some power, and that plays an important role in keeping harmony. It takes much more than just loving each other to have a lasting marriage. Love wisely and don't expect anything contrary to one's nature. We don't expect a rose to sing."

I did not know what that meant at that time; therefore, I did not say anything.

Roland must have remembered he brought me along, for I saw him coming toward us. When he pulled a chair close to me, he took my hand in his, apologized sheepishly and immediately I was relieved of that uncomfortable feeling. I tried needlessly to wipe away the look of happiness on my face. I felt like a fish suddenly thrown into its own water. Frau Erika knew that I adored him; it must have been that obvious.

I was completely contented now, but welcomed the suggestion made by Mr. Newman that "it was getting late and he had a rather hard day ahead of him tomorrow." Therefore, we thanked Frau Erika for her hospitality and left for home.

Mr. Newman and Mary got along well. He seemed nice and considerate.

Several days passed, and then I received a letter from home. My father wrote that he and my mother gave their consent for me to marry Roland Dewitt Smith. It was more a statement than a letter, signed by them under oath. I was happy, but again something was missing, no good luck wishes, no "God bless you both."

I told Roland I felt depressed about it. I said my mother could have at least sent her "God bless you both" wishes.

But maybe she had hoped that I had married Victor, a Catholic, because Mama was a Catholic.

Roland laughed a little and said, "Why, Corrie, your mother is not very religious, is she?"

"Oh, yes, Roland," I said, "My mother is very religious."

"Well," he answered, "I never had the idea that she even went to church, at least you never told me so."

"That's right, my mother has not been going to church in the last years because my father was a Protestant and my mother a Catholic, and it caused some confusion. Therefore, my mother just lived her religion quietly. She saw with eyes only a Christian woman could see, and she spoke with lips that only a God-fearing woman could speak."

Roland said softly, "Corrie, if she didn't to go church, she couldn't have been much of a Christian."

We had our first argument and I went in the other room. I just sobbed, feeling sorry for myself and guilty perhaps for having caused my mother grief, and at the same time angry with Roland. Who was he to say my mother wasn't much of a Christian? Just the thought of that alone made me bawl all over again.

I remembered as a fourteen-year-old girl, my mother and I had gone to Bussum, a small town about twenty miles from Amersfoort, to see my aunt and uncle. They had ten children and lived in a windmill. Making their living by farming on a small scale and grinding corn with the windmill, they did well for themselves by working hard and long hours. So, when my mother and I, on a weekday, set out to visit with them, dressed as was customary for city people (my mother always took extreme pride in our appearance), I felt so fortunate wearing my pretty clothes, my sheer hose and white gloves. I felt just a little superior when I compared myself with my cousins' plight. They wore the wooden shoes, black, thick, wool stockings (the itchy kind) and they had to milk cows in the cold. Their hands were red and rough. But, they didn't seem to mind at all because they seemed to do their work cheerfully.

My aunt had prepared a simple, but good and wholesome, meal. We were all sitting around the table, them tired from all the work, ready to eat. But not yet! First, my uncle would read a chapter out of the Bible, then a prayer, not too long, and finally we could eat. After they ate, again a prayer of thanks. The girls then would have to wash all those dishes, the boys bring in stove wood and coal. After the chores were done, they all would sit around the fire, my aunt knitting or sewing, one of the girls or my aunt would read from the Bible, or they played the old organ and sang hymns. But because we were visiting, they would just sit around and talk.

That evening as my mother and I sat in the train, going home, I told her that I really felt sorry for them, they never went to a show or had any fun after school, they just went to church on Sunday and to school during the week, and then worked. So, I said, "They sure live a miserable life, don't they, Mom?"

My mother did not answer right away, and I guess she felt sorry for them too, because they had to work so hard and there were so many of them.

She then said, just staring, "Oh, Corrie, they are so happy. They have riches and wealth you won't find in many families, it is such a good Christian close-knit family. I'm not sorry for them, I'll come closer to being envious." But I was secretly glad that I was not born there...all that hard work and all that Bible reading, before you could eat, "I'll never be jealous of that," I thought.

I sat there thinking about that time when I had been so young and carefree. But I know now one had to be a Christian to be truly jealous at that.

So, I opened the door, smiled and kissed Roland. Lucky for both that neither of us was stubborn.

Marriage

When Alexander came home we told him that he could go ahead and make plans for what we called our "American wedding."

We were married on the nineteenth of October in a small chapel by Chaplain Captain O'Henning. Roland asked Alexander if he would be best man, but he said he would rather not, but he would be host at our dinner at the Bristol Hotel, courtesy of the U.S. RDXR Division. A variety of whiskey and liquor was given as a present to Roland, valued at around two hundred dollars.

Mr. Newman and Mary were our only witnesses. Mary looked smart in a black Persian lamb coat and beige wool suit (the coat borrowed from Aunt Erika).

I wore my soft green crepe de chine dress, beige short veil, with real lilies of the valley sewed around the hemline that nearly touched my shoulders. I carried a small cluster of the same flowers and a white short ermine cape (Aunt Erika insisted that I wear it on this special occasion).

Several of the people who lived on our street were waiting by our front door for us to appear. They had heard that one of the Americans was getting married. Of course, the black chauffeur-driven limousine caused most of the excitement.

Roland was wearing his uniform and Mr. Newman a black tailored suit.

After Chaplain O'Henning pronounced us man and wife under the Law of God, Roland kissed me, his eyes warm and loving. There was no doubt in my mind for I knew Roland truly loved me.

At that time, I did not have a wedding band. He would have had to send for it from America. He said he would buy one for me when we were in America, a diamond. In Austria and Holland, women only had plain gold bands. But I could not care less, after all, I had him!

We returned to the house and had refreshments and a few drinks.

Roland was joking and said he liked the Austrian way of getting married better, at least he did not understand what had been said. But today, he said, he thought it should be changed from "and in sickness and in health, until death do us part." It should be more realistic, such as "and only in health until arguments, money troubles, and other women do us part." They all laughed, and so did I. In the first place I did not understand English too well unless they spoke slowly and made explanations.

Mr. Newman said he really should go to the office for a few hours, but he would pick us up around seven o'clock for dinner at The Bristol. Roland said he had to see Alexander about a few things, so he rode out with Mr. Newman, but he would be back shortly.

Mary and I intended to rest awhile, when the caretaker rang the doorbell. He explained there were four Austrian musicians, violinists and a cello, who would like to play for the American couple. Mary said she was sorry, but the couple had just left. The musicians were standing in the hall with their instruments, peeping inside, glancing at the appetizing looking food and refreshments, and most appealing drinks. Mary motioned them and the caretaker to come inside and help themselves to whatever they wanted.

They had not cared to play anyway and were filling themselves with everything available, and after about one hour of continuous drinking and eating, Mary had to order them to leave.

Shortly after that Roland came home with two wedding gifts for me, a white tablecloth with twelve matching napkins of the finest damask, made in Czechoslovakia, and a golden compact with the date engraved, gifts from the office crew. I told him I did not know how to express my appreciation.

At around seven o'clock Mr. Newman arrived, and we left for the dinner that was given in our honor at The Bristol, one of Vienna's finest hotels. At least twenty guests were present at our table, people whom I did not know, and if it hadn't been for Mary and Alexander I would have felt hopelessly lost at my own wedding dinner. Alexander whispered that a real Prince and Princess were among our guests, that even they, during this food shortage, welcomed an extravagant dinner invitation. He further explained that they were invited to most society affairs in leading hotels. We were told they were originally from Germany and had long since lost their royal standing among their own class because they had ignored certain standards even a penniless and homeless Prince was expected to live up to. But this couple had lived as they pleased, seemingly not caring for their titles and accepting nearly all invitations promising good free meals and drinks in acceptable company, of course.

As I glanced over the table observing the guests, a Colonel sitting across from me smiled so pleasantly and told us that he expected us one day next week to come by his club, as he wanted me to meet his wife. She had just now arrived in Paris from New York and was on her way to Vienna. He continued with a genuine gleam in his eyes, "You'll love her, she is a most fascinating person." Roland told him we would love to come.

Roland told me later that was Colonel McKee, a fine man. Besides the Colonel, most guests did not seem to know that this dinner was given for us. I did not enjoy the food. There were too many knives, forks, and dishes, too many courses, impeccable waiters, eight at our table alone, dressed in red livery, so well trained that before you spoke they already were at your service. Therefore, I passed up some delicious looking appetizers. I could not afford to make a mistake using perhaps the wrong silver.

Now and then I saw couples passing our table, women talking like queens, haughtily graceful. The waiters, carrying large trays, moved easily without making a sound. The place was chic, impressive, with red velvet carpeting and matching draperies, nearly too royal looking. An orchestra of violins and other string instruments, with all the musicians dressed in red livery, were playing soft waltzes on a large podium. After dinner everyone at our table moved to an adjoining room, a sort of hall with small winding stairways on each side leading to individual balconies closed in with ornamental handrails, where there was seating overlooking the whole dance floor.

When each individual party was seated, the orchestra playing softly, "The Merry Widow Waltz," the soft colored lighting created a most romantic atmosphere.

A chaise seat had been reserved for us; Mr. Newman and Mary, Alexander and an American girl from the office. I was thrilled and excited to be among so much splendor, and when Roland pressed my hand secretly under the table and winked at me, I knew that he also had been intoxicated by the surroundings.

Roland and I danced once. I was very proud of him and could have danced all night, but I welcomed the time when the music stopped, and we returned to our seats. A waiter came to our table telling Roland that the lady opposite from our table had given him the honor of the next dance with her. Alexander said he could not refuse because it was "The Princess" who had requested it. Roland rose and made a light bow in her direction, she slightly nodded her head and smiled. I did not necessarily like it, but Alexander as a gentleman talked to me all during the time they danced.

Roland, after returning her to her table, stood for a few minutes talking with her husband. I was proud of him as he handled every situation so naturally. Alexander complimented him on being a born social climber.

It was getting late and I was glad when at two o'clock the band stopped playing. As we were waiting for our coats by the vestiaire (a place for checking coats), the Prince approached us with outstretched hand and said in a very distinct accent, "It has been a pleasure meeting you and I wish you happiness for your future." I smiled at him, then at his wife, of course. I did not extend my hand, but nodded in her direction.

I was glad when we were on our way home; the strain not to say or do something wrong had been very tiring. Of course, Roland had imbibed enough liquor to be completely at ease.

It was nearly two o'clock when we were alone in our room and I at last had Roland to myself.

But in the early morning hours it occurred to me that something was wrong with Roland. He seemed to have difficulty breathing and pushed the covers on the floor complaining it was hot in the room and for me to open the windows. I put my hand on his head and it seemed to me that he had a fever. I slipped into my house coat and knocked on Alexander's door. It took a few minutes before Alexander opened the door. I apologized for awakening him in the early morning hours, but asked if he would please take a look at Roland because I thought he was sick.

Alexander laughed, putting on his bathrobe and said that I just had never seen any one with a severe hangover. But he agreed to take a look at him. As he entered he only glanced at him, then just stood there for a moment looking at him, then said seriously, "You are right, Corrie, he is sick, in fact he seems quite sick, much more than just a hangover."

He then called the U.S. military hospital and twenty minutes later, Roland was carried on a stretcher by two medics down the stairs to the ambulance.

Alexander then called the hospital to give the necessary information. He said I should not worry about staying with him, that it would be fine if we both locked our doors.

I was up and dressed early the next morning and Alexander told me which streetcar to take to the hospital. Visiting hours were from 10 o'clock in the morning until 4 p.m. and from 7 p.m. until 9 p.m.

When I entered the hospital, I was told at the information desk, by a U.S. nurse who answered me in a very cool, superior manner, that "Roland Smith was allowed no visitors." She then ignored me and went about her work. I was so stunned by her indifferent manner that the nerve to ask how he was, failed me.

I felt very let down as I returned to the apartment. I was glad when Alexander came home. He said he had called the hospital and they had told him Roland had a light case of double pneumonia and that for three days no visitors were allowed. I had not eaten anything, and Alexander brought me something to eat. I don't know how I would have gone through those three days if it hadn't been for Alexander and the cleaning woman. I called the hospital every day about three times and every time, the same answer. Then, in the afternoon as I sat in the living room reading, the telephone rang. It was Roland. He wanted to know if I was having such a good time that I could not come to see him. He kept on talking in a very angry voice, "fine wife was I, did not care whether he lived or died."

I then explained that I had been to the hospital and some nurse at the desk had told me that no visitors were allowed. I had called several times each day and so had Alexander, but we were still told no visitors.

Roland said, "I'll see about that. Now come on up here and tell them at the desk that you are my wife."

Immediately I got ready and arrived at the desk in about twenty minutes, thanks to the wonderful streetcar service in Vienna. The nurse at the desk was very nice now. She said I should have told them I was his wife and, of course, I could have been with him all during visiting hours. She led me through a hall to Roland's room. He was propped up on several pillows, looking well taken care of and spoiled. He acted stubborn, but I could tell he was happy to see me. There was one other fellow in the room. Roland looked good in his burgundy corduroy U.S. Army robe.

Roland's stubborn attitude left him soon after I explained everything in detail. He said Alexander had called and would come up to see him. He told me I did not have to leave at four o'clock, for me just to be quiet and say nothing. He even talked the nurse into bringing him an extra plate of food. The hospital was large with many patients, but very few visitors, and that's probably why they were so lenient.

Alexander arrived shortly after seven. Roland thanked him for getting him to the hospital and for looking after me. Alexander asked Roland if he could take me to dinner instead of bringing me my food, and with Roland's permission, he would like to take me to the opera the next night. Verdi's "Il Trovatore" would be playing. Roland said that would be fine with him, but he could not see what Alexander would get out of it because he did not understand the language. I told Roland neither did I, because it would be in Italian, but it was not necessary to understand the words. If you knew the story it was easy by gestures and expressions of hand and eyes to make out what the meaning was, and of course we would love the music.

Alexander was so cultured, not typical for an American. Roland and I both really liked him.

At nine o'clock the bell rang to let us know that visiting hours were over. I promised Roland I would be back early the next day, probably with Mary, because she had intended to spend the night with me.

When Alexander and I came to the house, Mary was already there. I had given the caretaker instructions to let her in the apartment should she arrive before we got back. Mary had brought me a book to read, "American History," in German. She said since I planned on making my home there it would be nice to read it because it would probably be many years before I could read a book in English. I thanked her for her thoughtfulness. She told me then that she was leaving the next week for Berlin, that she would leave Reino in Vienna, but she wanted to talk to her husband. I asked her if her husband could not come to Vienna? She said perhaps he could in a couple of years, but as of now, Germans were not welcome anywhere. She explained that because through her marriage she was still German, she would either have to move to Berlin or divorce her husband and get her Austrian citizenship back, that only then could she live in Vienna. That was why she needed to go to Berlin and talk with Hanz personally. It had been nearly three years since they had seen each other, and whether they could face it or not, it might not work for them to start a new life together. She said she had made up her mind that she was willing to try it if he at all seemed compatible. She said he did not know of her plans and she realized that he would be a very changed man, and that she had no hope of them being in love. She then added, "I can face whatever it is, but I hope he does need us, me and Reino."

I thought how unpredictable life is, no one knows how things will look a year from now.

"I will hope some day you will find the happiness you deserve, Mary."

"Corrie," said Mary softly, "You don't find happiness, you establish it, it depends on how you cope with misfortunes. Some people think I should have gone to Hanz the moment I heard he was alive, but that would have been disastrous. Too many people measure love by emotions and their own desires, calling it their duty."

She seemed very depressed and I suggested that because we both were tired that we might as well go to bed early. Of course, it was ten o'clock already.

Alexander had already left for work when we awoke. We made breakfast, toast with coffee and jam.

Mary went with me to see Roland. He was sitting up and said he was feeling well enough to come home, but he said that they had found that he had scabies (the "itch"). Of course, he was already cured, the hospital had disinfected all his belongings. He looked at me and laughed, saying, "You will have it, Corrie, and Mary probably, too, for it is very contagious." He then gave me a bar of dark soap and a small box of medicated powder that the nurse had given him to give to me. Now I should take the mattress outside on the veranda and sun it for several hours, then air out all clothes, change the bed linens, and sack them up for the laundry to have them disinfected, wash all furniture with Lysol. Then I was to take a hot bath with the dark soap, powder all over with the medicated powder, then roll myself in a clean sheet and go to bed. Next morning, change bedclothes again, discard the sheet I had used to roll up in, or boil it, then take another hot bath. After that I should be free of bacteria. I told Roland I didn't think I really had it for I itched very little, only on the inner part of my fingers and arms. He nodded his head, "that's the beginning."

He insisted I had better do as he said because a U.S. soldier had been having such a bad case, they thought his arm had to be removed and all because of his own neglect. Well, that did it! I promised I would do all that work. Mary said she would help me, so I promised her a carton of cigarettes from Roland because he was not allowed to smoke anyway. We would start on it the next afternoon; she needed to go home first to see about her trip to Berlin.

That night Alexander and I and an officer who lived one flight above us went to the opera. It was one of the most thrilling experiences in my life. Alexander let me use his opera lenses, bringing the stage close to my eyes. I was proud to be in the company of two nice

Americans, and having a husband who, though sick, allowed me such a wonderful evening.

Roland was kept in the hospital for another week, then released early one morning.

I had been busy getting rid of the "itch," and cleaning the apartment took longer than one afternoon.

Roland said he had missed me more than he ever could have realized. Now he had some news to tell me, which was good and not so good. He had received a letter from his brother, Ben, asking him to come home "since he was married now, why remain longer over there, that his parents were getting older and they had lost one son in the war, so would he please consider coming home with his wife."

Now he had made arrangements through Alexander, but there was one drawback. I could not go with him just now, it would take about six weeks to get my papers ready and there was no other way. I asked him, trying not to cry and also trying to control my voice, "Where will I stay after you leave?" He smiled and said, "There is a surprise for you." He said we were going to Holland together, then he could meet my parents and visit for sixteen days if that was all right with them, of course.

I took a deep breath. I was relieved—now that was really nice! Now I could hardly wait to leave Vienna.

We went to Colonel McKee's club one evening, and there I met the Colonel's wife. She was not at all the glamorous woman I had pictured her to be, but she was indeed a lovely person, kind, interesting, and she made me feel very much at ease.

Homecoming

We left Vienna on a cold, gloomy November day after saying good-bye to Mary's parents and Reino. Alexander brought us to the train; he had been such a wonderful person and good friend. He gave

Corrie Smith

Roland Smith

Form No. 87
FOREIGN SERVICE
(Revised October 1939)

Certificate of Witness to Marriage

(See section 72, title 22 of the United States Code)

FOREIGN SERVICE OF THE UNITED STATES

Vienna, Austria

October 28, 19 46

I, William O. Boswell, Vice Consul of the United States of America at Vienna, Austria, do hereby certify that on ~~this~~ the 19th day of October, A. D. 19 46, at The USFA Chaplain Center, IX Garnisongasse 14, in the city of Vienna, Austria, Roland Dewitt Smith, a CITIZEN ~~SUBJECT~~ of the United States of America, aged 21 years, born in Bessemer, Alabama, and now residing in Vienna, Austria, and Cornelia Maria Dijkhorst, a ~~CITIZEN~~ SUBJECT of the Netherlands, aged 23 years, born in Amersfoort, Netherlands, and now residing in Vienna, Austria, were united in marriage in my presence.

In witness whereof, I have hereunto subscribed my name and affixed the seal of my office at Vienna, Austria, this 28th day of October, A. D. 19 46, and of the Independence of the United States the one hundred and seventy-first.

L. S.

William O. Boswell
Vice Consul of the United States of America.

Service # 5390

Fee: One Dollar. To be issued in Quadruplicate.

me a souvenir, a golden medallion on a fine chain to put around my neck. He said a Jewish girl had given it to him. It was possible that it was valuable, but he wanted me to have it. It was odd looking, oriental, one side encrusted with small rubies and one nice-sized emerald in the center. I could not find words to express my thanks.

This was the first time in my life to travel first class (pullman compartment complete with shower and berths). In Holland I had traveled second class, just pullman, and during the war people were glad to be able to get on a train, mostly third class (coach). We had our meals on the train and we would not change trains until Frankfurt.

In Frankfurt we placed our luggage in a locker and went across the railway station to the Red Cross Restaurant where we had coffee and doughnuts.

At four o'clock that evening we got on another train to travel all night to Bremerhaven, arriving there sometime in the afternoon. We spent the night there in a hotel reserved for Americans only. To our surprise and joy, we found that there was space left on a chartered bus for Americans on leave, which would take us directly to Amersfoort. I had to ask the driver myself because such luck was hard to believe. He said the bus would leave at seven o'clock in the morning and would tour Holland for three days. We would be in Amersfoort after several sight-seeking stops, approximately around seven that night.

When we arrived at the old familiar station, I began to get a little nervous. Roland suggested that I call home first. There was a telephone booth directly across from Hotel Monepale. I dialed, and a soft voice answered on the other side of the line, saying, "Hello." It was my mother!

"Hello," I said, then, "Mama, this is Corrie."

"Corrie," she said, then silence. She asked, "Corrie, where are you?"

I replied, "I am here, Mother, at the station, here in Amersfoort."

After a moment she said, "Are you alone?"

"No, Mama, Roland is here with me. Can we come home?"

"Of course," she said, "come on. I will call Papa and turn the porch light on."

"Well?" asked Roland.

"Oh, Roland, she sounded happy. I told her you were with me." Now I had to fight my tears, but I managed not to cry.

"Yah," he said, "Your mother—I'm not worried about her, but I certainly hate to meet your father."

We took a taxi. As we rode along I tried to reassure him. Papa was going to be all right.

When we pulled up to the house, I could see that Roland was impressed with the not too large, but nice looking, white stucco house. The outside porch light was on. The taxi driver helped carry the luggage to the door. Roland paid him. I did not need to ring the doorbell as my mother already had opened the door. I hugged and kissed her, then Annie, Tillie, and Jan, my sister Annie's husband. They all were standing in the hall. My father and brother were not home yet. I introduced Roland, they all smiled at him and shook hands. The luggage remained in the hall, and after we hung up our coats, we sat down in the living room.

My mother smiled at me and said, "Corrie, this sure is a surprise. How is...uh...your husband?"

She, of course, did not speak English. I nodded, "Of course, Mama."

Roland said, "What did she ask you?"

I said, "She asked if you were my husband."

He laughed and said, "Yah, Yah," (trying already some Dutch).

He then said to me, "Corrie, I like your mother and all of them here, but I dread meeting your father."

I had to explain again to everyone what he said.

Tillie sat staring at Roland, then whispered to me, "Gosh, Cor, he is so knap (handsome), he looks like a gangster."

Roland said, "What did she say?"

I said, "She said you look like a gangster."

"A gangster?" Roland replied, frowning.

"Oh, Roland, that's a compliment here, like someone in the movies, a dignified looking gangster."

Roland said, shaking his head, "Some compliment!"

But Tillie looked so innocent and helpless, she had meant to say something nice about him. Roland then winked at her. Then Papa came in…

Roland and I got up, and as Papa and I shook hands, tears sprang up in his eyes when he said, "I am glad you came home."

I then introduced Roland, "Young man, I am glad to meet you!" They shook hands so firmly, I am sure it hurt Roland's knuckles. Papa hung up his coat in the hall, then sat down in the living room.

No one spoke, so to break the silence, Roland said to me, "Could I offer your father a drink?" (We had two bottles of cognac with us in Roland's saddlebags.)

I told my father that Roland asked if we could celebrate our homecoming with a drink.

"Sure, sure," Papa said, friendly like.

Roland, relieved, got the cognac, and Papa put three glasses on the table, one for Jan, Roland, and himself. Women, of course, don't drink cognac—perhaps a glass of wine or liquor, but not cognac.

After awhile, my father, Roland and Jan were trying to make conversation, through help of my translation. Jan spoke a little English, but what you learn in school does not enable you to carry on a conversation unless you specialize in the subject.

My brother came home and appeared surprised as well as pleased. He immediately was offered a drink to toast to our happiness and well-being. Roland asked me what my brother's name was, he had forgotten.

"Ap," I said, "short for Albert."

"ABB," Roland said, repeating, "Abb."

"No," I said, "AP."

"Abb," he said, "That's a funny name, Abb."

We all laughed, and he wanted to know why.

"Because they all like you, Roland, everyone always likes you," I said admiringly.

They had one more drink. In Holland civilized people would not allow themselves more than two drinks.

Papa asked me what Roland did before he went in the service, seemingly well pleased with Roland's appearance.

"Roland," I said, "Papa wants to know what you did before you went in the service." "Tell him I went to school."

"He went to school, Papa."

"Ah, he went to college," Papa said, more as a remark than a question.

"Roland, Papa thinks you went to college."

"Might as well, don't you think, since he seems to like me. Tell him I went to Georgia Tech."

"Yes, Papa, he went to college, he went to Georgia Tech."

"Oh," said my father, seemingly impressed, but I knew that he did not know, and I didn't know what and where Georgia Tech was. But anyway, Papa seemed pleased and didn't ask any more questions.

Jan spoke up now and said, "Are you from Georgia, Roland?"

"No, I was born in Bessemer, Alabama, and moved to Mentone, Alabama, then I went to high school in Chattanooga, Tennessee."

"Gosh," I thought, "how complicated!"

"But," I thought, "I do not like that Bessemer, Alabama, it doesn't sound pretty. After Roland leaves and people ask me where he was from, I will say Mentone, Georgia, that sounds prettier. No one will know the difference, and I have read some about Atlanta, Georgia, in my American History book, but I don't recall reading about Alabama."

Mama had made some hot chocolate. In Holland there wasn't much food shortage anymore because the countries that had suffered under German occupation, and were Allies, were supplied first. But still when we opened our luggage and brought out gifts such as nylon hose, soap, cigarettes, and cigars, they welcomed these luxuries.

I went upstairs with Mama to fix our room. The house had four bedrooms. Annie and Jan would give us their room and they would sleep in the attic which was nice enough but colder than a room. They assured us they liked sleeping in the attic. Jan said it reminded him of the time he had spent there during the war when he was in hidden by us from the Germans.

"Anything for our American liberators," he stood there grinning with his hands in his pockets and biting his pipe that never had any tobacco in it. But Jan loved that pipe! He was 23 years old and a graduate from M.T.S. (Middlebar Techinsche School). Papa considered him bright, with a good future. He was very advanced in architectural ideas. Jan and Annie had married while I was in Vienna. They already had all their furniture paid for and were now waiting for a house or an apartment. For the present they lived with Mama and Papa, and at times with his parents. They were either all loved up or arguing, seldom in between.

It was late that night before we retired.

The following morning Papa took Roland on his police motorcycle to Police Headquarters to show him off and let Roland register for both of us in the tourist file. Because I was married to an American, I had become a tourist in my own country.

The whole family took a liking to Roland, even Papa seemed

carried away, and in the afternoon, he allowed Roland to take a ride on his police motorcycle to go around the block, but Roland evidently had misunderstood because it was at least two hours before he returned. He explained where all he had been, and Papa said he had been completely around the city. We had been worried sick, I about Roland, and Papa about his motorcycle. When we first spotted him from a distance, Jan had said, "typical American, Corrie, just as unconcerned." We all thought it was funny because he and the motorcycle were still in one piece.

The days went by so fast. Mama, busy cooking, and Papa took Roland hunting and showed him around town, but it was cold at the beginning of December, so we stayed in a lot and talked. My brother Ap never had too much to say; even though he spoke English well, he mostly listened. Ap was quiet anyway. He wanted to get ahead in life and had a good chance because he already was manager of the sales department of Noack Royal Meat Works.

Several of my relatives came to visit us and to meet my American husband. My aunt asked me where Roland was from and I said, "From Mentone, Georgia." Jan, who had been sitting nonchalantly in Papa's easy chair with his hands in his pockets, his legs stretched out, biting his pipe said, "Not Georgia, Corrie, Alabama." I ignored him, saying calmly, "Mentone is close to Georgia. You have to go through Georgia to get to Mentone," I added. My aunt said, "Now isn't that nice; you are a lucky girl."

My aunt knew that America consisted of New York, the city of the skyscratchers, not scrapers; Chicago, where the underworld communicated; and Texas where the oil fields were. And, of course, Hollywood. Everybody had heard of Hollywood, but now where it was exactly, that was another question.

Now Papa and Roland were talking about the great American sport "football." Roland tried to explain it was played differently in America than in Holland. Papa understood, of course, that football is a game played kicking the ball only with the foot. Roland said, "No, not in

America." It was not clear to Papa and they did not understand each other. So, finally Jan entered into the conversation and explained it all.

"Jan, how come you know so much?" I asked.

Mama always called him "Jan-know-it-all." Only when she knew it would not offend him because Mama was for peace in the family.

"I've read a lot. I listen when people talk, and I've traveled," he said dryly.

"Traveled?" I said.

"Yes, traveled," he replied.

"Puh, you've never been to America," I said.

"You don't know where I have been."

"I know you have never been out of Europe," I argued.

Jan, remaining in the same nonchalant position he always had, biting his pipe, hollered suddenly "Ann... Ann....."

My sister, who was drying the dishes in the kitchen, came running, the dish towel in her hand.

"What, Janneman?" she petted him standing protectively behind his chair.

"Have I been to America?" Jan asked, remaining in the same lazy position.

"Did he tell you he has been to America?" Ann asked us.

"Yah, he said he has. He lies all the time," I said.

"Well now, just a moment," Ann said. "My Jan doesn't lie, my Jan exaggerates a little maybe, but he does not lie." And now, "Jan tell them you have never been in America."

Jan sat there looking unconcerned and amused, then said, "Ann said I have not been to America."

Jan was a person you might get mad at, scream at, nearly fight with, but you could never truly dislike him. He carried no grudge and was always willing to forgive and forget.

The time went by so quickly and sixteen days were past before we knew it. Roland had been to Maastricht in Holland to make arrangements for me to come to the U.S. as soon as possible. I dreaded to see him leave, but I knew it would not be long before we could be together. And now I was lucky enough to spend my waiting time with my own folks!

I saw Roland to the bus. He would travel with the same bus we came on, going to Bremerhaven and from there he would take the boat to America. He kissed me affectionately and promised to be good and he would write soon.

After Roland left, every member of the family began to realize that soon I would be leaving too, and more than likely never return, so they were all very nice to me, as they would have been to someone who would depart from life forever. Of course, I was on my best behavior also. Naturally those last weeks were to be happy ones! During the daytime after helping my mother with the household chores and writing Roland, we would visit with relatives or I would go to see an old girlfriend, or take in a movie. But my mind and conversation were usually on Roland and about going to America. Everyone seemed to envy me, as if I was going to the "Promised Land."

I could hardly wait to receive my travel papers.

One night Annie and Jan went to see his parents. Papa was gone somewhere concerning his work, and Ap had a date. So, Mama, Tillie, and I were sitting in the living room talking about the future, mostly my future. Then Tillie asked Mama if it was all right to tell me their big secret.

I said, "What secret?"

"Can I, Mama?" Tillie pleaded.

"Well, I guess so," said Mama.

Tillie moved her chair a little closer to mine; then she said in a very serious tone, "Promise not to breathe it to anyone?"

I promised.

Then she said, "You know, Corrie, I have been very lonely lately... and now Mama and I have decided on something. Papa knows about it...and he said it is all right with him now."

I thought she wanted to come with me to America. I knew I'd just have to be firm and tell her right then that it is impossible.

"Now," she continued, looking again at my mother, "We have decided to adopt a child, not a baby, but a little orphan about five or six years old. Mama wants it and so do I and Papa said it is all up to us."

"Well!" I said, shocked, but also relieved.

Mama looked at me and squinted her eyes, as if she was trying to see better.

"Well, Mama, you and Tillie are out of your minds. You mean to adopt a child, something for Tillie so that she will have someone to play with? Tillie is now thirteen years old and in two years she'll be thinking about boys; in five years she will be married, and then you will have that adopted child to look after. Look, Mama, you are not even in good health. I cannot understand! I cannot understand Papa! You all are just thrown off balance, it is peace now and you want to do something good, well, that's fine, do something good. But not adopting a child with Mama's health like it is...and before long Annie and Jan will have children, then Tillie can take care of them."

Tillie had said nothing, but then she looked at me, her eyes full of hate.

"I wish you had gone straight from Austria to America. We did not need you here. Mama and I had it all fixed up and then you have to come and try to talk her out of it, but you won't, do you hear?" She was crying now, her eyes all red and the tears coming easily; she looked so pitiful that I got up and gently placed my arm around her shoulder, but she jerked away and said to leave her alone.

She was bawling now and between sobs, she said, "I know that years ago you even tried to talk Mama into giving me away."

I moved in the big chair, away from Mama and Tillie...the very idea that I had tried to talk Mama into giving her away!

But then I remembered something.

Tillie had been about four years old. I had returned home from a tennis game. Not being a member, I had been asked to join, but it would cost seven gulden for membership. My allowance was only fifty cents a week and I knew there was no need to ask at home for seven gulden (seven dollars then) to join a tennis club.

But I had arrived home feeling left out of everything. I told my mother that my life wasn't worth living, that other girls from school had fun, they belonged to clubs and had lots of things I did not have. I had called my special friends' names off—Do-Jong, for example.

"Yes," said my mother, "that is an only child, there are here four to clothe and feed."

"Yes," I said, "that is too large a family, for a small income."

"But we have four now," Mama had said, "and there is nothing we can do about it."

I then had said, "We sure could have had more......with only two, instead of four."

"Yes," Mama had said, "it takes a lot less with only two children."

"Well," I had suggested, "why not give one away?"

I only had said that to let Mama know how deeply hurt I was, not to be able to belong to the tennis club and other things so important when you are young.

I had tried to look as if I really meant it.

Then to my surprise she had said, "All right, you just tell me which one."

I did not want to part with any of them, but I pretended and told

Mama that “I just have to think awhile.”

“You think about it,” Mama had encouraged.

I sat there awhile, seemingly wondering. I knew I would never want to part with my brother, after all he was the only brother I had. He was two years older than I was. He was fourteen then. Mama always did send him to the store at night instead of me, and I was always relieved about that because I was afraid in the dark. People claimed if you did mean little things, that a ghost would grab you at night in the dark, and I was scared. And Ap—a ghost would not get Ap—good little Appie! —Mama's pet. But, I sure would not like being without a brother.

And then my sweet sis, Annie—who could even think about doing without her? She was two years younger than I was and already helped with all the household chores—just the thought of not having her as a sister made me feel lonely already.

Then, how about myself...of course I belonged here...I would not be happy anywhere else.

I felt guilty when I thought how selfish that was, to wish that we only had Ap and me.

I would not even want to be without Tillie, though I had to tend to her lots of times when I did not want to. But after all, she was the baby, with big, blue threatening eyes, a rather spoiled brat, but a cute little mean thing. In fact, she had a little cruel streak in her, but I still would not want to part with her either.

I remember that once Mama had called me to go and find her, she was nearly four then. I found her all right—she was sitting behind my father's workshop seemingly playing with sand. As I walked up to her, she was squeezing something real tight in her hand, and she kept on squeezing. When I looked I saw that it was one of our goldfish out of the little pond in front of our house. She had squeezed the fish's eyes completely out. I looked at her and asked her why she did that.

“Did what?” she said.

I said, "Kill that goldfish!"

She said she wanted to see his eyes pop out more. I told her she had killed him.

She started to scream real loud and my mother came running, picking Tillie up (she now cried with big sobs telling my mother I had killed her goldfish.)

Mama carried her in the house, constantly soothing her, trying to get her calm, then she said, "Poor kid," and put her to bed with a sucker.

And the whole family had gone on believing that I was a goldfish killer.

So, when I looked at her I thought, "Only blood kin could love that mean little thing." At times she could be so lovely, even if it wasn't for very long.

So, I told Mama I guessed we might as well do without the luxuries I longed for and stay together because I didn't think anyone would want any of those three.

I looked at my mother now and said, "Why did you tell her that I once wanted to give one of us away?"

She said she had told the story to Tillie only to let her know that people cannot give up any one willfully from their families.

I felt sorry for Tillie, poor thing!

"Tillie," I said, "now listen, honey, if you and Mama really want that, go ahead! I am leaving anyway, so why should I care—but I must admit that I am strictly against it." I thought, "Poor Mama, she is going through the change of life and I had heard that women were unreasonable then."

The days passed and neither of us mentioned the incident anymore. I tried being extra nice to Tillie and gave her some of my things—

clothes—such as my winter coat.

Just before we left Vienna, Roland had bought me a nice sport coat, light brown mountain lamb. It had been advertised in the paper, a lady wanted to sell her coat in exchange for food. We had made the deal exchanging a variety of things, cigarettes, soap, and whiskey, which she said she could easily swap for food.

So, we all had been happy about the deal.

The coat, three-quarter length, looked good on me with my brown leather pumps and mist green scarf. Mama agreed I looked smart in the outfit. I liked clothes plain and finished looking. I did not care for furs, belts, ribbons, or lots of buttons. Ap, my brother, gave me a pair of Swiss Alpine sunglasses, black rimmed, closed in at the sides. He said they would make me look complete. I did not know whether it was a compliment, or if he was making fun of me, and I did not want to find out.

Two days before Christmas I received two letters from Austria, and one from Roland. He wrote me regularly and said he had written to the Governor of Tennessee to speed up my coming to the United States. One letter was from Mary. She had returned to Vienna for good. She said Hanz had asked her for a divorce. He had confessed that there was another girl, a German girl, and their love for each other had grown in their shared misery. Anyway, she realized he was a bitter man and she herself had not the strength nor the desire to win him back. She said they had come to an agreeable settlement that freed him from further responsibility concerning Reino. She said the sum of money was enough to care for Reino until he was twenty-one and would enable him to go to college if he should prove deserving of such an education.

She further wrote that she had signed up for employment in England for she thought she wanted to start out completely anew.

The other letter was from Victor. He wrote that he was glad I had returned to Holland and he looked forward to seeing me soon. It dawned on me that he was under the impression that Roland and I had broken up; therefore, I immediately answered him, telling in my note that I would be leaving in a week or so for America. I signed it "Corrie." I did not tell him that I was married; I figured he would gather that much.

It was shortly before my papers arrived that I received a note from Victor; it was just a poem. It read:

"Beneath a heap of dull, drab stones
I found one sparkling clear
And pure as crystal.
I hold 'm in the golden sunlight...
What rays reflect...what beauty glowing
In silence I observed,
Though I had seen fairer ones
But then as many sparks reflected
Into the soul I say.
Then suddenly it leaps, and as it waves and scatters,
From me it slipped, into a heaping pool of gravel......
Long I waited for its vision......
But gone was she......and past recalling
My bright and lustrous Bergcrystal."

I then wrote him a note asking if he would do me a favor and ask his mother if she would forgive me, for I had never met a finer woman and was thankful for the months I had the privilege of spending in the comfort of their home. And if she could forgive me I would like to send her something personal from America; if not, would he be so kind as to let me know before I departed from Holland.

I received my answer very soon; however, it was one from his mother and it made me sad and happy at the same time. She wrote:

> "Corrie Dear,
>
> From Victor we learned that you are soon to leave for America. We want you to know that we do not regret having had you in our home; not I, nor Father, carries any ill feeling toward you. We hope and wish that you adjust well in a completely new land. Hedi and Albert enclose their love, and we hope that you always regard us as friends.
>
> Deine,
>
> Therese Topitz"

I was very glad for receiving that letter. I wished it had come before Christmas because most people like being on good terms with each other to enjoy the Christmas spirit.

I wished Roland could have spent Christmas with us. In Holland families drew nearer during these holidays and relatives and friends that were not on speaking terms would often reunite then. We did not exchange gifts; as is the custom in some countries, our gift exchanging takes place on the evening of the fifth of December, Saint Nicholas Day. It is an old celebrated tradition that has no connection with Christmas. Hundreds of years ago, there was a Saint Nicholas from Spain who, according to the legend through the years, gave gifts to the poor children, arriving in Holland on December 5 by boat. He had a long white beard and was dressed in a velvet red cape. That was a big day for all the good children in Holland.

But Christmas was a day that had no connection with Saint Nicholas and was celebrated on the twenty-fifth of December. People donated money, clothing and fruit to the churches to make gifts for the sick and the poor. We, the children, would make baskets in Sunday school and fill them with fruit; then on Christmas Day we would take them to the hospitals, singing songs around the Christmas tree. At home we would have a big dinner and oranges and all kinds of nuts, and everyone was nice to each other. Even my father never raised his voice on Christmas. He would be nice and pleasant just like I was when we had a bad storm.

I remember well that during a storm I always had been good. Afraid, once during a severe storm I had asked Mama, "Why did God make it storm?"

She had said, "Because He is angry, He is warning the people, because they don't do His will, they won't listen."

So, ever since that time I was always good and obedient during a storm, that is if it was bad enough. Once Ap slammed the door on my little finger (I was about six years old then), and I nearly screamed and called him dirty names, but then it had thundered very loud, so I had told him "it was all right, just forget it, Ap." Then I had pressed hard on it until finally blood came, one real big drop. I had smeared it on a large white handkerchief and rolled the bloody spot on the outside so that Ap and Mama and God could see it. How kind I had been, not screaming or saying ugly words.

"To be afraid," Mama said, "was good—of course, not of people—but of God."

I remembered that once we all had been so afraid. It was when we still lived in the other house in the "Jan Steen street." I had been about eleven years old. We lived next door to the Wyetenburgs, a nice family. Mr. Wyetenburg was a bookkeeper for the Gemeente Bank and they had three grown children. Pete, the youngest, about eighteen, was a student at the Lycium, a school for bright young people only. It was then that they had taken in a boarder. Everyone on our street had sort of talked about it because he was a strange, rather odd man, very old—or at least I thought so—he appeared at least sixty or maybe older—what I could see of him. He was a cobbler, a shoe repairman, and had set up a small repair shop behind the Wyetenburgs' house. It was built from wood, just a plain little shop, then painted brown with only one window. No one paid much attention to him, but people still wondered.

Why did the Wyetenburgs put up with a shoe repair shop in the back of their house for a boarder, and then such a strange old man?

But, we were not the kind of people to meddle in other people's affairs. Because it was so handy, we started taking our shoes for repair to him.

Opentie was his name. No one knew whether that was his given name or his last name. He never talked, we just knocked very loud and after he said, "come in," then we had to put our name on a piece of paper already prepared and he would glue it in the shoe, or shoes. After three days they could be picked up. A sign on the door said, "All Repairs Finished in Three Days." He never talked, just looked up from his old, tiny glasses and listened to what had to be done for repair. But strange things were told about him. He was not an ordinary man, not just a plain shoe repairman people said; he was a communist. When he had moved there, he had placed pamphlets right there in the little shop. No one bothered them—they were still there, getting dusty and dirty. And old books were stacked along the wall. No one cared, no one looked—just books about shoes and things probably—no one asked. They said he washed his hands at least fifty times a day—people wondered. He would remain past midnight in that shop, not working, because even when listening close, you could hear no hammer or sewing machine. Not a sound came from that shop and people whispered strange things again. He was a socialist, they said now, a socialist or communist—what was the difference anyway? They said both were rebels, disobedient to law and order, disobedient to God!

But people still brought their shoes. He was very reasonable and did good work. Months passed, and the whispers had quieted down some.

Then, one evening in August, it had been unusually hot—smothering hot—no one had been able to sleep much that night. Suddenly, we were aroused by thunder. That was nothing unusual, but it had continued louder and louder and no rain.

We all had dressed and gotten out on the street; nearly everyone had been up and dressed. The sound of the thunder was continuous now, and the lightning one ball of fire. Everyone was frightened, even Papa, I could tell, because he stood on the street talking to people we seldom talked to before. We usually just exchanged greetings, but now people were standing fully clothed, and fear was written on their faces. Any moment we thought the sky would split apart. I stood close to my mother. Then we heard the church bells ring—it seemed so strange—the awful thunder getting louder and louder, and the sky so black, but still constantly on fire. Then people standing on the street began to realize this was not a warning this time. This was the end of the world.

The church bells were ringing louder and louder, beckoning people—and people responded. They began to leave their homes heading for the church—not their church—any church. They began to walk faster with their children and husbands. People began to pray; some of them who never prayed before. Others were crying, but most of them prayed, whether secretly or openly. Catholics entered Protestant churches and Protestants entered Catholic churches, and they prayed together, and they cared not what church they were in, if it was their denomination or not. They wanted to be in any church, in the House of God.

Some people remained silently praying in the streets. I knew Mama prayed quietly. And Papa was afraid, I knew because as I intended to walk for a moment to the other side of the street to talk to my girlfriend, he did not yell at me or shake me by the arm, he just said in a soft voice, "Corrie, let's stay here now," and I was afraid too, because I obeyed immediately, not as usual, mumbling "why?" or something.

There still was no rain. The lightning and thunder continued without slowing down and people realized this was more than a thunderstorm.

Then the door from the little shoe shop opened and Opentie walked out into the street. He looked at the sky, then turned facing the people and said in a soft voice:

"People, this is not the end of the world. It is an incoming thunderstorm from the sea, against another one from land, and the worst is yet to come. No rain is in sight yet. Go in your homes and open the windows, because reckless, destructive winds we will have."

A man looked at him and said, rather questioningly, "How do you know this is not the end of the world?"

This strange old man did not look at anyone and said, "The powers of the devil have not yet been at their mightiest, for the Bible teaches great misery shall come first and God promised that before His coming, every corner of the world shall hear about the Son of God. There are yet many places and people as good as you and I, and they have not heard yet."

"You speak of the devil's power as mighty?" the man questioned.

"Oh, yes," he said calmly, "For God's power is almighty!"

Most of the people had gone into their homes and opened their windows and the windstorm indeed did come, just as the old shoemaker had said. But several hours later the rain drops fell and the storm took to the sea after leaving its destructive mark all over the lowlands. But in days passing people did not want to talk about the storm, they rather forgot that they had been afraid. They were ashamed. Ashamed that they had fallen on their knees and prayed. Ashamed for each other, for the way they had behaved and shown fear. The world had not come to an end and they had gone to churches, not their denomination even, Catholics and Protestants had entered and prayed in the same church. Now they had that to worry about.

And then they had become alarmed at that strange shoemaker—to think that they had listened to him, even if he had been right about the winds. If they hadn't been so afraid, they would have known that themselves.

Now people said he was strange indeed. They claimed he spoke English, French, Spanish, Greek, Latin, and Russian. They said he had been all over the world: Australia, America, China, India, he had been to Palestine, the Holy Land, and from there he had gone to Russia. There, they claimed, he had been put in prison for no telling what, in a place called Sormovo, and there he had been taught how to repair shoes. Twelve years had he remained there in prison. Then, as by a miracle, they had set him free because they were convinced that he was not the man they had thought him to be, a genius, whatever that was, but he finally had them convinced that he was an unlearned boy, so then they had allowed him to return home as a shoe repairman. With incredible suffering he had made the difficult journey through Siberia, fighting the snow and the wolves. Now they said he had to repair shoes for two reasons, one to keep his mind from thinking too much about the things he had seen and experienced, and the other because the Communists may still get him and kill him or capture and maybe torture him, because they said now he grieved so much. I had asked Mama what she thought he grieved about, because we heard that he had no children.

"Hungry souls," she had said, "Hungry souls of mankind."

After that awful storm, Papa would often go to the little shoe shop and remain a long time. Mama had asked what he went there for and Papa had said, "to broaden my mind." He told my mother that "that man has knowledge, he has read everything about world history, philosophy, speaks many languages, and he worked for Pete a difficult mathematical problem in a matter of minutes, knowing every symbol."

Pete said it was astonishing what he knew about meteorology.

But people just brought their shoes and kept away from him. And then not too long after that he was found sitting in his chair, his bony hands lying lifeless on his lap, and a few hours later his body was removed by an undertaker.

But people seemed not to care; they had no pity's sake.

Then, a newspaper man came and made pictures of the little shoe repair shop, and well-dressed men accompanied by fine dressed women came just to look, and the men took off their hats and some of the ladies even touched the hammer or his chair, and a few of them wiped away tears, they looked so sad, just shaking their heads.

Then the people in our street had made up for flowers just as if they had liked him, some of them even acted as if they would miss him, and they said, "how good he had been for mankind" and "that his soul would be among the archangels in Heaven."

Hypocrites, I thought, they never even stopped to talk to him when he was alive and now they called him a good man. People, I thought, just like you better after you are dead, so they can feel superior.

Papa just sat in his chair, puffing on his pipe, then he said to Mama, "I've always had the feeling he was someone very special."

Then a government car came and loaded all his tools, books and his chair in the car for the museum, they said. No one called him a shoemaker any more, they called him Professor of Christian Science, Dr. C. L. Opentie.

America

It was not long after that the day came for me to leave for America. I was to go to Paris by train, Pullman first class, daytime from Amersfoort, Amsterdam, Brussels, Paris. Reservations for a night's lodging were made at Hotel Terminus Nord close to Gore du Nord, and from there I was to contact the R.T.O. Railway Transportation Office and then travel from Paris by train to Frankfurt, Germany. How complicated! I thought, simpler for me to travel direct to Frankfurt. But Jan (Know-it-all) explained that probably Paris was the meeting center for all war brides to concentrate and from there in group form to travel to Frankfurt.

I had to have a certificate signed by a doctor that I was in good health and not pregnant.

I was all right, in good health and all, but I had a fever of 102 degrees. The doctor could find no cause for it. I told them at home it was travel fever. My father said, "Now isn't that something. Went all through Germany in the middle of a war to Austria and now has fever about going to Paris in peace time."

I said, "That was because I did not speak French."

I tried to be casual when I was packing my clothes. My mother had been busy ironing and getting my things in tip-top shape. I did not take everything because once in America I would be able to buy a few new clothes.

Mama had given me $200. It would buy some American clothes, Mama said, and she would want me to be able to dress as other American girls. In Dutch money, that was equivalent to 676 gulden, which was quite a sum after deflation.

Several weeks before time for me to leave, we had agreed that Jan, Annie's husband, would see me to the train. We were just going to say good-bye in a casual way. I told them there was no reason to get all upset; I was not going to prison or somewhere against my will.

My mother said that because they had met Roland they felt much better about my leaving for a new land and strange people, especially because Roland had told them his father and mother were Christian people. So, Mama said it gave her a feeling of security because she said Christian people were inclined to do the right thing.

I went upstairs to have a last look at my room and placed a letter on my bed because I knew I could not tell them what I wanted to say without breaking down and upsetting myself and probably them. I said in my note that "I loved them all very much and would miss them, and Mama was the dearest, most unselfish mother anyone could have wished for, and please don't worry about me because I am so lucky to leave to be with Roland. Your loving Corrie".

I was now packed and dressed. Jan stood silent, waiting in the hall beside my suitcases.

"Well, Cor," he said, "we better go now."

"Well," I repeated, "I guess I have everything now, my papers, my passport."

I counted them off on my fingers, then I looked at my mother. A spasm of pain caught my throat, but I managed to say in a clear voice, a bit too loud perhaps, "Thank you for everything, Mama, you've been so good to me, all of you." I said, "Now don't worry about me and I will write all along the way from Paris, from Frankfurt."

No one cried, thank God! I did kiss Mama, but just said a casual good-bye to the others. I knew this way would be easier for all of us, no hugging and kisses, and turning around to wave good-bye.

But then as Jan and I walked through the door, I, carrying my small suitcase and Jan the large one, as we were walking a piece into the street (I wanted to walk, it was only about one and a half miles) thoughts began to run through my mind such as "this is probably the last time you walk here."

Then Jan—dear Jan—began to complain about the suitcase being too heavy and it cleared away the dryness in my throat and I blinked my eyes a few times. Jan kept talking about unimportant things.

Then as we came to the station, he said, "Cor, I am getting a ticket to Amsterdam. Your mother wanted me to see to it that you had the right train when changing trains from Utrecht to Amsterdam."

We both laughed. "I am glad you are, Jan," I said, and I meant it, he was such a dear!

In Amsterdam he placed me on the train to Brussels and said, "You think you can make it now alone to Mentone, Georgia?"

"Oh Jan, I am going to Chattanooga, Tennessee, didn't you know that?"

He didn't, he said.

"Well, anyway," he added, "be good and don't take off with any strange man in Paris," he joked.

He kissed me on the cheek. After he left the platform, I opened my pocketbook and put my Swiss Alpine sunglasses on. I had to.

There were only two other passengers in my compartment. They did not say much, and it was quiet except for the monotonous noise of the train.

In Brussels I exchanged trains and entered a coupe that was empty. A short time later another passenger entered, a man. He glanced at me, smiled, and placed his hat and valise in the rack. I returned the smile. He then opened a newspaper and started reading. I noticed it was a French newspaper. As the train began to move, I either looked out the window, or pretended to read a Dutch pocket novel. After about one hour of continuous reading, he started folding the paper carefully into a small neat package and put it inside of his trench coat, which was hanging on a coat hanger in the compartment. We were traveling first class; diesel in a daytime compartment.

While he was reading, I had observed him. He was approximately in his late thirties, was very well dressed in a brown expensive looking suit, brown tie and socks, and brown calf leather-looking shoes that were polished, but not to a shine. His fingernails were well manicured, and he was wearing a ring with a seal. The reason I had observed him so closely was because there was nothing else to do and no one else in the compartment.

He was looking out the window now and automatically opened a cigarette case, then smiled again at me, presenting the opened cigarette case. It contained very thin cigarettes rolled in beige paper with golden mouth pieces, smiling he said, "mademoiselle."

Knowing only a few words of French, I said, "Tress been, merci monsieur."

I also shook my head.

He smiled and lighted a cigarette, elegantly inhaled and leaned back against his seat. He said something in French I did not understand, and I said, "No parle Francais."

I asked him in English if he spoke English or German or Dutch? He smiled and said, seemingly regretfully, "No parle Anglais, no comprenez."

"No comprenez," I answered him.

He then smiled again, and I returned his smile. After awhile he looked at his watch, then pointed at it, then to his mouth and the locomotive. He arose, offering me his arm, then said, "Mademoiselle, avez-vous dejeuner."

I realized he wondered if I was going to eat in the diner. It was one o'clock and I was starved, and nodded, "Oui, monsieur."

I did not know whether I should sit with him, but once in the diner, I had no choice. He just smiled at me, then I realized again by exchanging expressions, that he would order for me. I was uncomfortable but managed to eat without spilling anything or getting choked. I explained I was on my way to Paris. I then wrote down on a piece of paper the name "Hotel Terminus Nord," and made a question mark.

He smiled and drew two small circles close together on a piece of paper, pointing at them he said that one circle was Gare du Nord, the station on which we would arrive and the other, Hotel Terminus Nord. He placed his finger on his watch and said, "two minutes apart."

He was so nice and seemed a gentleman, but I would be on guard.

It was close to five o'clock when we arrived in Paris. I was rather nervous. He pointed at my luggage and carried it from the train and immediately a red cap arrived loading the suitcases on a push cart.

During the war we had been accustomed to carrying our own luggage and it seemed strange now to trust someone with my precious belongings. I walked closely beside my luggage, having no intention to let it from my sight.

As we passed through the douane (customs), I saw that my traveling companion was definitely a gentleman, for as the dauane officer opened my suitcases, he politely, not obviously but casually, turned the other way. When the inspection was completed, he pointed at the suitcases, then at himself, and I took it that he wanted to help me carry them to the hotel. I felt uneasy, but I knew nothing to say. I wished I could speak French and then I could have explained in a nice manner that I would rather walk alone and carry my own luggage, but he seemed so nice, and I did not speak French.

Once outside the station, he stopped and pointed across the street, and as I looked, I saw the big neon sign "Hotel Terminus Nord." He smiled and motioned for me to walk beside him. He seemed to want to take me across the street to the hotel.

If I just knew how to tell him nicely that I really preferred to enter alone!

But, he had already pushed against the revolving door and walked, after setting my luggage on the floor, over to the check-in desk. He said something in French and the desk clerk looked in a book, then motioned for me to sign the register.

I had never been in a hotel before and felt uneasy, but I tried to act as if I had been accustomed to signing the register all my life.

The Frenchman then said something else, and a young man in a uniform came toward us.

"Oui monsieur," then to me he slightly bowed. My companion showed him some papers and his passport and the young man in uniform listened to him talk. He then looked at me and said in English, "I am the interpreter of the hotel. The gentleman wished that I introduce him. This is Mr. Eugene Paeff; he is employed by the French Government, Department of Commerce."

He paused, then looked at me and continued.

"Monsieur would like to show you some of Paris, or perhaps," he then pointed to a billboard in the lobby, "take you to La Traviata."

I looked at Monsieur Paeff and smiled, then, glancing at my luggage and facing the interpreter, I said, "That is very kind of monsieur, but I am sorry I have not the proper dress at hand. You see, I am on my way to America, to my husband, and will have to contact the R.T.O. and state my arrival."

He said the hotel management would assist me in any way possible. I asked him to thank Monsieur Paeff for his kindness; he had been a great help to me, and I should always have a high opinion of French gallantry.

He smiled as the interpreter gave him my message.

In the meantime, a bellboy stood waiting to take my luggage.

The interpreter then told me monsieur would be disappointed if I did not have one "Speciality, La Paree" with him in the hotel bar, to wish me "Bon Voyage," and he would wait for me in the lobby. "Boy," I thought, "the French are different; they don't take no for an answer!" I agreed to return after freshening up and getting things settled, such as toilet articles and nightclothes; aside from that I did not intend to unpack.

The bell boy picked up my things and said in Dutch, "Wilt U my volgen als u blieft, Madame" (Will you follow me, please, Madame)?"

He went ahead of me to the second floor of the hotel. As he opened the door to a small, but nicely furnished room with adjoining bathroom facilities, he turned on a light and placed the luggage on a rack. "Als U iets wenscht, Madame, ik ben tot U dienst," he said, speaking Dutch. I tipped him one gulden (about thirty-eight cents) and told him everything seemed fine.

I had five thousand francs, but I did not know the equivalent value. It was approximately ten dollars, but I did not need it for anything except taxi fare and tipping and perhaps something to eat. My travel papers warned against exchanging unnecessary amounts of money, for our hotel and meals were all included in our travel papers.

I cleaned up but remained dressed in my olive green wool dress. It was soft fabric and as flattering as anything else I had. I checked by telephone with the R.T.O. I was relieved when the voice on the other side answered in English. He took down my name and informed me that my train would leave from Gare de l'Est to Frankfurt, Germany, at 4 p.m. the next day. I asked him if it was far from Gare du Nord, and he said it was not far. I planned to take a taxi early enough and make myself familiar with the departing gates.

I was rather thankful that Monsieur Paeff would be waiting for me in the lobby. As I entered, he immediately rose and then, instead of going into the bar, he said, "Aves-vous diner?"

I understood only "diner."

I had dreaded eating alone and even though I could not talk with him, I welcomed the invitation. After we were seated at a small round table for two, covered with spotless white linen and shiny silver, I thought as the waiter served us wine, about what Jan had said, "don't take off with any strange men in Paris," and here I was only six hours later in company of a complete stranger. But, after all, I would not leave the hotel, and shortly after dinner, I intended to excuse myself and return to my room.

The dining room was nearly full now, and as our food was served, I felt indeed fortunate not to be alone. If not for him, I probably would have remained in my room and ordered a sandwich. I would have felt miserable and lonely.

It was rather a pity that we could not talk to each other and I wondered why he was being so nice. After we finished dinner, he had the waiter bring us a 'Specialty La Paree.' I was secretly worried that it perhaps contained some intoxicating liquor, then felt somewhat ashamed for having such thoughts when I found it to be no more than a tiny cup of strong coffee, mocha it was called. It was indeed different and delicious. The time had come to tell him in a nice way that I enjoyed dinner, but I must return to my room.

But, then to my surprise, he motioned for the waiter and paid the check. Then walking to the lobby, the interpreter came toward us and explained to me "that tomorrow monsieur would like to show you through Paris before you sail for America." He explained that it was his duty as a born Parisian.

I felt ungrateful, but I informed him my intentions were to leave by taxi about ten o'clock in the morning, that I already had checked with the R.T.O. I asked the interpreter to thank monsieur; it was kind of him.

He explained what I had said, then replied that Monsieur would meet me at the R.T.O. for dejeuner (lunch). I told him that would be nice.

Monsieur bowed, then smiled and said, "Bon soir, Madame."

I said, in English, "Good night, monsieur, merci boucoup."

As I returned to my room, I locked the door and felt pleased with myself. I set the clock for 7:30, rolled my hair, and went to bed. I slept well and awakened the next morning by noises in the hall. I took a bath in the smallest bathtub I had ever seen, then dressed and applied makeup with extreme care. I would try to be as attractive as I had heard girls in Paris were.

I skipped breakfast. I felt uncomfortable not speaking French and eating alone. I was not hungry anyway. I called the desk and asked them to call a taxi and send someone for the luggage. I walked down the stairs. Checking out, I felt insecure. I tipped the bellboy carrying my luggage another gulden.

The taxi driver talked in French, but I did not understand him, and he delivered me safely at "Gare de 1'Est." I paid him with one thousand Francs, expecting some change. After he carried my luggage into the station, he politely tipped his cap, but he did not return any money.

"Oh, well, I did not care," I told myself.

I looked around for the sign R.T.O. Then I spotted it on the right after entering the station. A French man first answered the window, but after I spoke English, an American soldier came. I explained who I was and showed him my papers. He told me I could leave my luggage there, that it would be taken care of and placed on the train leaving for Frankfurt. He said if I intended to look around in Paris, to be sure to return there by 3:15. He smiled and that was that!

I looked around, then sat down at a bench in the waiting room. "Well," I thought, "if nothing else, I won't miss my train." It was now 11:30. I watched people enter and leave. Everyone seemed to know where they were going. I had been sitting there approximately twenty minutes when someone touched my shoulder. I looked up and saw Monsieur Paeff.

I was glad to see him, as if seeing an old familiar friend. He smiled so pleasantly. He then pointed to the R.T.O. and motioned for me to follow him. There standing in front of the R.T.O. window, he explained to the man speaking French that he intended to take me to see the famous Eiffel Tower, the Champs Elysees and the Arc de Triomphe. He also showed them his passport.

The American at the window assured me monsieur was perfectly in order. He explained that the French were promoting tourist relations with the Americans and building their reputation as considerate and charming.

I felt completely at ease now. Outside the station waited a chauffeured car seemingly completely at Monsieur Paeff's command. As we rode along, he explained that we were now driving along Haussmann Boulevard on our way to the Arc de Triomphe. Then we drove through Avenue des Champs-Elysees, where people were sitting at sidewalk cafes in the cold weather, sipping wine or drinking coffee. As we drove along, he pointed out the American Embassy, then the Grand Palais, the Petit Palais, and from there the Eiffel Tower. We did not have time to go up; I did not care to anyway. We passed the musée du Louvre. More than the museum itself, I was impressed by the beautiful gardens, looking as if a carpet was spread on the streets.

It was nearly two o'clock and he said we would eat in a small café near Gare de l'Est. From the café I sent a postcard home.

Even though Monsieur Paeff was very nice and attentive, I felt relieved when he delivered me at 3:15 at the Gare de l'Est. He extended his hand and said, "Au revoir."

I thanked him and told him in English that thanks to him, my stay in Paris had been pleasant.

As I walked into the station, I saw several girls standing and sitting near the R.T.O. I walked toward them and asked the American in uniform who seemed to be in charge if these girls were all en route to Frankfurt. He looked up and said, "Yes, there should be fourteen to be complete."

He then said that we just as well leave for the train. Now and then some of the girls spoke to each other in French or Italian, but I could tell by their manner that no one knew each other. The American soldier, a sergeant, stopped us before entering the train, then he said in English that this train would carry us to Frankfurt, Germany. He told us he was our host, and should we need anything concerning our trip, we should ask him. Food would be served in the diner on the train. We were given sleepers, two girls to a compartment. He would call our names and compartment numbers. Our luggage was already placed. No other persons would be allowed to travel in the passenger car, only war brides on this transport. Our safety was guaranteed, he laughed.

He started calling names, our maiden name and married name. All girls were either French or Italian. No other Dutch girls on this transport, of course; only a few Dutch girls had married Americans since Holland had mostly been occupied by Canadians.

My name was called and another girl's, a French name, Collette Le Paurre. I entered the train looking for the compartment number. I then saw my luggage and turned facing the French girl. She seemed friendly.

"Comment allez vous?" she said, and shook hands with me, smiling, showing some pretty, white teeth. She then stood in the doorway saying something in French to passing girls, and they answered her in rapid French. All of them were talking to each other, carrying on in excited voices.

I sat down on the lower berth; she turned to me and smiled. I smiled in return. I supposed this was going to be a smiling trip, just smile, and smile again.

They were all talking to each other, laughing and talking. I did not like any of them. I envied them and their knowledge of French. You cannot envy them and like them, too. I thought they seemed to have understood the American Sergeant, so when she turned and said something to me again in French, I replied in English, "I do not speak French; I am from Holland."

"Ah," she said, "Hollandaise!"

She was not a typical French type as most of the others. This girl had pink outdoorsy cheeks, hardly any makeup, blue eyes, and brown, clean-looking hair, which was parted and combed to one side. She was more plump than slender, but not fat. She was dressed nicely in a pale blue wool sweater and navy skirt, and loosely hanging over her shoulders was a trench coat.

I asked her then, "Do you speak English?"

"Oh, yes," she said, "a little."

"Well," I thought, "that's better than Monsieur Paeff."

I said, "I will be so glad when we start moving; I am hungry."

"Yes," she said, "I do."

Then the American sergeant came and asked if everything was all right.

"Yes," we both said.

He told us we would depart in a few minutes. After five o'clock we could enter the diner and order whatever we wished from the menu. She looked at me and said sincerely, "Is that nice, not?" I agreed it was nice indeed.

She looked at me smiling and said, "I have in compartment you, I do like, nice much than other French girls, they from Italian border."

Then, after looking at her, I added, "The other girls are different. You look more like a German girl than French. Please," I added, "forgive me."

But she smiled and said, "Thank you, I do not like looking typical French girl." Then she added, "I'm partly German. I lived in Lotheringen. My grandfather was German."

I thought a moment, then I asked, "Do you speak German?"

"Yes," she said, "I have attended German schools."

"Now," I said in German, "I am so glad, at least we can talk without difficulty, because it is so hard to express yourself if you don't speak the language well."

I felt much better then. We left for the diner and I learned she was the only girl that spoke German. I asked her in the compartment if her folks minded that she was leaving them. She explained she had not been home in months, and after her husband left for the U.S., she had been living with her aunt. She said her mother had been a widow since before the war and she had only one brother, twelve years old. Her mother had screamed and carried on badly after learning that she was married to an American and would leave her, but she said in time her husband would make it possible for her mother and brother to come to America. She said her mother, a seamstress, had to provide for herself and her son, that she received only a small pension because of her deceased husband.

We drew matches for which one was to sleep in the upper berth. Collette was the one, and in a short while we prepared to go to sleep.

The sergeant announced we would arrive in Frankfurt at about eight o'clock in the morning. Breakfast would be served at 7:30 in the diner and everyone should be packed whether they intended to eat or not.

Everything went as planned. After leaving the train, a bus took us to an army camp, where preparations were made before sailing to America.

Four girls were placed in one room. Showers were in the hall and meals served on schedule. No one was to leave the premises. A PX was on the grounds, a movie theater, ice cream parlor, and a beauty shop. We received our smallpox shots and a limited physical. I wrote a letter to Roland and one home.

Three days later we sailed on the General Howze, a former Navy ship, which now belonged to the army. Again, there were four girls to a cabin. I didn't get acquainted with any of the other girls, for some had their husbands with them on the ship. They could only see each other on deck or in the dining room, for no male, husband or not, was allowed in our quarters.

The weather was bad; it was February, and most of the time we spent either sick in bed or on deck trying to get some fresh air. The food served was excellent, anything and as much as we could wish for, but no one had any appetite. We managed to eat some oranges and crackers in our room. Eating was a must, otherwise you really got sick on an empty stomach, which could be fatal.

One day, Collette and I tried to see a movie in the ship's theater, but right in the middle of the picture, the ship started rocking and rolling and we had to hurry out of there.

We were told that if you would stay outside on deck, you would not get so nauseated, so we dressed warm, wrapping our heads in scarves, and took army blankets to keep warm, and we made for the deck. It was raining and the wind blowing heavy. We managed to find a corner where we stayed partly dry. No one was on deck; they claimed even some of the crew were sick, in bed. As we sat there awhile, two MPs on duty came walking toward us. (We were guarded as if we were harem girls to be delivered to some king or something).

They asked us if we thought we were going to make it to the United States of America. We asked them, suddenly alarmed, "Why, are there rumors that the ship won't make it?"

We were sitting there close together, wrapped up in our blankets, but still cold and now scared! The soldier shrugged his shoulders, looking around at the waves, his collar up high around his ears, he then said, "maybe, and maybe not!"

Then he asked me where I was going in America.

"To Tennessee," I said, "to Chattanooga."

"To Tennessee," he repeated, saying it real slow, dividing each syllable. He then looked at me, then at the other soldier who had not said anything so far.

"Chattanooga, Tennessee!" he said again, as if speaking of some fearful place.

Then, as if saying something confidential, he added; "I hope you make it, you know going over the Tennessee River will be difficult, you could not hire me to go there!" Then, looking at the other MP, he said, "Would you?"

"It'll be rough," he claimed.

"But, why?" I said, puzzled, "My husband never mentioned it."

"Of course not," the first one said, "he realized you wouldn't have come. You never have seen pictures of Tennessee?"

"No," I said, "I saw it on the map."

Shaking his head again, he said, "You see, in Tennessee they have that Great Tennessee River (putting emphasis on great) and a lot of other rivers, but no bridges, no windows in the houses, just little bitty windows. Oh, man!" he said, as if speaking to himself.

I asked him, "Well, how do people get over the river?"

"With what they call a ferry," he laughed a little, "have you ever been on a ferry?"

"Yah," I said, "that's okay, nothing wrong with a ferry."

"Yah," he said, shaking his head. "But a Tennessee ferry, this is not like any other ferry. They do allow people on there all right, but no luggage. Do you have luggage? A lot of luggage?"

"No," I said, "Just two suitcases."

"Oh, well, they probably take them over in a small boat then," he said reassuringly. I didn't have a big trunk; a big heavy trunk would sink one of those small boats in Tennessee.

"How did you come to marry a guy from Tennessee?"

"When I met him I didn't know he was from Tennessee," I said, feeling sort of let down.

"Well," he said, "don't worry about it, it'll probably be all right."

Collette had said nothing. Then she asked him, "What about North Carolina?"

"Is that where you're going?" he asked.

She nodded.

"You're all right, you have nothing to worry about."

"I wondered," she said, because she had one trunk and two suitcases.

"No," he said, "getting to North Carolina is no trouble, you go by railroad, over a railroad bridge."

"North Carolina," he added, "is a pretty good country."

Collette asked them where they were from.

"Brooklyn," he said, "Brooklyn, New York," as if that was someplace everyone wished to be from.

I didn't say anything, but silently wished Roland hadn't been living in Tennessee.

I asked him one more question.

"Couldn't I go from New York by train to Chattanooga?"

They both said, "You could go by train as far as the Tennessee River, but that's as far as the train goes."

"Why," I asked, wondering, "didn't they build bridges?"

"They ran out of money," he said, making sort of fun.

"Good God!" I thought, "what a country I am going to!"

I became sort of depressed and suggested to Collette that we go inside. That night I could hardly fall asleep thinking what if my luggage turned over in that small boat. I decided that tomorrow I would take all my papers out of my suitcase and carry them in my pocketbook.

Only a few girls appeared for breakfast; most were in bed sick. We had been sailing for six days, and the last two were rough.

The following morning as we entered the dining room I told Collette that I was getting used to the ship because I felt good, and had a tremendous appetite. She laughed and said, "No wonder, we are anchored in the harbor of New York; look out the window and you can see the skyscrapers.

After breakfast, we went on deck and saw in a dim, hazy background, tall buildings touching the sky. It was fascinating, and everyone was somewhat alone with their own thoughts. A great moment! And I was a little envious of the girls who were sharing this experience with their husbands.

We were asked to pack our things, because in two hours we would be leaving the ship. Some girls would be met either by their husbands or relatives of them. Others like myself, would travel alone to their destination. The Red Cross would place us on the train and give us further information.

We were to be the last to leave the ship. Everyone seemed excited. Handshakes and good luck wishes were exchanged.

Collette and I had plenty of time, but we had dressed completely as advised and emptied our cabins. The ship's crew was anxious to clean the ship so they could go ashore. We were sitting in the lounge watching people leave. Names were called on loudspeakers of passengers who had relatives of husbands awaiting them. I paid no attention, then after awhile the voice said; "Repeating, Mrs. Roland Smith, repeating, Mrs. Roland Smith!"

Colette jumped up and said, excitedly, "That is you, is it not?"

"Yah," I said, suddenly alert. It dawned on me—I had not been used to being called by that name.

She said, "Someone must be here to meet you!"

But a soldier came to me and said, "If your name is called, you are ordered off the ship."

I hastily hugged Collette good-bye. A little frightened, I walked down the gangplank. There was a young man standing alone, with outstretched hand.

He said, "Corrie?"

"Yes," I answered, and putting his arm around me he said, "I am Ben, Roland's brother."

I had it on my lips to ask him where Roland was, when suddenly Roland popped out from behind a stack of boxes and hugged and kissed me. "Welcome to America, Corrie," he said, smiling.

"I am so sorry to be late," I apologized, "I did not expect you to meet me, Roland. That's why they had to call me several times."

"I was not worried," he said, "I knew you were on the ship; the Red Cross notified us by telegram."

"Are you glad I came to meet you?" he said, teasingly, his eyes twinkling.

"It has not dawned on me yet, Roland; it's such a surprise, and to think that I now really am here in your country!"

We had to wait a few minutes for my luggage, then left the

boardwalk and headed for the car. Roland asked me if I would like to see something of New York, perhaps the Empire State Building, or if I would rather get on our way to Tennessee. At that time, I was not interested in sightseeing; all I wanted was to be near Roland. I felt complete, sitting beside him in his new blue Chevrolet.

Ben had been silent so far. Then, looking at me, he said that I was as pretty as Roland had told them and he added, "Roland is a lucky boy!"

I smiled happily.

Ben asked me what I thought of those tall buildings in New York. I told him I was fascinated, as well as frightened, and all that traffic! I nearly panicked as it seemed that we barely escaped several collisions, and my admiration for Roland's driving grew with the minute! How calm and handsome he looked!

They took turns asking questions about my trip, and I told them everything they wanted to know, including my fear of going over the Tennessee River. Roland and Ben assured me there were bridges over every river in Tennessee.

Ben said, "Some of those dumb Yankees who never had been out of New York, except for going to war, really thought that way about the Southern states."

I was glad when we were traveling on the highway, leaving New York behind us. Everything was so overpowering, the fast-moving cars, so many people, confusing traffic lights. I was amazed by the stores—they were filled with clothes—and the fruit stands right on the street had bananas on the stem. I asked Roland to stop and buy some bananas. I had not seen nor tasted any in at least five years. So, they stopped and bought a pound.

Driving along the highway, I commented that I could not see how people lived in such tiny houses.

"Where?" Roland wanted to know.

I pointed to several small houses in a row. Roland explained that they were motels for tourists to spend the night.

How practical, I thought; just imagine spending the night right on the highway! I wondered what they looked like on the inside.

We stopped in a restaurant to eat and I bought a postcard to send home. We planned to travel to Washington where Roland wanted to show me The White House.

Arriving there shortly before midnight, we admired the gleaming mansion from a distance. In the night, the floodlights reflecting on it added to its elegance and beauty. I would have liked to spend a day or so in Washington, but Roland did not seem to have much money, because after leaving New York, he borrowed $50 from me for expenses such as gasoline and motel rooms.

I was not stingy, but I knew the money my mother had given me she had saved over a period of years. Of course, Roland would not understand that you need three gulden and eighty cents for exchange of one dollar.

When Roland and Ben stopped at a bar on the highway, I told them I did not care for a drink. I just wasn't going to waste my mother's money on anything except what she would approve of.

We spent the night in a motel, ate breakfast on the road at a small restaurant, and were now well on our way to Tennessee. I was mostly impressed by the lovely homes, often painted white and surrounded by a yard. In Holland, only a few people in the city had been that lucky. The country is so overpopulated there would not have been room enough to build each house individually.

I asked Ben if his wife had objected to his coming with Roland to meet me.

"Well," he kind of hesitated, then added, "Corrie, Jewel and I are not getting along too well. At the moment, we are separated." He then added that she was rather unreasonable because of her pregnancy.

"Oh," I said, suddenly alarmed, and disliking him a little, "leaving her alone to come on this trip, it would not have been necessary."

They took turns with the driving.

Chattanooga

I was sleepy and tired, but refused to let myself fall asleep. I loved the neon lights, the beckoning signs, the friendly waitresses in the restaurants. It was about five o'clock in the evening when Roland said, "this is the Tennessee River; we are entering Chattanooga."

A sign on the bridge said, "Welcome to Chattanooga, the Electrical Center of the South." It seemed so strange that here they beckoned people, they wanted them to move to their city, where in Europe we had only been tolerated long enough to just pass through.

"In about five minutes now, you will be home."

We drove up on what Roland called Cameron Hill, and after a few turns, he stopped on Boynton Terrace in front of an apartment house that was badly in need of repair and painting. But it did not bother me. Roland had explained that a place to live was difficult to find and we would temporarily live in the downstairs apartment of his sister Vera. His parents and his seventeen-year old brother, Jack, lived upstairs in the same apartment. He said his parents owned a modest home in the country, in Mentone, but because Mr. Smith was employed in Chattanooga, they had moved here.

Roland's mother was now coming toward the car. She smiled and hugged me. She then said that she had been looking for us all that day and was glad we made the trip home safely. Roland carried my luggage into the downstairs apartment. His mother apologized that the place was not as clean as she had liked it to be, but Vera, her daughter, had moved with a girlfriend. Roland and I could use the place until we found something. The small living room was nicely furnished, a peacock blue couch and chair, a wine-colored rocker, two end tables, a coffee table, and a floor lamp. The furniture was Roland's. His mother said he had bought it that week.

She looked at me and smiled. She was a woman of large frame, with a lovely face and soft, nearly white naturally wavy hair, and brown serene eyes. Roland resembled her in looks in many ways and I felt it would be easy to like her.

I wanted to make a comment on the living room furniture. I felt nearly hypocritical when I remarked how pretty it was when peacock blue was the one color I disliked intensely.

The bedroom suite and kitchen outfit were nice, but belonged to Vera. The bedspread, a white chenille, was Roland's, along with a set of dishes and silverware. His mother invited us to have supper, as she called it, upstairs, after we washed up a little.

After she left, Roland pulled me close to him and kissed me, then he said, "Corrie, I hope you can be happy here. Of course, before too long we will look for something nicer."

How I loved him! And then I thought guiltily, "what is an apartment, or even a peacock blue couch, when I have him."

Looking at Roland, I said, "I am so happy!"

He sat down for a moment on the kitchen chair and said seriously, "We are going to eat upstairs with mother tonight, but only tonight. We will have breakfast here tomorrow morning, and we will get some groceries, so we can cook here right from the beginning."

"Sure," I said.

We climbed the stairs and entered the apartment. His mother had the table set and nearly everything prepared. When we were seated I didn't show very much appetite, and Mrs. Smith asked me what I liked to eat.

I thought a moment, then I said, "Only turkey or chicken."

Ben, who was still there, and Roland laughed as if I had said something real funny. I asked Roland what was funny.

He said, "Nothing, but mother meant in the line of vegetables."

A short while later, Mr. Smith came home. He was a nice-looking man, but of smaller build that I had pictured him to be, because Roland was so tall. He seemed a man who took pride in his appearance. He greeted me warmly and asked several questions concerning my trip and what I thought of the United States.

I told him many people in Europe had envied me to make my home in this country, and that I concluded by just traveling through, that this was indeed a land of plenty.

The following morning, I emptied my suitcases, placing the contents on hangers and in drawers. I took a bath, then made the bed while Roland cooked breakfast.

After we ate, we went to the supermarket to get some groceries. That is where I met his brother Jack. He worked there in the meat department. The night before he had not been home. He was nice and clean-cut looking, in a white shirt with bow tie. Roland proudly said he did not smoke or drink. I did not think that was anything special because of course, a boy, seventeen-years-old, did not drink!

That afternoon I met his two sisters, Vera, the oldest, and Eveline, who could pass for Roland's twin sister, and her husband, Junior. Then, there were Dennis, his nineteen-year old brother, and Irma, his seventeen-year old wife. They all were full of life, laughter and gayety. They complimented Roland on having a pretty wife, admiring my hair and complexion. In Holland or Austria, people may call you pretty to others, but not to you in person. But I was not immune to flattery, and I liked them for it.

One of Roland's cousins from Dalton, Georgia, came to see us in a very pretty car. She brought me a gift, a large white box, fancily wrapped with a pink bow. I opened it. It contained a beautiful white silk slip, among other lacy intimacies. She said if the size was wrong I could exchange it. It had been purchased at one of the finest department stores. I wished I could have expressed my joy as I felt it, but I thanked her sincerely. She invited us to Dalton where she and her husband owned a nice home. They had one son, eight years old.

Roland up to now had not been working. He drew $20 a week from the government until he started to work. He said he would look for a job.

Mrs. Smith and I went shopping while Roland placed applications at various places. After entering the first store, I bought two nightgowns of the same color and style. The saleslady said they had more styles to choose from, but I was easily pleased. Then I tried on a dress. The saleslady commented how well the dress looked on me, what nice size I was, and how becoming the style and color. She didn't need to flatter me to sell the dress. I had no intention of leaving the store without buying it. Mrs. Smith whispered to me not to buy all my clothes in one store, that there were other stores where they had more to choose from. I told her I didn't want to leave; the other stores might be sold out by the time we got there.

I bought Mrs. Smith six nice bath towels because she was looking admiringly at them, and I bought some for my mother to send home. For Victor's mother I bought a silk slip and two pair of nylons. For each of my sisters, a slip and nylons. For Mary, the same, plus a pair of patent leather shoes with ankle straps. For Roland, two white shirts and two pairs of pajamas. Also, one pair for my brother, because his pajamas were patched so many times that it was hard to decide whether they had been a stripe or print when new.

There was so much of everything in the stores, so many items, so many things I needed—wanted—and all could be had with money. In Europe, even if you had money, the stores were still empty. But I did not want to burden myself with the miseries overseas, I lived now in America, and must make my comparisons only with those around me.

We were waiting for Roland, loaded with packages. He picked us up in front of a store.

"It looks as if you've spent enough," he said as he greeted us.

I told him I had about $40 left, and, "Of course," I said, "You still owe me $50; I have not forgotten that."

He promised to pay me back as soon as his check arrived.

He had good news; he had found a job at Combustion, starting out at $1.60 an hour.

After he went to work we were on a routine. Roland left every morning at 6:30 for work. I then washed the dishes, made the bed, washed and waxed every piece of furniture, washed the walls, cleaned the windows, and scrubbed the kitchen. Everything was spotless now!

Then a few weeks later, Vera said that she and Lawrence planned to get married and would need the furniture, but we could keep the apartment. Roland decided to sell the car and get an older make, then use the money for a down payment on the new furniture.

We bought a breakfast room set, a bedroom suite, and a gas stove. We could do without a washing machine because sheets, shirts, and towels we sent to the laundry.

I asked Roland if he thought it possible that I could find a job. His cousins told me that I might find employment in a department store as a salesgirl, either in the jewelry or cosmetic departments, but I feared I did not speak English well enough. Roland's sister, Eveline, suggested I should try McCallister, a hosiery mill, that would not require knowledge of English. She promised she would go with me and place an application, also. They hired us and said we could start to work the next day. So, in the same afternoon we got my Social Security card.

I liked the work; it was clean and easy, from seven a.m. until three-thirty p.m. and off on Saturdays. I made $28 a week, which I found to be a lot for doing so little. I spent most of it buying small items for the house and some clothes. Two dollars a week was saved for bus fare and I packed a lunch. Maybe before too long we could start putting $10 a week in the bank to save for a home.

During the week we stayed home at the apartment; sometimes over the weekend we went to Dalton to visit Roland's cousins. Occasionally we saw a movie or visited other relatives in Chattanooga. I wrote home often, telling about America and Roland's family. His mother, I realized, was an undemanding woman who had been easily led by her husband's rather dominating ways; he was a good man, of high morals, but persistent to have everything go his way.

I was an excellent housekeeper, but my cooking wasn't anything to brag about, and what was worse, I did not make any efforts for improvement. When criticizing remarks were made, I just laughed along with them. My cooking didn't taste so bad, I just had no variety. Every Sunday, fried chicken, potato salad, and banana pudding. During the week either pork chops and beans or salmon loaf and beans. Roland said he wondered how many cans of pork and beans it would take to kill a man. I told him I was not fond of beans either.

But Roland seemed happy, he never complained, always willing to help around the house, drying dishes, emptying garbage, washing his car, and together we got the groceries. We paid on our furniture regularly and I never regretted that I had left my people and country behind. People asked questions sometimes concerning the war in Europe. When I told them things that did not take a long explanation, they often remarked how lucky women in the United Stated had been, escaping all the suffering.

I did not agree that they escaped all the suffering; perhaps they'd had a different kind. For a good wife, who faithfully awaited her husband's return, suffered just as much as we did overseas. And there was also the suffering of parents worrying over their children. I developed a great deal of admiration for American women. They were practical, ambitious, taking much pride in their appearance, keeping house, cooking, being a mother, and often besides kept a job requiring eight hours a day.

Troubling Times

One Saturday I was cleaning house and Roland left to get our weekly groceries. But after awhile Jack, his brother, delivered them and told me Roland would be home shortly, he was getting a haircut. I kept waiting and it was getting late. Finally, I went upstairs to his parents and told them that I was worried because Roland had not come home yet and it was now nearly seven o'clock. His father, who was looking out of the window, said, shaking his head, "there is no telling when he may get back."

After awhile I decided to go downstairs and wait, feeling blue. About a half hour later he came in. He smiled and let himself fall in the wine-colored rocker, blinking his eyes. He looked at me and said, "Hi-dy!"

I did not smile, but said, "Where have you been since ten o'clock this morning?"

He said, "I think that a man who works all the time has the right to be out once in awhile."

"Oh," I said, "Sure they do, that is, in the proper way. If you had told me before that you wanted to shoot some pool, or drink a few beers, or go hunting, I would not care."

He just looked at me, raising his eyebrows.

I then added, "Sending Jack with the groceries while you stayed out was inconsiderate."

This was our first real argument.

He said that he had been henpecked long enough and he was getting tired of it, everything had to go my way, every cent he made had to go "on the house."

"What about a man having a beer now and then?"

He was tired of being henpecked and he might as well tell me right there and then, he was going to have a little fun every now and then, I could like it or not like it.

I started saying things that did not exactly sound lady-like, so he suddenly jumped up and said, "I am not going to listen to this, I am getting out of here!"

He got in his car and took off.

I could not believe that he would really do that to me, and I figured that in about fifteen minutes he would realize where he had been wrong and come home. But fifteen minutes passed into one hour, and then past midnight. Finally, I went to bed, and some time around two o'clock I heard a car drive up the hill and stop.

I jumped up to look; it was Roland!

I returned to bed and pretended to be asleep.

The following morning, he told me he was sorry and that he had not meant to take off, but he just could not stand to be nagged. It was easy enough to forgive him, he was so soft-spoken, and lovable!

The following Sunday we made plans to visit his cousin Elsie and her husband. Roland had washed his car the day before. It was an old car that used more oil than gasoline, but it moved, and usually got us anywhere in town.

We walked out of the house, Roland dressed in his nice summer suit and I in my new dress, when suddenly Roland discovered that he had a flat.

"Well," he said, "I am sorry, honey, but I'll have to change the tire."

First, he changed pants, then softly whistling, he went to work on the tire. In about twenty minutes he had changed back into his good clothes again, and we were ready to take off.

It always took a little time because that old car had to be warmed up like an airplane.

Then suddenly he said: "Uh oh."

I asked, "What now, Roland?"

"I am afraid we have another flat." He got out of the car, and said, "Yep, it's the rear tire now."

I became afraid that we would maybe have to stay home, so I said, "What are you going to do now?"

"Oh," he said. "I think I can fix it, I'll try to patch it. Don't worry, it won't take long."

He again changed pants, and while taking the tire off, his hands all dirty, he looked up and asked me, "Honey, could you get me a pan of water?"

And I thought how blessed I was, he had changed clothes twice, fixed two tires on that old car, and never uttered one bad word. It is something to have a husband with that mild a disposition.

Finally, the tire was fixed and we took off to Elsie's.

There was a young couple visiting them, they stayed a short while and then when they were ready to leave, the woman said to me that they were glad to have met me and for Roland to bring me over sometime. So, I smiled and said, "Does Roland know where you live?"

She just ignored me and never told me where they lived, or that Roland knew.

I was wearing my new dress and Elsie complimented me on it. I didn't say anything, but I smiled at her in return for the compliment.

We were all sitting in the living room talking when Elsie said she was going to fix supper and she invited us to stay. In fact, when Roland protested, she insisted that we stay to eat. And Roland, knowing how I hated to cook, said, "No thanks, Elsie, we've got to get home, Corrie already has things fixed."

"I don't have anything fixed, Roland," I had protested.

Then, I had asked him, "Why don't we eat here since they have asked us?"

Roland finally gave in, but he did not eat much, but I did. Everything was prepared so well, and of course, I didn't mind helping with the dishes.

I thought the day had been pleasant, but on the way home in the car, Roland said, "You really embarrassed me, Corrie."

"Why," I said innocently, "What did I do?"

"You know," he said softly, "that this is the last time that I take you there."

"What did I do wrong, Roland?"

"First," he said, "You should know that when people ask you to come to see them sometime, not to take that seriously, because they only say that to be polite.

"And I thought you knew that when anyone complimented you on your dress, it would be nice if you said, 'Thank you, I will let you wear it sometime.'"

"Wear it sometime? When I know it would not fit them? That would be silly!"

"You should say it anyway, just to be nice. And listen, Corrie, from now on when people ask us to eat, unless we are specially invited for dinner, you learn to say no."

"Why," I said, "When they ask us?"

"They always ask people here, Corrie, that is customary, but it is not customary that you take them up on it!"

I nearly cried, but instead got mad.

"How am I to know what is customary, or polite, or when they mean it?"

"Most of the time it is either customary, or politeness; that way you are safe."

By the time we came home, Roland was in a good humor again.

A couple weeks later, now on Friday night, it seemed that Roland had the urge again to "live a little and have some fun."

It was already past midnight and not a sign of him, at least not at home. I did not worry anymore, I just got mad. I could not sleep. I kept waiting, hour after hour.

At about four a.m. I heard the key turn in the front door. I pretended to be asleep, and it seemed the moment he came in the house I calmed down, falling asleep a short while later.

Of course, the following morning I was ready for a good argument. But his father came downstairs early and asked Roland "if he hadn't intended to treat me right, why had he brought me to this country away from my people?"

Roland kept silent for a while, then said, "I intend to treat her right" in a flat tone.

"You're setting a nice example, if you call that right!" Then he added, "You are running with the wrong people, Roland!"

"I am not doing anything so bad," Roland said in a smug tone.

His father, as he walked out, mumbled, "Birds of a feather flap together!"

Roland wasn't feeling good and stretched out on the couch. I didn't care if he wasn't good company, at least he was home.

But at four o'clock I had to wake him because we needed to get some groceries. He claimed he did not feel like it, but he did wash his face and we walked to the car.

But, as I came close, I looked, frowning, at the car, my face turned red from anger, all over the car words were written with lipstick, such as "SEND HER BACK HOME, WE LOVE ROLAND, SEND HER BACK!"

Roland narrowed his eyes and I saw he was stunned, but as I looked at him, ready to burst out in tears, he said, "Honey, believe me, I don't know who did this!"

I opened the car door and sat down on the front seat. I closed the door because I did not want anyone to see me.

Roland put his arm around me and said, "Corrie, there is no other girl I care about but you; I want only you."

Finally, I calmed down. "Why would someone want to do this to me? I haven't harmed anyone."

He promised that from now on he would take me with him whenever he went somewhere.

We got the groceries and went to a show that night. He had convinced me that he didn't care for anyone else, and therefore, it did not matter who wrote that on the car.

A couple days later he told me he was leaving Chattanooga to work in West Virginia in the coal mines for a while. As soon as he had a job and place to live, he would send for me. At first, I did not like the idea, but then I tried to accept it.

His brother Ben was already working there, making $23 a day. He planned to send for Jewel, his wife, soon, because besides their two boys, twelve and ten years old, they now had twin girls.

Roland sold the old car for $150 and gave me $70.

West Virginia

After he left I continued my regular routine and worked every day. I received word that he arrived in Marianna, West Virginia, and had already started to work. He was trying to find a place to live so I could join him. He was living at the mining company's boarding house. Less than two weeks later he called me at work and asked me to come up there.

I preferred to work out a notice, but Miss Green, my boss, said that under the circumstances it was all right to quit suddenly.

I left Chattanooga the following day by Greyhound bus at 5 p.m. and arrived in Pinneville twenty-one hours later, where Roland met me. He seemed very glad to see me and I felt good in my newly bought light brown suit with shoes and bag to match.

Roland said he had gotten acquainted with several people and thought I would like them. They were simple, but very accommodating.

We stayed that night in Pinneville, but left early the next morning by a county bus for Marianna, getting off in about thirty minutes at the company store, something like a commissary. They sold everything. From there we had to walk the rest of the way and what I saw was not very enticing. On each side of a dirt road were three and four-room little wooden houses; "shanties" they were called.

Roland had rented one of those little shanties at $3 a week from the mining company. He said we would have to buy a few pieces of furniture, just enough to get by with. The floors were of unpainted wood, but clean. Each room had two small windows for which Roland had bought new shades.

After I changed clothes and shoes, we walked back to the company store to purchase a bed and mattress, a wool blanket, a card table and four chairs, a wash pan, mirror, and hot plate, two cups and four plates, one skillet and cooking vessel, paper drapes and curtain rods. I had brought two sheets, towels, and washcloths.

We wrote to Mrs. Smith to have her send our pillows, blankets, and bedspread.

A young woman from across the street came over and offered us the use of her icebox, introducing herself as Mrs. Louise Dancy, and she offered to help in any way she could. Her husband, Johnnie, worked on the night shift with Roland.

Our household goods were delivered right away and in one hour everything was placed. We ate some sandwiches Mrs. Dancy had fixed, and then it was time for Roland to go to work. I hated for him to work in the mines, such hard work, and dangerous and dirty, but maybe it would not be for long.

Mrs. Dancy asked me to come on over to her house because it would be 12:30 a.m. before Roland returned from the mines. She asked me to call her Louise and I said for her to call me Corrie. She was a very attractive dark-haired girl of small build. Her three-room shanty was nicely furnished and spotless. She told me most people living in the mining camp in Marianna were young and likeable. I soon learned that she was right. The people were simple, but not coarse. They were decent hard-working people, who lived with regard for each other, as if living in a world apart from the rest, at least in this community.

We had been living there several weeks when Roland and Ben were called to Chattanooga to attend the funeral of their brother who had been killed two-and-a-half years before in Belgium. His body had been shipped back to the United States. While Roland was there he stored the furniture, and gave the apartment up.

In the meantime, Louise and her six-year-old boy were company to me and I had gotten acquainted with another young woman, Geneva, the wife of Ted Stoots, also a miner. They had three children.

We lived there nearly two years and had our furniture in Chattanooga paid for and Roland had bought an old model car for which he paid cash.

Ben's wife, Jewel, had moved up there with her children and between several more acquaintances, I wasn't often alone.

Several weeks I spent wallpapering the whole place and painting woodwork, then lots of my time I'd spend reading and knitting, mostly for people in the neighborhood.

Then, our son, Billy Ray, was born. Roland seemed very proud of him and allowed me to buy for the baby whatever I thought he should have. Roland was on day shift now and only occasionally took off, either to play poker or drink beer in one of the neighboring taverns.

Often on Saturday nights I would get someone to take care of Billy, and Roland and I would drive the old car to Pinneville to see a movie. We planned to stay in Marianna perhaps another year before moving back to Chattanooga, until Billy could be placed in a nursery, should I return to work. But then unexpectedly we were forced to leave Marianna.

It was on a Saturday shortly past noon that Roland, Ted, Johnnie, and Fred Cook (I did not know him) left in Roland's car to shoot some pool and drink a few beers. It was already ten o'clock at night and no one had returned. I was over at Louise's and kept waiting a few hours, but then I decided I had better take Billy and go home because they probably would return sometime in the early morning hours.

But all-day Sunday passed, and Monday morning.

Louise learned that they had left the tavern Saturday night and headed for Welch, a fairly large town, to have some fun. Louise said she would like to get someone to drive us to Welch because they more than likely were in jail. Geneva Stoots, Ted's wife, said she could not go because of her children, but Louise took her boy with her, and I left Billy with Jewel. We got one of the neighbors to drive us to Welch. When we arrived at the jail, the neighbor said he would inquire about them. Louise and I were sitting in the back seat with her boy in the front, and we waited in the car.

Then after quite awhile, our neighbor returned with a strange look on his face. He entered the car, took his place behind the wheel, then he turned around facing us and said, "Louise you must prepare yourself for a shock. There has been a terrible accident."

He then added, "Johnnie is dead, Louise, he and Ted were killed instantly as they went over the bank 300 feet down the mountainside."

"Oh, God," Louise cried.

Turning to me, he said, "Corrie, Roland is in jail. He is slightly injured and in a state of shock, and charged with manslaughter."

I did not answer. I did not feel I had the right to ask any questions concerning Roland.

Then Louise started to cry and said, "Poor Geneva, with her three children!" She asked if they would let her see Johnnie, but the neighbor shook his head. He said they were at the funeral home, but she would not be allowed to see them. She then said she wanted to talk to Roland.

Our neighbor went inside to ask for permission.

We were allowed to talk to him and I was astonished at Louise. At first neither of them could speak, and then instead of accusing him, she comforted him.

"Poor Roland, don't worry," and as he broke down, she added, "don't cry, Roland, it was an accident and I don't want you in jail."

But then they had to take Roland away because he went completely to pieces.

I didn't say anything, I just felt numb, as if the ground had moved from under me. We drove home in silence except for Louise now and then breaking out in uncontrollable sobs.

Everybody had heard about it when we arrived in Marianna. I picked up Billy at Jewel's.

Ben and Fred Cook were released from the hospital where they had been treated for minor cuts and bruises. Jewel said Ben had gone over to Geneva's to help her with some funeral arrangements. He also intended to talk with Louise because he was representative for the local coal miners' union.

I took Billy and went home, putting him to bed with a bottle. Then I sat down on the bed and finally broke down. I did not leave the house all day that Monday. I kept my shades down, but I did see from the kitchen window people enter and leave the house of Louise and Geneva. I knew that they must have brought the bodies home.

Then, someone knocked on my door early Tuesday morning. It was the company store manager. I really had been afraid. After all, these people would stick close together, they blamed Roland, I could sense it as they passed this house. The way they looked at it, I didn't know how they felt about Roland. The store manager asked if he could come in for a moment. He looked at me with compassion and asked if there was anything he could do in the name of the company, if I should need clothes or money or anything else to attend the funeral.

I started to cry. I didn't even know whether they wanted me at the funeral. I didn't know what to do, and Roland was still in jail. I hadn't even been to see Geneva or Louise, in fact, I hadn't been out of the house, I had been so ashamed.

He placed his arm comfortingly around me and said, "I'll see what I can do." He then left.

About ten minutes later there was again a knock on the door. It was Louise. She had been crying a lot, her eyes were red, but she was calm. She simply said, "Corrie, I want you to come over and see Johnnie, and meet his people."

She then said the store manager came and had told her why I hadn't been over there.

I told her I wanted to stop at Jewel's and have her keep Billy. Louise said she would walk over there with me. Jewel said Ben had not yet had time to get Roland released, but as soon as he could, he would see what he could do. Louise said she would make bond herself, if Ben didn't have Roland released within a few hours.

All of Johnnie's relatives were nice to me and seemed to have no hatred toward Roland. They all said Roland needed to be released from jail.

We then went over to Geneva's. She seemed in a daze but was composed and talked quietly and about how nice and peaceful Ted looked, "as if he was asleep." She even apologized that in her hours of grief, she had forgotten all about me.

"Good God," I thought, "How glad I would have been to comfort her and Louise, but I thought they didn't want me to, that I didn't have the right, because they held Roland responsible for the accident, and he had been spared." I had been guilty with the thoughts that they would rather not have me around.

I asked Geneva if there was anything I could help her with. She said the children didn't have clean clothes, everything was dirty. So, Jewel and I did her laundry over at Jewel's and I later ironed everything.

Roland came home late that afternoon and everyone treated him very nice, but he was extremely depressed and seemed unable to control himself.

We both attended the funeral and after that Roland was unable to work for days.

But then we began to wonder what they really would do to Roland. Some people predicted that perhaps he would be getting five years in the workhouse. Others said that maybe he would go to prison for nine months and then out on parole. Of course, he would never be allowed to drive a car again, especially because he had no insurance. It would be two weeks when they would have his trial.

Geneva's mother asked me if I would keep Geneva company as much as possible until she moved to Pierpoint, where she would build a small house on her parents' lot from the $3,000 she received from the coal miners' insurance, in addition to a small pension for as long as she remained single.

Louise moved to Beckley, her hometown, in less than three weeks. Her parents lived there along with lots of people she knew.

Roland had relatives living nearby in Wyco. A cousin, Johnnie Hulgan, was also married to a coal miner and had four children. She came to be present when Roland stood trial.

Roland's car had been a total wreck, so an acquaintance of his took us to Welch and Jewel kept Billy.

Roland's name was called, and he disappeared into a small room. We all three were tense as we waited. A few minutes later he returned, then he said to us, "Let's go!"

I asked him if it was put off and he said, "No, it was dismissed from court because the investigation showed it could not have been prevented, and proof showed the shoulder of the road broken off."

They even returned his driver's license, unmarked. I still could not believe it, and sat quietly for a while. I then said to Roland, "You mean it is all over now? They are not going to put you in jail then?"

"No," he said quietly, "no one pressed charges."

How lucky we had been.

Ben, since the accident, had made a complete change in his life. In fact, he said he would never drink again, he had accepted to live according to the will of God. He seemed very serious about it. Then, several months later he had an accident in the mines, losing one of his eyes. After he received the insurance, which was approximately $3,700, he and his family moved to Cleveland, Tennessee, where he took a part-time job and enrolled in college to become a minister of the gospel.

Roland, at the insistence of his cousin, decided that we would move to Wyco, one of the nicest coal mining towns in that vicinity. The company kept the homes in excellent condition; a white painted fence surrounded each house; the streets were paved and had sidewalks.

To our advantage, Roland's cousin had been living there for many years, which added much to our making friends, and without any great effort we were accepted in the community. I was very satisfied living in the nice three-room house, because it was such a clean, attractive place. We had our furniture moved up there from Chattanooga by

Arrow Transfer and Storage Company, and with a few new additional pieces, such as draperies, an electric stove and washing machine, we had a nicely furnished home. The peacock blue couch and chair now were more attractive with slipcovers in light gray with small tangerine designs.

Billy was now nearly twenty months old. Roland did not drink, and we got along fine, making several nice friends. One woman, a schoolteacher, Mrs. Ginny Brown, whom I had met through Roland's cousin, became a close friend of mine. I admired her very much, especially for the way she managed her children and controlled her temper always. "Temper," she said, "is a form of selfish emotion."

We remained in Wyco nearly one year, living peacefully. We seldom went anywhere, but now and then when Roland went hunting, he would take Billy and me to stay with Geneva in Pierpoint.

Roland bought another car, a 1942 Fleetline Chevrolet. The mines had slowed down to only three days a week, and after waiting two months, Roland decided that as much as he hated leaving Wyco, he had to find work elsewhere.

We left Wyco and moved to Corrine, only about ten miles from there. Roland worked five and six days a week. We lived in an upstairs apartment, two small rooms and bath, clean, but nothing compared to the nice place in Wyco.

Roland was on night shift again and started keeping company with people whose influence awakened every weakness in him. He started coming home late and sometimes stayed out all weekend, either gambling or drinking. He seemed discontented and bored at home. Instead of matters improving, it got worse, he was so restless and pleasure seeking that he gave me $50 and insisted that I leave for Chattanooga, and stay for awhile with Elsie, his cousin, so he could "live a little."

Elsie had once told me if Roland and I ever had any trouble, I should feel free to come to them. Of course, I realized that was said so I would not be desperate in case of any rare emergency.

I was so disturbed about Roland wanting me to leave that I packed and let him drive me to the bus station. After he dropped Billy and me off, I ran into our former neighbors, Ethel and Parker Renalds from Wyco. They asked me if I was going on a trip. I was so forlorn and unhappy that I could not control myself any longer.

I explained to them the situation. They persuaded me to return with them to Wyco and spend the night in their home and that I should not let Roland run Billy and me out of the house.

Early the next morning I had them drive me to my own place. Roland had not been home since I left. Later in the afternoon I heard him come up the steps with a man he called Rufus. They were annoyed to find me there and Roland demanded the $50. I told him I had already mailed the money on bills that were due and only had $5 left.

"Let me have that then," Roland said in a nicer tone.

I walked into the kitchen and asked Roland to come in there a moment, that I wanted to talk with him.

Looking indifferently at me, he said, "What?"

I handed him the $5 bill and said, "Nothing." Then I turned around to keep from facing him.

As they were leaving, I sat down in the living room with Billy on my lap, rocking him.

I did not know what to do, all my tears didn't bother him, a man without a conscience you cannot reach; they do what they want to do. I realized he had no regard for me, nor for Billy, really for only himself. And still life without him...I could not stand the thought of it.

About an hour later I heard him climb the stairs......alone. I still was sitting in the rocking chair with Billy. I must have been a pitiful sight, with my swollen eyes and makeup smeared.

He entered and then sat down in the chair opposite me. He

appeared sober. Then, as if remembering something, he suddenly arose, digging in the bottom of his pants pocket. Then he placed a crumpled $5 bill on the coffee table.

"Here," he said, "it is yours—you can have it, honey."

I did not answer, but started rocking Billy faster, and tears dripping on his little blonde head, I got up, put Billy in his baby bed and got a towel for my face.

But Roland followed me and picked Billy up and sat him on his lap, letting his head lean on his shoulder. He then kissed Billy on his hair, saying:

"This is Daddy's little fellow, yes, sir."

Billy did not move, just laid quietly, enjoying it. But Roland continued, "Daddy is going to be better...he is going to start treating Mama right."

He looked at me, then said, "I mean it, honey. I am going to straighten up," he continued. "I know I've done you wrong, honey, but I'm going to straighten up. I mean it, Corrie, because hell! I've been awful!"

He looked at me again, then added, "I really mean it this time, Corrie!"

I was fighting my tears and he came over to me, putting his arm around me. I felt as if I saw the sun appear after long weeks of rain. To forgive him was easy enough, because when he was kind, he was as kind as he formerly had been bad.

Weeks passed in complete harmony and the only time he left the house was either to work or to go hunting for a day or so, but he returned home at the promised time. When he went to drink beer somewhere, he was back within three or four hours.

There were times that we were invited to a house party and he would take me along.

Then he asked me whether I would like to return to Chattanooga to make our home. I was not completely in favor of it, but perhaps he had matured enough to stay on the right track.

Return to Chattanooga

We left West Virginia in the car, taking only our clothes. We intended to look for a job first, then for an apartment, and return later to pick up the furniture.

We had no trouble getting a job. Roland was hired by Somerville Iron Works and I at the United Hosiery Mills, starting in two weeks. I first had applied at Dupont, but they told me to come back after I became an American citizen.

We rented a cheap apartment upstairs on McCallie Avenue for $22 a month, two small rooms and a kitchen and bath. The place was filthy! The former occupant had dumped the coal in a corner on the floor of the living room. The rent being so low, with $100 I could clean it up and make it look nice.

Roland went to work while I cleaned, scrubbed, and painted. I painted the kitchen bright yellow, with white curtains that had a yellow ruffle. I put in cheap light-colored linoleum and new white shades.

Roland and Ben went after the furniture in a U-Drive-It truck. After everything was placed, no one would have recognized the former apartment. A couple months later, the owner of the house, Mr. Burger, wanted to see what we did to that apartment. He was amazed and said that he knew it could be made into a nice place, so, he upped the rent from $22 to $35 a month.

Roland and I kept silent. After he left, Roland said, "We are moving out of here as soon as we find another place."

I dreaded moving, but Roland found a newly decorated place above the apartment of one of his cousins, Leon Smith, who lived there with his wife, Janell, and child, Vicky, a girl the age of Billy.

Janell and I got along fine; she didn't let anything upset her much. They were not home much on the weekends; they visited with one or the other of their parents to keep the grocery bill from running so high.

Roland drove me every morning to work, then dropped Billy, who was now three years old, at the Pro Re Bona nursery. We were out of debt except for a large gas heater, so Roland traded his 1942 Chevrolet for a 1949 Buick.

I didn't have proof, but plenty of reason to believe that Roland ran around with women. When I mentioned it, he assured me "that women were the least of his worries."

Well, I didn't doubt that!

The early months of fall were boring, and I was very lonely. Roland worked during the day and at night went to school on the GI Bill, and on weekends he usually was out "living," leaving Billy and me alone. Sometimes on Sunday night he took us to a drive-in theater. While he recuperated from the night before, I watched the movie. Billy would be asleep in the back seat. Of course, watching the movie that way was no fun.

Then Christmas came. He was so nice and considerate, especially on Christmas Eve morning. I had the Christmas tree decorated, several packages wrapped in red and green paper with colorful bows adding to the festivity and atmosphere. Everything in the house was spotless and oranges, nuts, and a fruitcake were on the kitchen table.

Roland always saw to it that a nice supply of "cheer you up" was in the refrigerator. Billy's tricycle, among other toys, was safely hidden in the closet. To top it off, Roland gave me $30 to spend as I wished for something for myself.

Secretly I had hoped that Roland would surprise me with a wedding ring, as I was still wearing the old one my mother had given me to wear on the boat until Roland would get me the nice one he had promised. But this was not the time to become sentimental over a ring.

I asked if he could not come along to town with me this one time. But he said he had something to do. I brought Billy to an aunt of Janell, a Mrs. Vessy Smith, whose daughter, Gloria, would look after Billy for a dollar, so I could shop in peace.

With the $30 I bought several pieces of lingerie and had them nicely wrapped. Because I was in such a happy Christmas spirit, I decided to pick up a few extra groceries on my way home; it was only a few blocks out of my way. I usually bought the groceries, then had Roland pick them up later.

It was such a beautiful sunny day, cold, but so pleasant......I wished everyone could have such a nice Christmas. I had not been as content in a long time. Then, as I walked along Market Street, I suddenly stopped. I could not believe my eyes, but it was true. There before my own eyes was Roland in the car, waiting for the traffic light to change, and a woman sitting beside him—very close.

I don't exactly remember what happened, but a man handed me my packages.

In a daze I walked home—it was not far—about fifteen minutes. I sat down in the chair in the living room. I just sat there staring; I did not cry, I just did not move.

He had some things to do he had said, and had given me $30 to buy my own Christmas present!

It wasn't long before I heard a car drive up. He turned on the light as he entered the living room and acted as if he was unaware that I was home.

Surprised, he said, "Hi there, I didn't know you were sitting there in the dark."

"No," I said, "You didn't know I would be on North Market Street either."

"What do you mean?" he said, frowning.

"You know exactly what I mean, Roland; I saw you."

"Saw me where?" he said, opening his mouth half way, as if he could not place where.

"You know where—and with whom—with that woman in the car."

"I don't know what you're talking about, Corrie."

I broke loose in hysterical sobs.

He squatted beside me, taking my hands in his. Comfortingly, he said, "Honey, there is no reason to get all upset over nothing, because I can explain everything. I know it looks bad, but there was nothing to it. That woman was the wife of a friend of mine and she had to go to work and did not have a way."

"Oh, stop it, Roland! Stop it. Stop it. Stop it!"

But then I thought he might leave me again, and if a man lies to cover up for things you know he is guilty of, that is the same as an apology, and I would just make matters worse if I let him know I didn't believe him. If I kept on accusing him, he wouldn't even feel guilty and a man won't stay with an unpleasant woman. I realized he was guilty, but this was Christmas Eve and I could not stand to be left all alone. "I'll do anything to keep him from leaving me tonight," I thought.

So, I managed to stop my tears, and I said, "I do believe you, Roland, but you should have stopped when you saw me."

"But I didn't see you," he continued.

"Well," I said, "since it was as you said, let's forget it; after all, this is Christmas Eve." I added that just for extra security to remind him.

He said softly, "Let's go after Billy."

In the car he kissed me and said, "I love you, honey!"

That was all that mattered.

Then spring came. Everything looked pretty, people seemed happier, too. I looked forward to the summer and trying to get a tan. I tanned nicely for a blonde.

Roland traded cars again, this time for a convertible, still a Buick, black with a white top.

But, the summer didn't turn out as I had hoped it would. It started when one day I was called to the nursery from work. Billy had a temperature and I was advised to take him to a doctor.

Roland was now working for the Chattanooga Linen Company, so I called his place of employment. The girl answering the phone told me that Roland Smith was off sick.

"Sick!" I thought. I said then, confused, "Are you sure?"

"Yes," the girl said, "his wife called this morning reporting that her husband was sick."

I thanked her and hung up.

There was nothing to do but take Billy on the bus. I didn't think he had anything serious, but the nursery required you to take children to the doctor or home when running a temperature.

I took Billy to the doctor and he said that Billy had a light infection in his bronchial tubes. He handed me a prescription.

Roland came home as usual around 4:30. After he sat down in the living room, I told him Billy was sick; I had taken him to the doctor.

Roland was always tenderhearted to Billy. He picked him up, setting him on his knee, then petting him, he said, "Is my little fellow sick?"

I remarked about the weather being so hot and that I was tired.

He put Billy on the couch. He then started taking off his shirt, complaining about the heat, too.

I noticed that he was blistered from a sunburn on his back, so I asked him where he got his sunburn.

He said, "Yah," touching his shoulder, "I do have a burn, don't I?"

He sat down in the chair, picking up the paper, and started unfolding it; then he said, "You know what they had me do at work today? See, there was no work for me in my department, so rather than let me go home, they asked me to mow the lawn."

"Roland," I said, "you're lying. I called up there today and they told me your wife had called in, reporting you sick."

He looked at me then said, grinning, "that's strange. You mean I did not work? Huh? I feel just as if I did put in a full day's work."

We had a terrible argument, from one word came the other, and finally for his own safety, he had to run. He said he was moving out, he was not going to live with a hell-cat. His parents had moved to North Chattanooga, and that's where he said he was going to stay.

Roland's parents never interfered in our arguments, though they did not uphold Roland in his wrongdoing.

I was miserable, not happy with him, but I was sure I would be more lost without him.

I would ride the bus to work, dropping Billy off at the nursery, which was only one block from the hosiery mill.

Then, four days later when I came home from work, I found Roland in the kitchen peeling potatoes. I did not speak, but had to admit to myself that I was pleased. I still did not know what he was up to. He told me he realized that he hadn't appreciated the things he had gotten used to and he came back to show some appreciation.

I hated my own weakness and wished I could tell him, without hurting myself, that I was through with him. But it seemed every cloud had disappeared from the sky!

Several happy weeks followed, and I wanted to hold on, not let contentment slip away. But when fear overrules strength, you lose nearly every time.

I asked Roland the following Saturday if we could pack some food and drinks and spend the afternoon on the lake. But he said he didn't know any other couple to join us and that just the three of us would be no fun. I didn't know anyone either; at work I hadn't gotten acquainted with any girls on a personal basis.

It was such beautiful weather, I dreaded staying in all day, upstairs in the hot apartment. So, I asked him to take Billy and me to the lake, that he would not have to stay with us. Billy Ray, looking at him with big pleading eyes., begged "Please, Daddy, take us!" He already had his bathing trunks on.

Roland agreed to take us. I wore my bathing suit under my skirt and blouse. I did not take any ice or food along; I wanted to hurry before he changed his mind about taking us.

Roland went downstairs to let the convertible top down, and I told Billy to go help his Daddy and sit in the car, because Roland might take off alone.

But we arrived at the lake in about fifty minutes. He let us out, Billy and me, a large beach towel, suntan lotion, a book, and my purse. We were not on what the public referred to as the main part, but rather a grassy spot off the highway.

Roland promised to come after us about six o'clock or a little later. It was not quite twelve o'clock.

I didn't mind; it sure beat sitting home cooped up. Billy was no trouble, sitting contentedly on his towel beside me, his eyes squinted. I let him play in the water for a while, where it was not deep. It was a very hot day and Billy began to whine for a cold drink. A little girl who was sitting near us with her parents, brought Billy a Coca-Cola. I nodded to the mother, thanking her.

It was of course my own neglect that I had not taken time to bring ice and drinks myself.

Billy was getting tired and sleepy, so we moved to a shady spot under a tree. Billy stretched out on the beach towel and fell asleep in a short while. I was reading a Dutch book, "Henne"; I spoke English easily enough, but reading a book was still too straining.

It was past sundown now, and nearly all the people had left. I began to get a little uneasy. What if Roland didn't come after us? It was past eight o'clock. But the people with the little girl were still there, with an older couple. They were roasting wieners, so I knew they were in no hurry. They were having a good time; now and then they roared with laughter. I noticed they were drinking beer.

After awhile, I got up and stretched a little, trying to see if Roland perhaps was trying to find the right spot. The mother of the little girl hollered at me, "Hey, come over and join us, have a beer." She motioned with her arm. She was a jovial cheerful type, who probably made friends easily.

I welcomed the invitation and said, as she handed me an opened beer, "I am sorry, but I don't like beer." I quickly added that I had nothing against beer, I just did not like the taste of it. She offered me a Coca-Cola, which I gratefully accepted because I felt dehydrated.

They asked me to sit down. I glanced over at Billy, and the man, probably her husband, offered to get him so he could be near me. She said in a friendly tone, "Sit down, make yourself at home."

She was fixing Billy a roasted wiener. He was sitting close to the man, sleepily rubbing his eyes. Billy liked strangers, that is if he could see me. I thought these people were waiting for an explanation as to how I was there without a car or anyone.

She handed me a roasted wiener, without asking if I wanted it. I felt as if I had been rescued from a lonely island.

I explained my husband had brought Billy and me to the lake while he was gone to have the car worked on. I added that I guessed he ran into more trouble; otherwise, he would have been back by now. They told me not to worry, that they would take me home.

She then remarked to the others what a lovely accent I had, then asked me where I was from. When I just had managed to become the center of attention, right in the middle of my conversation, a car stopped, and Roland sort of weaved out. But, they all had an adequate amount of "joy fluid" as Roland called it, and welcomed him as if he were an old buddy. They had plenty of beer on ice, and Roland carried several cartons from the car.

But, I enjoyed it, these people were families, I had nothing against drinking a beer now and then, but I hated the tavern type, the family destroyer. Here, I felt included. Most of Roland's beer drinking friends didn't include me, they always made me feel an outsider.

The woman offered me a Coca-Cola every time Roland had a beer. In a good-natured way, she would say, "Here, keep up with him."

It was nearly eleven o'clock before we went home, and I wasn't going to ask Roland what caused him to be late because I wasn't letting anything, or anyone, destroy the pleasant atmosphere.

But, you cannot capture happiness any more than you can store daylight. He started staying out again more and longer hours. My disposition began to suffer, not only in Roland's presence, but in general. I wondered if maybe I was a bore?

One day over the weekend when Roland was out again, I visited his sister, Eveline. She had a good husband—not real handsome, but dependable. He did not drink, and never went anywhere alone, except to work. I asked her how she did it, getting along so nicely without distress. She was not smarter than I, nor prettier.

She laughed, a deep sounding chuckle, and said, "Corrie, I love my brothers, especially Roland, but they are all irresponsible. Not any of them is "husband material. I love Junior for his stability and that's why I married him. You didn't marry Roland for that, did you?" She then added in a deep low voice, "Junior is good, real good, but dull, real dull. I love him because he is so good, but I make sacrifices. Junior is narrow-minded and self-righteous, not much fun, but his goodness compensates for that."

I guess there was a lot to consider about Roland, his non-criticizing disposition, his good looks, and mildness of temper. I could not recall that he ever had used profane language. But I also began to realize that an exciting, handsome man was nice to look at, but in my case, did not compensate for a life of loneliness and discontentment.

And my wants were so few. I didn't mind having to work. I never complained about not having much money.

Coming Apart

Roland came home on Monday evening, after staying out the whole weekend. I asked him where he had been.

He said, "If I told you, you would know more than I do."

He then sat down on the couch, smoking, blowing the smoke in little ringlets to the ceiling. He seemed more restless than ever before. I knew there was something on his mind.

Finally, he said, "You know, Corrie, you are not happy with me now, are you?"

"Happy?" I said, "Happy, the way you treat me, leaving me alone nearly all the time?"

I started to cry.

He just sat there silent, smoking, then he said, "You think I am treating you pretty bad, don't you? In fact, so bad, you can hardly stand it any longer."

"Well," he continued in a low voice, "it is going to be worse, Corrie, because I am not intending to stay home. I realize our marriage is a mistake. I'm just not ready to settle down, and the only thing we can do is separate."

I could not control myself any longer and started to cry hysterically, but he calmed me down. He brought me a glass of water and then said that he hadn't meant it, he was all mixed up, and he didn't know what was wrong with him. After I calmed down enough to talk, I asked him if he was in love with another woman.

But he said, definitely not, it wasn't another woman, the problem was women and since he was so interested in other women in general, he realized he didn't love me. He said he hadn't been happy either.

I asked him if he didn't think he had to contribute anything to receive happiness.

"Just because we at one time appealed to each other, do you think that secures happiness?"

Most people realize that you must sacrifice for anything you get in life, for an education, a good job, but happiness, they think, it is just given to you, without effort, or restrictions of their wants.

He said that he just liked to be free, to do as he pleased.

I told him that I did not think any decent person, no matter how rich they might be, could do as they pleased and have what they want, except at the expense of others in one form or another.

He insisted he just wanted to be free.

I cried nearly most of the night and was unable to go to work. Roland suggested that I see a doctor. I realized I should because I was a nervous wreck.

The doctor's report was that I had a goiter and thyroid trouble, and he advised an operation as soon as possible.

But that evening when I came home, Roland had packed and left; I did not know where he'd gone. I called his parents. They were sympathetic, but there was really little they could do. I told them I was to have an operation, and if they saw Roland, to tell him.

Roland had gotten acquainted with a nice-looking young man, who was married, and lived on the same street where we lived. This young man and Roland often took off together, 'to live it up'. So, a few days later when I saw Roland's car leave from there, I decided to talk to his wife.

I took Billy and went over there. After I rang the door bell, a very attractive brunette opened the door. I introduced myself and she said she was Peggy, Wallace's wife. She was very young and slender, and with a pleasing smile. She invited me to come in. I asked her if she had any idea when her husband would return because he went off with Roland.

She looked at me, round eyed, raising her eyebrows and shrugging her shoulder, and said, "there is no telling."

She seemed so relaxed, so at ease, that I asked her how she accepted it so easily.

But she smiled in a comforting manner and said, "I might as well make the best of it, I have three children, three babies, and sitting here worrying about him will not change matters, it only will make me old before my time."

It didn't take me long to realize that she certainly did not drown herself in self-pity. When I left, she told me to come back whenever I wanted to, and I thought I would some time. She seemed sensible, a little distant, maybe reserved, but not indifferent.

Roland stopped by the following evening to tell me that he was leaving Chattanooga for Detroit. He asked me what my plans were. I told him I did not know. He suggested the best thing I could do was to return to Holland. He allowed me to take Billy or leave him with him, whatever I thought best.

I told him I had no intentions of returning to Holland. I didn't want to worry my mother with things she had no control over. I told him I had become accustomed to living here and it would be difficult for me to return to Holland, divorced with a child, unhappy, and pick up the pieces from there.

I intended to apply for American citizenship and then file for a divorce. I also reminded him that Billy was a native-born American. I wanted him to grow up and think American, that if I returned to

Holland now, Billy would never be a whole-hearted American, a boy must from his youth up be taught to believe in, and cling to his own country. I wanted Billy to be able to sing the Star-Spangled Banner with American sentiment and he needed to be able to visit and see his daddy. If I took him abroad now, he might exaggerate the fact in his mind that he never got to see his daddy. If I stayed here and he didn't get to see his father, then at least I was not to blame.

Roland said everything sounded all right with him, because he wasn't in any hurry for a divorce. He promised to send money as soon as he got a job and was established.

After he left, I felt hopelessly alone, but I had to face reality.

First, I had to find someone to keep Billy during my confinement in the hospital. I called Vera, Roland's sister, and she agreed to keep Billy for at least fourteen days. In the meantime, I had made friends with Janell's aunt, Vessie Smith, who was not a relative of Roland. She was a great help, had been divorced herself, and knew what I was going through.

I could not afford to keep the apartment, so I stored the furniture at the cost of $9 per month. Vessie said I could stay with her the first two weeks after I would be released from the hospital.

I did not write home about anything; there was nothing they could do, but worry. The only unbelievable thing was that strangely enough, I still loved Roland.

Mr. Smith demanded that Roland remain in Chattanooga until after my surgery.

Vessie went with me to the hospital and left after the visiting hour was over. An intern who made routine check-ups asked me if something was bothering me, but I told him everything was alright. I had come to the point that it didn't matter. If I lived, fine, if I didn't, well, I would not know about it.

A girl named Caroline, with whom I had become acquainted at

work, stayed with me during the first day after my surgery. She was a wonderful person, of unusual consideration, but through her genuine sympathy and devoted kindness, I became more aware of my own miserable situation. Caroline told me that Roland's father and mother came shortly after my surgery, and she told me that Roland had been to see me also. Physically I was getting along fine.

Roland came once more but didn't stay long. This visit left me depressed. He was sympathetic, but he didn't show any affection, nor did he seem concerned.

I was released after eight days and stayed with Vessie. I received $36 the girls from work had collected for me. Caroline and I went to pick up $77 Roland had left me at his place of employment. I was getting along well and in four weeks able to return to work.

I needed to find a place for Billy Ray until I would be able to afford a place where he could stay with me. Vessie was working; otherwise, she would have kept him. The winter was coming and taking him out of his warm bed at 6:30 in the cold morning, waiting for the bus, was not advisable. I managed to find a couple, a policeman and his wife, who took care of Billy for $14 a week. He received excellent care and love as well.

I rented for myself a small, unheated room for $4 a week next door to Vessie. I had to share the bath and there were no cooking facilities. But Caroline asked me to take the early bus to work and stop at her house for breakfast. Two months later the duplex of Vessie's house became vacant. Moving in there solved many problems. Vessie had quit work so she could keep her grandchild, and because she would be home anyway, she could keep Billy for me for only $5 a week. Of course, I would furnish his milk and food.

Vessie lived in the other side of the duplex with her two children, Gloria, who was sixteen years old and attended high school, and Mack, her nine-year-old son. Her two older children were married and Vessie was going to keep Myra, her daughter's little girl, so Sally, her daughter, could work. Myra, who was three years old, made a good playmate for Billy.

Things were working out nicely because Roland did send $20 weekly. I enrolled in a course to make application for American citizenship.

Shortly before Christmas, Roland's mother called. She said Roland had been in an accident and his face was all cut up. He was out of danger now, but she thought it her duty to let me know about it. She asked me how I was getting along, and she told me Roland had inquired about Billy and me in a letter, and asked her to find out how I felt about him. She then said Roland would like to call me. He also had sent $50. I told her I wished him no harm and if he wished to call me at Vessie's (since I did not have a phone) that was all right with me.

He called a few days later and talked like a different person. He told me how sorry he was and that he missed us, Billy and me, and if I would just give him another chance he would spend the rest of his days making it up to me. He asked me if I could come to Detroit; if so, he would send me the money, and if I liked it there he would get an apartment for us and send after the furniture. I told him to send the money and I would think it over. But I already knew that nothing could keep me from going if he wanted me.

Vessie kept Billy because things were too uncertain to take him along.

Roland met me in Detroit at the railway station. He was so attentive and considerate, he told me several times that he loved only me and Billy, that the three of us belonged with each other. His face was still badly scarred, but it didn't hurt his looks, I thought. He said he would get quite a sum of insurance money and then he would buy me something he knew that I always wanted— "a nice diamond wedding ring."

I was moved. I realized I still loved him very much! I stayed a week, then I told him to find a nice apartment, then send the money for me and Billy to come on, and to transfer the furniture; I then would quit my job and come up there. That it would take about $200.

When he took me to the train, he said he wished he could just send after the furniture and have his parents bring Billy. I asked him, "Why? People need to plan things first."

He told me that he was worried, I might change my mind, or he might get lonesome, and with the wrong company.

I told him if he did not have any more willpower than that, I had no business moving up there, then, because temptations are everywhere.

Ultimately, I did not go to Detroit. Roland was laid off, and he came to Chattanooga. He waited to be called back to work and after two weeks, they called him to return to work at four o'clock Monday afternoon. We had enjoyed being together and I thought seriously about moving to Detroit.

I saw him to the bus station, but I did not wait until he departed because sometimes buses didn't run on schedule. I did some shopping and had my hair shampooed and returned home about three hours later.

Vessie told me that Roland had telephoned and left a number for me to call. I dialed the number and asked to speak with him; from the music, I assumed he was in a beer joint. He said he had missed his bus when he stopped close to the bus station to have a beer. Now he had several hours to wait, so he wanted to know if I could join him while he had a few more beers. I really was flattered, he was changed, because never had he asked me to join him in a tavern. Even though I did not drink beer, I did not like the idea of him sitting there all alone. I promised him I would be there as soon as I could.

Immediately I called a cab. I leaned back in the seat smiling—to think he wanted to be with me a few more hours.

As I entered the bar, I felt somewhat ill at ease. I wasn't accustomed to visiting taverns. But after all, he was still my husband, though we had lived separately.

There was an older couple sitting opposite from him in the booth. Roland introduced us, but I did not pay any attention, because I really wanted to get away from there, and eat, but in a place where Roland still could drink beer.

Roland immediately moved over, and putting his arm around me, he said, "This is my baby. What do you want to drink, honey?"

I told him I did not care for beer, but a Coke would be fine.

"No," he said, hugging me tenderly, "I want my baby to be happy. I'll get a half pint of Canadian Club."

I protested, but he got up and said he would be back in a minute—he was so nice!

The woman said, "I feel so sorry for Roland, he is so worried that he missed his bus."

"Oh," I said, surprised. He didn't seem worried to me, but I did not say anything.

She continued, "Yeah, if he is not at his job Monday evening, he may be fired."

Roland returned, a half pint of whiskey in his coat pocket. He sat down beside me and poured me a stiff drink.

"Now, Roland," the woman said, "don't be so stingy!"

But I placed my hand over the top of my glass.

She then said, "Let's drink to Roland getting to his job on time."

We all drank to that.

Roland was sitting beside me, looking at me, smiling. I thought how good-looking he was, even when drinking. He then pulled out his billfold and said, "Let's see how much money I got left." He started counting out loud—$9—the bus ticket is $14.80."

I did not say anything, but then I thought and said, "Where is your bus ticket, Roland?"

"Well," he said, "I still have my bus ticket, but the bus won't get me there on time, I probably will have to go by plane."

"By plane," I said, getting kind of upset," do you know that people with $9 in their pocket don't ride planes?"

"I know it," he said, emptying his beer glass. He looked real pitiful when facing the couple across the table. He said, "Do you know, I have never ridden a plane?"

No one made any comment.

Then the woman said, "Roland, I could let you have the money. How much do you need?"

Roland thought awhile, they he said, "Oh...about thirty dollars."

Picking up her purse, she said with a real determined look on her face, "I'll let you have it, Roland, if you are sure now that your wife doesn't mind. You know some wives just would not stand for other women mingling in their affairs."

I just remained silent, thinking plenty. Then, after finishing my drink, I said, "You know—that Canadian and Coke makes a pretty good drink."

The woman looked at me, ignoring what I had said.

Then she said, "You sure you don't care if I loan your husband the thirty dollars he needs so he won't lose his job?"

"Oh noooo," I said, "Why should I care? I think it is nice of you."

"You're sure now? You're sure you don't mind?"

"No, of course not. I think it is real nice of you. You are a real friend."

They saw they were not getting anywhere. Then Roland said: "Corrie, will you call the airport and ask what a ticket costs? Wait, here is a dime, honey."

Well, I thought they really wanted some money out of me!

The telephone was at the end of the bar. I laid my handbag on the counter, where the bartender was wiping the table. Coming close to me, he said in a soft tone, "I don't know what the guy is to you, but they are pulling your leg, ma'am; there is a girl in the back booth waiting on him."

"Thanks," I said, "I thought something was going on, but I hadn't figured it out."

I dialed the number and asked what the fare to Detroit was, coach, $26.80.

I thought, "That bunch of scum! They must think I throw my money around like they do." Returning to the table, I said, "$26.80, Roland."

Sounding well sober now, he said, "That's $26.80 too much."

They must have had a discussion while I had made the telephone call. Roland came straight out and said, "Corrie, could you let me have some money?"

The woman interrupted and said, "Of course, Roland, if she has it, what wife would not help her husband when he is in a predicament?"

I hated this type woman; the only way she could feel superior was by wrongdoing. But, I intended to play my side of the game; so, I said I wished he could have contacted me earlier. "You see, I went on a shopping spree, I just bought a television today."

"A television?" ...... Roland said frowning.

"Yah," I said, "a television. And a camera. I paid cash for it, $399."

I was just making that up. I had bought it on credit, but I said, "I still have enough left for Roland to get to Detroit."

I noticed Roland's face and he nearly smiled, but he controlled it and said, "Let's go to the airport."

"No," the woman said, "you can get tickets at the Patten Hotel."

All four of us left in a taxi for the travel office. I acted more embarrassed than I really was, and I said to the woman, "Roland is in no condition to get on a plane; in fact, they won't sell him a ticket."

Roland was looking at me now, but his eyes did not focus.

I said, "Roland, you are in no condition to travel. I will get you a plane ticket tomorrow, but not tonight."

I then walked toward the door, and got into a taxi. Roland got in the cab with the other couple.

After I got home I told Vessie what happened. She laughed and said, "I knew that, but I had to let you go, no one could have told you, you had to find out for yourself. But, you're doing fine, you are growing up."

I began to realize that depending on Roland showed my lack of intelligence. I would not say that I was not hurt by Roland's behavior, because I was, but not in the same way as when we had our first breakup. It was now my pride that was damaged, my faith in him completely destroyed. And still when he called me a couple of days after he arrived in Detroit, I could not deny that I was pleased to hear from him. He claimed, of course, that it was not true that he just wanted money from me that night to have a good time. Well, I did not want to argue about it anymore, and I told him I soon would be an American citizen and then I would file for a divorce.

Now and then I visited the neighbor, Peggy, whose husband, Wallace, had left for Michigan also, and was now in Battle Creek. I liked her very much. She had an inner self-assurance that I lacked. She had no self-pity, even though she only had the bare necessities and three children to care for, the oldest five years of age. She told me the only thing a woman in our situation could do is cling close to her children because that is about all the happiness there is for a woman married to an irresponsible husband. She was a person who, without any effort, would make you appreciate anything good that ever happened to you. Her mother and sisters effortlessly made me feel part of their family.

But then one day, when I went to see her, she told me that Wallace had wired her the money and asked her to come to Michigan. She said she would try it again, because there were three small reasons.

I got a sort of let down feeling after she left because she had been someone I could talk to with reason, someone like Mary.

I wrote home and said Roland was working in Detroit now and that I planned to stay in Tennessee. They probably would advise me to join him, if I could, but I did not intend to write home all the details, at least not yet.

From Roland I received money for Billy regularly. I wrote him that soon I would get my naturalization papers, and then I would file for a divorce.

Late in November I became an American citizen. It was rather sad, that on this special occasion of becoming a legal part of a country, I was so alone, without a husband, or relatives. When I saw the girls with whom I had taken my naturalization course, with corsages pinned on them, and receiving well wishes from their husbands, I felt instead of acceptance, and a feeling of belonging, a sudden terror. The terror of being without anyone who really cared. And as I walked home, I thought of a German song I once heard, this is my translation:

"When there are no stars in heaven, and fate played you an unkind part,

Your hopes and dreams all have vanished...

And empty loneliness in your heart,

Look in the gardens, for shady places...

Where tiny flowers bloom...

They held out through the long cold winter

Still yearning for the sun...

So, please do not take for granted, the little things in life...

Believe in all, that's good and humble, then clouds do not survive."

New Beginning

I hurried home; I had lots to be thankful for. Vessie was nice, not a bit sentimental. And, of course, there were Roland's people, but there was little they could do. In fact, I hated to worry his mother with my troubles, she already was a worrier.

But, now, I did have another problem coming up. Vessie could not keep Billy any longer because she would soon start to work. Her daughter had bought a home and intended to quit work. I thought about moving closer to my work, so I could walk and leave Billy during working hours in the nursery.

I placed an application for a unit in the Boone-Hysinger government housing development. The management tried to talk me into sharing a nice apartment with a girl who worked for the Electric Power Board. I met the girl. She was also a divorcee, with a small child, but I realized she had a very good income and I would not be able to carry my share of the expenses of her nice place. So, whether I liked it or not, the only thing I could afford would be in the housing project. It would take about three weeks to see whether I was eligible. They told me I needed to get a divorce first, so the rent could be based on my income.

One day as I was sitting in Vessie's swing on her porch, a car drove up and a very nice family stepped out. At first, I did not recognize them, but then I saw it was Peggy and Wallace and their three children. They stayed awhile, asking me how I was getting along. I told them I was doing fine, and then Peggy asked me if I planned to move to Detroit. I told her, no, I had no intentions because I was situated here, and I didn't know what the score would be once I would move to Detroit.

I asked Peggy if she liked it in Battle Creek, Michigan. She smiled happily and said they were doing fine, and Wallace said he did not think he ever would move back to Chattanooga. I told her I was glad for her.

Of course, a little jealousy came over me, they all looked so nice, and happy, so well taken care of, dressed so nice, and the pretty new car!

They had to leave, we said goodbye, and I watched them as they walked to their car, lucky happy family! Peggy said something to Wallace, who was already sitting behind the wheel, she then turned around and came back to the house. I stood in the door, she said in a low voice, "I want to talk to you just a moment, because I am not going back with Wallace, I am staying here with the children. She whispered, "He is not changed...and I hate Battle Creek!"

I asked her if Wallace knew about it, but she whispered no, he did not, it was going to be a surprise. She then said "bye," and as she came to the car, she turned around and waved.

Two days later she called and said Wallace had returned to Michigan and she had rented a little place only two blocks from where her mother lived. She had asked Wallace to send the rest of their things. I asked her if he was angry when she had told him she and the children were not going back with him. She said that if he hadn't liked it, he didn't let her know about it. She said she didn't think he really cared one way or another.

I filed suit for divorce and shortly after receiving it, I moved to the housing project. Every morning at 6:30 Billy and I left the house walking. It was about twenty minutes to where I dropped him off at the nursery. I then went to work, picking him up again at 3:30.

Fortunately for me, I lived in a nice block. People were clean, the apartment was nice, my furniture, draperies, and wool rugs made the place look cozy and warm. I did not get familiar with many people. There were several nice families living there. Some were there as a matter of circumstances; others, victims of their own laziness.

Shortly after Peggy divorced Wallace, I persuaded her to move to the project, also. In the years that I lived there, I never visited with anyone, except her, and two girls from work, and another girl who worked at the hospital. Billy Ray was happy there; there were Peggy's children to play with, among many other youngsters. I thought it very important for children to have playmates, other than their own brothers and sisters.

I now dated and learned that there was nothing wrong with my personality and that I was not a bore. Nearly every Sunday in the hot summer, Peggy and I took the children with our dates to the lake, or to the park. I was not lonesome as I had been when married to Roland. But, at first, people had pitied me, then as I began dating and seemingly had more fun than they, their pity vanished and some of it even turned to envy. But, it did not matter, pity is worthless, though I should have welcomed comfort at times.

I wrote home simply that Roland and I had divorced, without any details. I told them Roland and I were just two different people and that it was best that he and I went our separate ways. Of course, my mother did not accept it that easily. She became so worried that plans were made to send my sister Tillie to come over to the U.S. to see how I really was getting along. My sister arranged to get her passport and bought a ticket, but then she could not get a visa, because she was single. Many girls had made misuse of a visiting visa and gotten married to Americans once they were over here, and that way had legal permanent residence without going through the difficulty of immigration. They informed my sister she was eligible and could apply for immigration papers. But, Tillie was not interested in immigration. I kept hoping and she managed to get as far as Canada.

I wrote letters to the naturalization and immigration offices in New York, but every time it was refused for the same reason. So, without seeing each other, she returned to Holland.

My family then got together and arranged for Billy and me to come to Holland by boat on the Holland-America Line. All arrangements were made through a travel agency.

I kept my apartment, had my telephone disconnected, paid up my insurance, and sent my trunk ahead to New York.

Billy, who was now six years old, and I left by train. Peggy and Vessie brought us to the train station. Billy and I spent one night in New York at the Governor Clinton Hotel, directly opposite the Pennsylvania Railway Station. Early the next morning we went by bus to New Jersey, to the Holland-America Line docks. We were to sail on the Watermann. A Dutch passenger liner, it was not a luxury liner. Most passengers were either young honeymooners, exchange students, artists, or underpaid diplomats—mostly people who wanted to travel on limited funds.

It was mid-April, but still cool. I had Billy dressed in a brown English tweed suit with leggings, and I could hardly wait to have my mother see him. I was brought to my cabin by a steward and found that I was to share my cabin with a German girl, also a former war bride. She was going to Germany to visit her parents and she had her five-year-old son with her. During her visit her husband remained in Florida. She said he just was generous enough to let her, Paula, and Johnny come on this trip.

Most passengers seemed a little nervous and excited. I was glad it was a Dutch ship; at least I could understand everyone. They spoke either Dutch, German, or English. It gave me a feeling of security. Our trunks were placed in the bottom of the ship, and there were certain hours that we would be able to get into the vault, if for some reason we had to get something out of our trunks. Suitcases and small pieces of luggage were kept in our cabins. Passengers were divided into three groups so there would be a place for everyone in the dining room. My cabin companion and her son were to have the same table as Billy and me. She and I got along right from the start, and Billy Ray and her son, Johnny, already were exchanging marbles for pictures of basketball players.

Announcements were made on loudspeakers when lunch, dinner, tea, and snacks would be served. The bar would open the moment we were out of the harbor. Drinks were tax free, which made a martini cost about fourteen cents.

After lunch, Paula, Johnny, Billy, and I remained in our cabin for awhile. I liked her very much; she was full of fun.

We were now heading out to sea and the boat began to rock a little. The ship's rule was that from two o'clock until four o'clock, all children under ten years of age were to be either in their cabin asleep, or in the playroom that was a large hall-like room where children would be entertained under supervision, supplied with all kinds of acrobatic equipment. The reason for that was because during the midday hours most members of the ship's personnel were then taking their siesta. Some of them had been on their feet since four in the morning.

Paula and I decided to take Billy Ray and Johnny to the playroom. She and I got a deck chair and we were sitting there rolled in wool plaids, watching the waves reach their height and then splatter apart. It reminded me of a quotation from a German philosopher: "Die wellen des lehbens sind wie die see, when die am hochsten reichen zurbrechen sie—immer," meaning, "The waves of life are as the sea, when they reach their peak, they break—always."

It was so pleasant sitting there, watching the waves…so unreal… nearly all were strangers, but connected, in a little world of its own, surrounded by water... just water everywhere. Then, a steward came toward us and called my name. He told me to report to the purser's office. I could not imagine what could be wrong. I hurried down below deck. The assistant administrator was sitting behind a desk.

"Mrs. Cornelia Smith?" he asked as I approached the desk.

I said, "Yes."

He then asked me to have a seat. As I sat down, he told me there were a few questions concerning my papers. I told him I thought I had filled out my papers correctly and accurately. He smiled and said there were just a few minor questions. I was a little annoyed, because I had taken special effort to fill out my papers correctly. But, he smiled again, leaning back, relaxed in his desk chair. He was now looking at a paper in front of him, going over it with a pencil in his hand. Then, he said, "Here you are: you did not state your destination after leaving Rotterdam."

"Oh," I said, "just Rotterdam."

"I see," he said, "you are from Rotterdam?"

"No," I answered, "but my people will meet me there. The reason I did not state my going any farther is because I will have transportation."

He was a very good-looking young man, in officer's uniform of the Rotterdamsche Loyd. He kept smiling, then he said, "Where, then, is your destination?"

I protested, "Why? I did not see anywhere on my forms that I had to give that information."

"I am sorry," he said, then, "Please tell me where are you from?"

"All right," I said coolly, not in the least impressed by his good looks, smile, and uniform. "I am from Amersfoort."

He laughed, and standing up now, he extended his hand.

"Are you the sister of Ab Dykhorst, Corrie?"

"Yes," I said, "I am. But who are you?"

"I am Wimm the Krieger, they call me Bill now, and I am a very close friend of your brother."

He sat down again and said, "There was nothing wrong with your papers, but I just kept looking at that name, Smith, from Chattanooga, and Cornelia to Holland, and I just had to find out."

"I cannot understand why Ab had not mentioned to me that you would be traveling on this ship," he said, puzzled.

I told him they did not know that I was coming on that ship.

"Corrie," he said, "could we meet in the bar tonight and have a drink, so I can give you news about your family?"

I agreed that would be wonderful.

Returning on deck, I told Paula about it.

After dinner we put Billy Ray and Johnny in bed. There were always stewards in the hall looking in on the children if you wished them to. Paula and I dressed for the occasion and then went into the bar. It was a combination dance hall and bar. It was nearly filled with people and shortly after that, a small band started playing and couples began dancing.

Bill already was waiting there. He ordered drinks, and I introduced Paula and Bill to each other. Then, Bill told us about my parents. His wife, a girl I knew, was also a personal friend of Nell, my brother's wife. He then told about my sister, Tillie, and Annie, and all the town's gossip. Bill lived about ten minutes from where my parents lived.

That was one of the most exciting evenings of my life!

Bill then told me I was a special honored guest because he usually did not spend that much time with one passenger, he was assigned to look after the welfare and contentment of all the passengers.

The following day Billy Ray and Johnny were promoted to junior MPs, and each was given a cap to wear and a band around his arm.

There were a few days that Paula and I were unable to leave our cabin, as the waves were high and rough and nearly all passengers were sick, including some of the ship's crew. While we were sick in bed, an alarm was given for the customary drill. All passengers had to put their life-saving jackets on, find their place on deck, close to their sloop (life boats). We were so sick we were unable to go (or so we thought), but no matter how sick you were, they made you get up because whenever there should be trouble, it is usually in rough weather. Even though we did know it was just a drill, it gave us an uncomfortable feeling. Aside from that, we had a wonderful time. We had harbored in Halifax, Canada, then in Southampton, England, and just before we anchored in Le Havre, France, we had three engagements on board. Bill made the announcements. I told him I should take a couple of trips and surely on one of those, I should have a chance to meet someone myself.

He laughed and said confidently, "Pay no attention to engagements on ships. It is customary for three or four couples who meet on the ship to become engaged, but they only last until we reach land. It is something of the mixture between land and water and much fresh air. It stimulates some people. They don't get seasick; it has this sort of effect. Of course," he said, "it is not lasting, but we love it." He claimed it was good advertising, making the other passengers happy.

We had now been sailing for nearly seven days. Then, on Friday night, we entered the harbor of Rotterdam, but no one was to go ashore until early Saturday morning. Most passengers seemed excited. I told Bill that because of him, my trip had been so nice. He helped me a great deal, telling me how much to tip each crew member, such as the head waiter. The table waiters, Malayans from Indonesia, with their yellow skin, short stature, and straight black hair, ate only rice while seated on the floor, their legs folded under them. They worked for very small wages.

I tipped the head waiter $5 sealed in an envelope, and put $4 in the box for the group of table waiters; the room steward got $5; the deck steward for getting my blanket and chair every morning, $3; and the girl in the playroom for the children $5. Some passengers tip in the beginning of their trip and then again at the end, but I only tipped the Friday night before leaving the ship.

Saturday morning, we knew it would take a long time before the passengers were allowed to leave the ship. Bill came to our cabin and he said that he had spotted the whole family; they were all there to meet me. He took me into the hall to let me look through the porthole, but I did not see them, there were so many people there. Bill saw how nervous I was, so he gave me a little nerve pill. He told me most of the people had been waiting on the outside since eight-thirty that morning, and it was now eleven. Bill said he would like to take us off the ship and deliver us to my folks. They knew by now that I was on the Watermann because I had sent a telegram from the boat.

As we walked down the gangplank, I held Billy Ray's hand tight in mine. I just looked into the crowd because I knew if I should spot my mother, I would not be able to look my best. Then Bill, who walked beside us carrying my luggage, said to turn left. And there they were, all of them! I hugged Mama first, then Papa, then Tillie, Annie and Jan, Ab and Nell (I did not know my brother's wife except from pictures. I had only seen her when we were still school children.)

Of course, they all adored Billy Ray! I kept talking to my mother, how happy I was to see them all, how wonderful that they all came to meet me, how lucky I had been on the boat to have Bill.

Then, my mother said, stopping me, "Corrie, we don't understand one word you are saying."

I had not realized I was talking in English. Bill had warned me that I should practice some Dutch on the boat, but every time I had finished the sentence in English. So, I had to repeat everything.

Billy Ray was still holding my hand very tight. The he said, "Mama."

I bent down to him to hear what he wanted to whisper in my ear.

He said: "Mama, are they your people?"

I said, "Yes, darling, these are Mama's people." Then, suddenly, he started to cry.

"Honey," I said, "what is the matter?"He stood there wiping his eyes, whimpering. "They are your people, but they are not my people."

I told him they were his people, too, but his lip quivered, and he said, "No, they all talk so funny."

But then my brother came to him and said, in English, "Now Billy, this here is your Granny and your Grandpa, and I am your uncle, and we all love you."

I could tell that made Billy feel somewhat better then because he said, "I didn't know you could talk like us too."

They all said Billy and I looked so good, were dressed so nicely, and my mother seemed so relieved.

Bill rode home with us in my brother's car; they had two cars. My sister Annie and her husband, Tillie, and my father would ride in one car; and Ab and Nell, my mother and I, Bill and Billy Ray in the other car.

There were flowers all over the house and I had not felt so wanted in years.

My sister Annie had two children, Wilma and Renee, a girl and a boy. My brother also had two children, a girl and a boy, Myra and Hans. Soon Billy Ray felt at home with his cousins to play with. There was only one misunderstanding between some other children from the neighborhood and Billy Ray.

Billy wanted to play in the sand about a half block from where my mother lived. New homes were being constructed and the children there played in the nice yellow sand. So, Billy Ray walked up there and just stood there looking. One of the children said: "He hoe heet jy?" ("What is your name?"), but pronounced He hou hate ji, so Billy Ray said, "I hate you, too." Then, he came home about to cry. He told me that the children had told him that they hated him so, I went with Billy Ray over there and I asked the children what they had said to him. One little boy told me he had asked him his name. I told Billy they did not hate him, they just had asked his name, but it sounded much like "I hate you." Then they told Billy they would let him play with them.

But, Billy Ray was a typical American boy; he did not like to have them tell him how to play, he wanted to show them how, so the playtime did not last too long. However, a few days later they got along just fine, and they learned from each other.

....

Even though the large picture of Roland had been removed from the hall, only members of the immediate family knew about my being divorced from Roland. It was my mother's wish not to explain anything, and to pretend that I was still married, and my husband was awaiting my return to the Unites Stated. Divorce in Holland was then not completely accepted, especially not by people who practiced religion.

It was not pleasant nor easy to behave as the loved and faithful wife, and of course, I didn't have any dates or go anywhere such as the theater or restaurant for dinner, unless in company of members of my family. After all, Amersfoort is a small town with about fifty-five thousand inhabitants. In case I should decide to remain in Holland, we would blame it on extreme homesickness.

My brother's wife, Nell, and I went to visit Bill's wife. She was a lovely person and expecting a baby. She said she was alone so much because Bill was most of the time at sea. She said she hoped I would come back to see her, and I visited with her a couple more times.

Among some of my other girlfriends, I asked about Jo Ponsen and Tillie informed me that Jo had married a doctor from Hungary and they had left for South Africa where he planned to serve as a missionary. They had taken Mrs. Ponsen along with them.

I smiled when Tillie told me that, for Mrs. Ponsen must have been happy. After all, doesn't the Bible teach that if you bring up a child in the way of righteousness, in their old days they shall not depart from it?

Friends of my brother and his wife gave a house party and they invited me, also. I was flattered, as my brother and I never had been very close. When we were in our teens, he always had his own group of friends and they never had included me. He had been a studious sort of fellow and now had worked himself up to personnel manager of the import and export department of Noack Royal Meat Works, one of the largest and finest meat packing factories in Europe, with branches in Canada, Indonesia, and the United States. My brother's job was mostly public relations, checking on wholesalers (not selling) in Germany, France, Belgium, and Holland, to find out if there were any complaints on their products.

They were nice to me at the party, but soon I learned that I had nothing in common. My life had gone in a different direction to theirs, and I began to feel that my home was in the United States. I was just a visitor here. Later my mother realized it, too, but she was glad, and she said it was now easier to accept than before I had been home.

Everything was nice and peaceful at home now. Papa, after thirty years of service on the police force, was drawing his pension at the customary retirement age of 55. Because I had lived in different countries, I learned that the police do not always function by the same rules and regulations. The police force in Holland is not controlled by politics. Not only is it necessary for every police member to have completed two years of Law Enforcement Training School, but requirements before being accepted were high. One had to be of certain height, weight, and intelligence. His past record must be void of any crime or other undesirable actions.

Principles of the school are first to set a good example to gain the admiration and respect of the people. A policeman's conduct must be disciplined and of high morals, whether in uniform, on or off duty.

Further, the course consisted of fundamental study of the law, and testing of emotional stability to be able to control others in critical situations. There was instruction on how to carry arms, and how and when to use them, to learn to use the method of having been adequately trained successfully and to your own advantage, even while unarmed, against those well armed, but inadequately trained.

After completing the course, one year had to be served as a trainee before being appointed permanently.

My father's long-time service on the police force provided us with a certain amount of respect from the townspeople.

Since my father's retirement, several months during the spring and summer he operated a tennis court. It was a private club and it didn't pay a lot, but it kept him busy and he really enjoyed it, he said.

Billy Ray and I, visited my sister, Annie, who lived in Arnheim for a couple of days. Her husband had lived with us several months during the war to escape being sent to Germany to work in war industry. He later married my sister.

I was very fond of him and always had considered him more as a brother than an in-law. He was an architect employed for "Het Ryk" (The State) and my father had forecasted long ago that Jan had special talents, and now he was among the few others to be decorated by the Queen.

He was presented with a medal for deeds of non-military character, for leadership and extreme devotion and his ability for saving cost on designing; and for speedy rebuilding of war-destructed areas in the Netherlands. He was given the choice to either accept "The Order of the House of Orange," or a nice lump sum of money.

To his regret, he admitted, and because of his financial standing, he had to choose the money. In fact, he said there was no choice to it from his side, but had he been a man of financial means, he certainly would have chosen "The Medal of Honor," which is also more or less a letter of introduction signed by the Queen, and it would help a recipient gain admittance in many circles in Holland, and several countries would honor its Royal medal also. "But," said Jan laughingly, "the few places I will be going, there they recognize money as well."

I always loved Holland, but I realized I had pulled my roots from there. I was glad that I found out where I really belonged. Some people never know, once they live in different countries. I felt that I had many ties in America and was glad to return "home," as I now called it. Every one of my family gave me gifts. Clothes, pretty, wool sweaters, souvenirs, and Papa gave me $300 to get on my feet after returning to the States.

My brother and his wife brought me to the boat; they were so thoughtful of Billy and me. They were allowed to come on board. My brother had sent red roses, and they were in the cabin. I was not on the Watermann, but on a much more luxurious ship, the Maasdam.

I did not have a pill when they left, and it was not easy, but, we just pretended that I soon would be back again.

This boat was much nicer, the weather smoother, the people richer, but I did not have a good time as on the Watermann. Nothing could ever make me forget that trip!

When Billy Ray and I arrived in New York, we had immediate connection to Chicago and from there to Chattanooga. Everything in my apartment was undisturbed and Billy Ray went out to play with his old buddies. I went over to see Peggy and I rattled on and on before she stopped me to tell me I was talking in Dutch.

Up until that time I had not been thinking of ever getting married again. Over the years I had dated several boyfriends, and two of them definitely were interested in getting married. It was nice of them that they wanted to marry me, but I did not want to get involved with anyone. I suppose I was afraid of getting hurt again, but I guess secretly, I kept hoping…waiting....

Roland had sent a lump sum of $100 right after Billy Ray and I returned home from Holland. Everything was going its old routine. Several years passed, and Billy finished grammar school. Roland now had married again, and Billy went to Detroit to spend a couple of weeks during the summer months.

Time passed. Of course, I seemed happy to others, and I was to a certain extent, but I was alone, especially on holidays, such as Christmas. When you have no real ties, no one to call your own, no one to belong with, you are just alone with your agony.

I corresponded with everyone at home. Billy's father sent money regularly.

Then, I got a letter from my sister Tillie. She wrote that she planned to get married and that they had chosen Chattanooga for their honeymoon. I could not believe that I was reading that right, but I was. It was one of the happiest messages I ever received. It would only be one more month. I was busy getting things in order. I was trying so hard to get things just right, between flowers, and housecleaning, my work, and an occasional date, that when they arrived a couple hours earlier than I had been led to believe, they found me not home. I was in town picking up flowers and some goodies. They had to wait about fifteen minutes at the neighbor's house.

They loved my apartment, even though they did not like the project. But, I told them a person gets used to it and it was close to my work, and the best I could afford.

My sister's husband, Jan, was a wonderful person. They were Catholic and since I did not have a car, they hired a taxi several times a week to attend early mass.

A girl from work and her husband took us sightseeing. I had been in Chattanooga nearly twelve years and never had seen all the beauty there is to see on Lookout Mountain. My sister's husband, who had traveled many places the world over, because he flew for the KLM Royal Dutch Airlines, said that Rock City was truly one of the world's masterpieces of nature. A friend of mine took us later to have dinner at the Panoram Restaurant." Tillie and Jan were tired from the long trip abroad, but were enjoying everything Chattanooga had to offer in scenery and beauty.

I hated to see them leave, but was thankful that something so unbelievable had become possible—my own sister and her husband visiting in Chattanooga.

After they returned to Holland, I received a letter from Tillie. She wrote she had been visiting my mother when the doorbell rang. Mama went to the door; there was a beautiful car parked in front of the house. A young man standing at the door said to Mama, "Mrs. Dykhorst, how do you do?" Then, "Do you know me?" Mama had just looked at him and told him, "No, I am sorry, but I don't know you."

In the meantime, my father had come to the door, and the young man said, "Do you remember me, Mr. Dykhorst?"

My father had tried hard, but said, "No, I can't place you either." Then Tillie, hearing the conversation from the living room, came into the hall, and he then said to her, "Tillie, do you recognize me?"

"Yes, you are Victor," she had said.

They had asked him to come in, after all, it had been nearly fifteen years. He remarked how much Tillie looked like me. He had explained he was visiting in Holland with his wife and daughter and had been determined to come to see them.

My mother had invited him to bring his wife and daughter and have dinner that evening. They had returned, the three of them, and they had talked and then he had asked to see pictures. His wife, so Tillie wrote, was a school teacher, and very attractive and likeable.

I just sat quietly reading the letter. He had married a school teacher. Naturally, I was glad. A school teacher was more suitable for him than I any way. They had a daughter, just one child.

Then a few weeks later, at Christmas time, I received a card from Austria, from Victor. He told me in his card that he had visited in Holland during the 700-year festival, that he met Tillie, and it brought back old memories, from the time he had spent during the war. He asked me to write to him, saying that he often wondered how I had been getting along since I left Austria.

I answered him, telling him in my letter all about my son, my work, and America. I also added that his card had brought me much joy, and I would like to hear from him again, but if it brought even one moment of friction or unhappiness between him and his wife, then I had rather he did not answer.

I did not hear from him again.

Time passed in the same old routine. I had become acquainted with a man who thought very much of me and Billy. He was older than me, and very settled. He offered me a good home, the kind of home I had always hoped for, and I thought it possible to live with in a Christian way.

As I thought on those days…long ago in November
When the skies were gray…and I was alone
Sad whispering winds…and raindrops were falling
And my happiness all gone

And, as I stood completely unaware of what the future be
Had been arranged a miracle so just...so kind to me...
I watch the cloud...she breaks...and then the sky...
So pure...so blue...I see...
My heart stood still from sudden happiness
My faith restored...my joy renewed...
It had been brought back to me...
And at that day...at that time... I then thanked November.

And, I hoped that God would guide me in the right direction, for I realized that no matter how much security or money you may gain, if you don't turn to God you are still alone. Then I prayed, leaving behind all feelings of petty pride. God granted me this husband, and I vowed to put forth all my effort to make a good life for the three of us, for I had gained much understanding, and I didn't expect a rose to sing, because I learned that happiness isn't something we receive; it is only accomplished by proper living, loving, and much giving.

Corrie and second husband W.F. Cotten

Corrie and second
husband W.F. Cotten

Epilogue

My mother lived an interesting and challenging life and faced many hardships. As her son, I cannot remember her ever complaining about any of the hardships or celebrating any rewards. As the saying goes, "she maintained an even strain". What I do remember is how she grew stronger from the challenges and felt blessed with the rewards.

Roland and I never developed a father/son relationship. My mother never spoke negatively to me about Roland. She would only say he was not a bad person, that he loved me but that he lacked character in some situations. She made sure I spent time with him when I was young by sending me to Detroit, where he lived and worked, for two-four weeks during the summer. He tried to be a father to me during this time but you have to be a dad more than a couple of weeks a year, especially with a young child.

The man that was a father to me was my step-father, W. F. Cotten. He was there to see my ballgames, the man who took me hunting as I was growing up, was there when I left for the Navy with tears in his eyes and a big hug when I returned. He was the man who showed me what character is, that your word is your bond and taught me what a strong work ethic can accomplish. He was a wonderful father and roll-model and someone I greatly respected and loved.

I remember my mother writing this manuscript in long-hand at the dining room table after a day's work at the Buster Brown hosiery mill where she was employed for thirty-five years. This was in the mid-sixties and I was in the tenth grade. I asked her why she was writing it and how she could remember it all. She had kept a detailed diary and once reading it again, it all came back to her. She said the manuscript was for me and felt that with our family being so small and separated by great distance that someday I may want to know and understand more about her earlier life. What a real treasure for me! I have read it many times and realize she never ran from adversity. What a great adventure she had. What a life.

After high school, in the sixties, I joined the Navy. Upon my return, I enrolled in college under the GI Bill majoring in radiation physics. Upon graduating and working in that field of study for a few years, I returned to Chattanooga and became a general contractor in residential construction, like my step-father. After forty-plus years of building, I am currently retired and married to Gail Hunter. I have two children, Chad who is also a general contractor and is married to Marci Mechling. Kelli, my daughter, owns her own company and is married to David Schwind. They all live in the Chattanooga area.

Roland died in 1986 with cirrhosis of the liver due to alcohol abuse. I was told he never missed a day of work or drank on the job. Mr. Cotten, my step-father, died in 1993 of natural causes. My mother died in 2003 of natural causes with me by her side.

My mother's parents visited us once in the United States before they passed away. Mother and Dad (step-father) were able to visit Holland several times. Aunt Tilly and her husband, Jan, visited many times over the years from Holland. Uncle Jan has passed but Aunt Tilly still comes to visit. She was here in 2017 at age 85 and we hope to see her again next year.

My mother seemed to always look through to the other side of hardship and realized she could get through with a strong character and deep faith in herself and God.

Thank you for reading Treasures of Sadness. My mission in sharing this book was not only to honor my mother but to also offer it as an inspiration to others that may be facing adversity.

I appreciate and invite your comments. Please visit our website at www.treasuresofsadness.com.

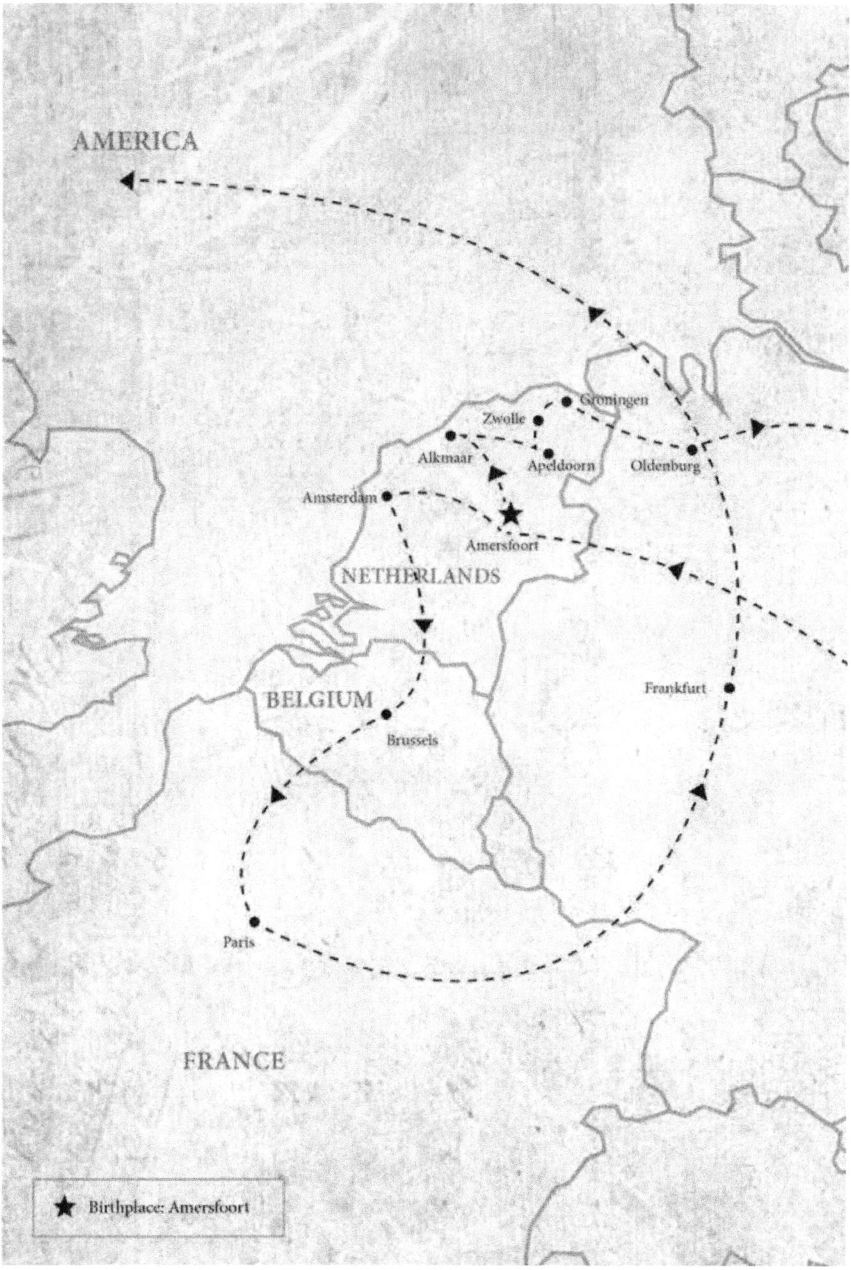
AMERICA
Groningen
Zwolle
Alkmaar
Apeldoorn
Oldenburg
Amsterdam
Amersfoort
NETHERLANDS
BELGIUM
Brussels
Frankfurt
Paris
FRANCE
Birthplace: Amersfoort

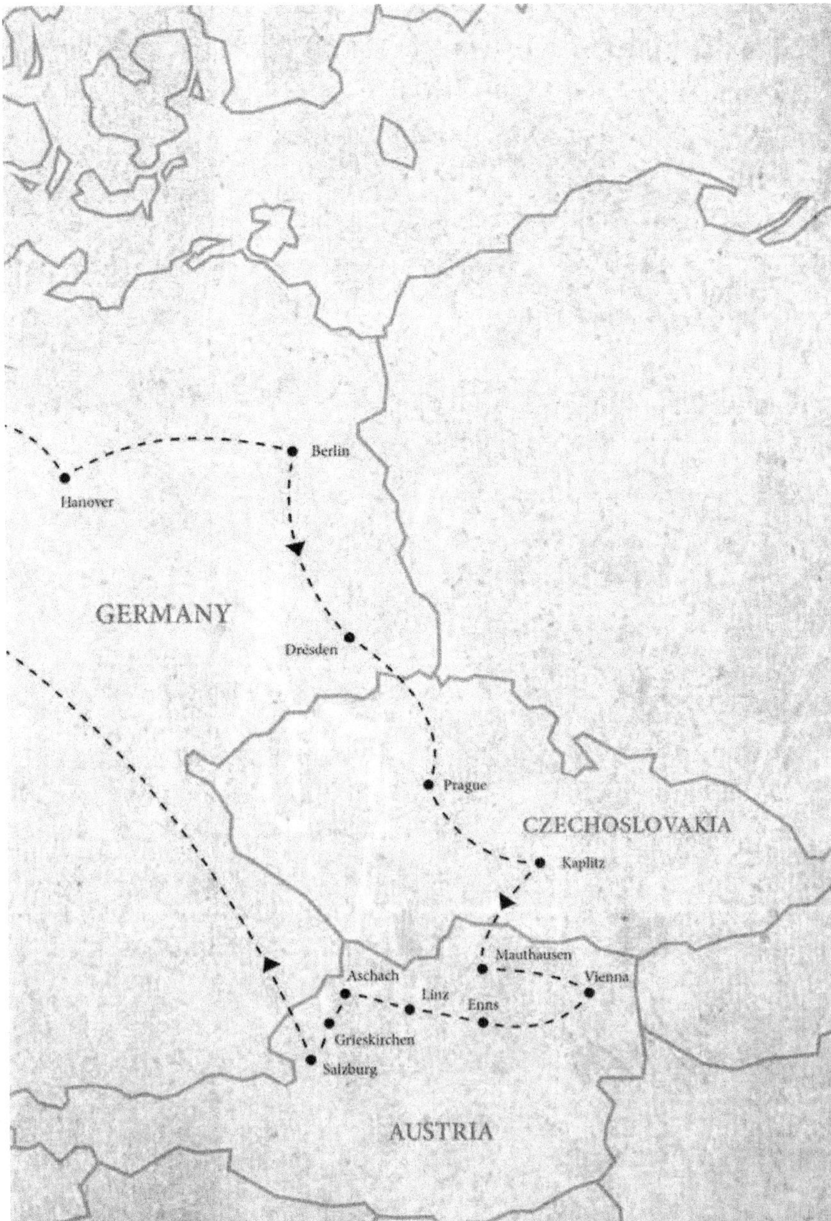
Berlin
Hanover
GERMANY
Dresden
Prague
CZECHOSLOVAKIA
Kaplitz
Mauthausen
Aschach
Linz
Enns
Vienna
Grieskirchen
Salzburg
AUSTRIA